THE **BIGGEST**
BEETROOT
IN THE WORLD

Giant Vegetables and the People Who Grow Them

Michael Leapman

First published in Great Britain 2008
by Aurum Press Ltd, 7 Greenland Street, London NW1 0ND
www.aurumpress.co.uk

Copyright © 2008 by Michael Leapman

A CIP catalogue record for this book is available from the British Library.

ISBN 978 1 84513 319 1

10 9 8 7 6 5 4 3 2 1

2012 2011 2010 2009 2008

Typeset by SX Composing DTP, Raleigh, Essex
Printed and bound in Great Britain by Cromwell Press, Trowbridge, Wiltshire

Contents

For Zac: his turn

Acknowledgements

I could not have written this book without the wholehearted co-operation and generosity of its five main characters – Gareth and Kevin Fortey, Peter Glazebrook, Ian Neale and Gerald Treweek – who allowed me unrestricted access to their homes, gardens and greenhouses for most of 2007. My thanks are due to them, as well as to the host of skilled vegetable growers who gave me their time and attention along the way, notably Joe Atherton, Alf Cobb, John Evans and Ian Paton. There are too many others to list here, but most of them get a name check in the text. In the initial stages, John Trim was invaluable in putting me in touch with the right people and Peter Seabrook helped me track down Bernard Lavery, the chief progenitor of today's giant vegetable cult.

As I travelled around Britain, several good friends allowed me and my wife Olga to stay with them, often adding the luxury of driving us to the shows. So, many thanks to Brenda and Edward Vaughan, Annie and Bob Macdonald, Sarah and Tony Thomas and Robin and Michael Lake.

My visit to Alaska owes a great deal to Jacqi Todd, the British representative of the state's tourist authorities, and Condor Airlines. Once I was there, Scott and Mardie Robb gave me a notably friendly welcome, as well as valuable insights into the way things are done across the Atlantic.

The seeds of the book were sown by Karen Ings and Graham Coster of Aurum Press, who have nursed it sympathetically through to its final flowering.

Michael Leapman
June 2008

Chapter 1

Abertysswg

Early afternoon on a balmy September Saturday in Abertysswg, an old Welsh mining village not far from Merthyr Tydfil. Wales are playing Australia in the 2007 rugby World Cup in Paris, and the lounge of the Working Men's Club is packed with men and women mesmerised by the wide-screen television, where their muscular heroes are about to slump to defeat, despite a brave second-half rally.

Meanwhile, in the bar upstairs, trestle tables groan under the weight of mammoth leeks, onions, beetroot and swedes. For, unluckily, this is also the day of the village's annual giant vegetable show. 'When we booked the date we didn't know about the rugby,' laments Neil Burridge, one of its principal organisers.

Rugby is a team game of fast, aggressive action that commands fierce national loyalties – especially in Wales – and watching it in the company of compatriots is a powerful manifestation of solidarity and common identity. By contrast, cultivating enormous vegetables is fundamentally a solitary pastime. At the top level there is certainly a strong competitive element, but the overriding satisfaction comes from a sense of personal achievement: of overcoming all the hazards and disappointments inherent in trying to outsmart nature by making something grow bigger than anyone has done before.

As a spectacle, it can't compete with the afternoon's showdown in Paris. That is why there are fewer than the usual number of enthusiasts for horticultural overkill queuing on the clubhouse stairs, impatient to feast their eyes on the swollen and elongated marvels behind the closed doors. But there is plenty of tension and excitement among the principals, the men and women who for months have been pampering their produce day and night to get it to the peak of plumpness for this, the Welsh Giant Vegetable Championship. This is the most historic show on the British circuit: there is no consensus about the origins of the biggest-is-best phenomenon (which nowadays regularly commands a whole page in *Guinness World Records*), but some assert with conviction that this is where it all began.

Abertysswg is one of a string of distinctive villages lining the dramatic Rhymney Valley, north of Cardiff. Ribbons of narrow terraced houses cling to its steep sides, the parallel streets separated by short, steep climbs. Little evidence now remains of the coal mines that were responsible for the creation of these villages a century ago, even though it is barely thirty years since their rapid decline began.

When I arrive at the club's front entrance at around 10 a.m. I wonder for a moment if I've got the date wrong: why no sign of people unloading their monstrosities and taking them in? I know that entries close at 10.45, so this should be a busy time for arrivals. All becomes clear when I get inside; I am directed to the first floor, where – with some difficulty – the exhibits are being hauled into place. Like everything in the village, the club is built on a slope, and its back entrance is some twenty-five feet higher than the front. Carrying a gigantic marrow or swede down the back steps makes a lot more sense than struggling up the front stairs with it.

By the back entrance – high on the ridge, where there are ravishing views over the valley – I greet Ian Neale and Peter Glazebrook, two of the most assiduous of the giant vegetable fraternity. They are among five growers whose progress I have been monitoring since the beginning of the year, when their monsters were no more than fragile seed leaves cosseted in heated greenhouses. Ian – a tall man with a soft Welsh lilt to his voice – runs a plant nursery near Newport. Like many competitors here, he is pessimistic: the lack of sunshine and dismal weather all over Britain last July, when the vegetables should have been piling on weight, means that nobody really expects any record-breaking specimens at this year's shows.

'It's the worst season I've had for about twelve years,' he says. 'The stuff came up and looked at you, and looked at you, but it wasn't going to grow for you. There were hardly any flowers on the marrows and cucumbers for me to pollinate.' Still, he usually does well with big root vegetables. Indeed he is pictured in the 2007 *Guinness World Records*, holding up the 51-lb beetroot that earned him inclusion in the book – the holy grail to which all giant vegetable growers aspire.

Peter and his cheerful wife Mary, with their friends and fellow growers Joe and Carmel Atherton, have driven here from Nottinghamshire, a round trip of around 350 miles, to display their prowess in this specialised area of cultivation. The tall, gaunt Peter was, until last month, the world record holder for the longest carrot – he grew one of over 17ft for a one-off contest organised by the BBC and shown on television earlier in the year. For him and Mary it has been an especially strenuous weekend. Only yesterday they were in Harrogate, competing in a heavy onion weigh-off (Peter came second); they had to drive home in the afternoon, dig up and prepare today's entries and then make yet another pre-dawn start.

Joe, a small and wiry former miner, has a magic touch with carrots and radishes. It was he who took the long carrot record from Peter at Shepton Mallet just two weeks earlier, exceeding his friend's best by some two feet. Then a week ago, at another Welsh show (at Llanharry, near Bridgend), Joe triumphed with a 12-lb carrot and a radish about half a pound heavier. He has brought the same carrot today, with 'Rocky' written on it in felt-tip pen to mark its slight resemblance to a prize fighter – an uncharacteristically whimsical gesture for such a serious grower. And today, he tells me, he has brought an even bigger radish than last week's.

Peter and Mary left their home near Newark at 4.45 this morning, while Joe and Carmel, who live near Mansfield, had to get up almost as early. Mary and Carmel are certainly not giant vegetable widows: they help their husbands where they can and enjoy the September shows as social occasions. Following their established custom, the four met for breakfast at a motorway service area and arrived at Abertysswg at 9.15. By the time I get there they have already unloaded their bulky cargo and plan to take advantage of the sunny weather to head into the nearby Brecon Beacons for a bracing walk and a pub lunch, returning in mid-afternoon to see how many of their entries have won the £20 first prize in each of the classes: enough, they hope, at least to pay for their petrol.

At 10.30, as they are about to set out, a car turns into the narrow street and pulls up sharply. Out get Kevin and Gareth Fortey, brothers in their twenties – close friends of Ian Neale and two of the youngest growers on the regular giant circuit – whom I have also been visiting regularly since the spring. With their even younger friend Kyle they have come from Cwmbran, only an hour's drive away; so they could afford to cut it fine.

They swap cordial greetings with the Nottinghamshire quartet, sympathise over the season's unhelpful weather, and begin to unload their produce. When I ask them, 'Any winners?' they say that, in spite of the heavy rain and the general lack of sunshine, they have high hopes for their cucumber and celery and, with luck, their marrow. Watching them struggle down the steps with the 80-lb marrow, then with the two enormous clumps of celery – careful not to snap off any of the leaves that make up the bulk and weight – I can share their optimism. Each competitor is allowed two entries in each class. Peter, though, limits himself to one at the Welsh shows. He feels that, as an Englishman, he is an outsider and should not try to hog the prizes at the expense of the locals: a typically self-effacing approach.

At 10.45 sharp, the doors of the upper hall are closed and the long and literally burdensome process of judging begins. At the biggest shows the entries are weighed as soon as they are unloaded by the growers; the monsters can then go straight from the scales to the exhibition bench and stay there until the end of the show. This minimises the number of times the vegetables (some weighing over a hundredweight) have to be lifted and moved. However, it also reduces the competitive tension, because the growers, if they stay around long enough, will know straight away how much their exhibits weigh and whether any of their rivals' are heavier.

Here at Abertysswg the procedure is to take the vegetables into the hall for the judges to weigh later, in the contestants' absence. This means recruiting a team of muscular volunteers to shift the produce on to the scales and then back to the benches. The root vegetables and marrows, although heavy, are quite straightforward to handle; but the men have to be particularly careful with the leafy stuff (the cabbages, cauliflowers and celery); if they break any leaves off they could spoil a grower's chance of winning. The technique is to manoeuvre the vegetables onto a large bed sheet before carrying them to the industrial weighing machine borrowed for the occasion. The sheet has already been weighed separately, so its weight can be deducted from that shown on the scale for each vegetable.

Two men preside over the judging: Alan Burridge – who effectively runs the show along with his brother Neil – and Ray Davey, a familiar face on the circuit, who judges at the annual British championships at Shepton Mallet and has been presiding here since 1989. Alan notes down the weight of each entry in kilograms, the unit used on the scale, although most of the growers prefer pounds and ounces. Ray's wife Beatrice, sitting at a table in the back of the room, records the weights and writes the tickets to place on those exhibits that have won prizes.

After the weighing comes the measuring. The Welsh show does not have classes for the longest carrot, parsnip and beetroot – something of a specialisation for Peter and Joe, who grow them in split drainpipes – but it does give prizes for the longest pea and runner bean and the largest sunflower head. And Abertysswg has its own distinctive procedure. In other shows that have classes for the longest bean, measuring is done in a straight line from the tip of the bean to its toe. Here a flexible tape measure is used, following the bean's contours – which can (and in this case probably does) make a crucial difference to the result.

Downstairs, before the rugby starts, Kevin and Gareth and Kyle are playing snooker. When I had visited them in Cwmbran a few weeks earlier, the excitable Kyle confided that the Abertysswg show was his favourite on the circuit, both because of the club's fine snooker table and because just down the road is a shop that sells, by his expert reckoning, some of the best fish and chips in Wales. As the lunch hour approaches we stroll towards the centre of the village, where its few remaining shops and another working men's club surround a small green that is mostly taken up with a children's playground. The fish and chips from the Wah No takeaway (they do Chinese as well) are as good as Kyle maintained – fresh and crisp in a feather-light batter – and Neil and I and the Cwmbran crew eat them perched on a seat on the green, looking down over where the colliery used to be. Mining began here in 1897, in two pits owned by The Tredegar Iron and Coal Company and named McLaren 1 and McLaren 3, after Sir Charles McLaren, a director. It was a typical company village. The pit owners ran everything, including the village shop – still at the same location – and the pub at the colliery gate, called the McLaren Arms. Some of the streets are named after the boss's sons – Alfred, Charles and Glyn. The mine closed in 1969, the pub more recently.

It was at the McLaren Arms that the seeds of this giant vegetable show were sown. Back at the club after lunch, I meet two members of the organising committee, both former miners, who were there when it all started twenty-six years ago. They tell me there was already a regular flower show in the village, at which the produce was judged on its quality, not its size, and women entered their home-made cakes and jams. The keenest vegetable growers, though, would meet in the pub in the early autumn and boast about the size of their leeks, onions and the rest: 'Braggers' Corner', they used to call it. And then one of them had the idea of organising a show devoted entirely to oversized produce, just to see whose boasts could stand up to scrutiny.

The first show was held in the pub itself in 1982 and was called the Welsh Giant Vegetable Championship, because, so far as anyone knew, there was no other contest of its kind in the country. Two years later it moved to the Working Men's Club. An early visitor was Bernard Lavery, now regarded as the father of the giant vegetable movement in Britain. He helped establish a rival show in his home village of Llanharry before he broke away from the organisers and found a sponsor for a show in Cardiff, then moving it on, first to the Alton Towers theme park, then to Spalding in Lincolnshire, and finally as an adjunct to the big Amateur Gardening show at Shepton Mallet, Somerset, where it is held today. Despite this big-time competition, the Abertysswg show has survived (it is now sponsored by Castlemaine XXXX beer) and has also outlasted the original village flower show, which expired a few years ago for lack of support. There have been one or two modifications to the original format. There are now three classes judged for quality rather than size (for onions, leeks and parsnips) and, as pumpkins and squashes grew bigger over the years, the organisers decided that the difficulty of taking them down the steps into the hall, and the amount of space they took up once inside, made it impractical to continue to show them.

There is no universally accepted explanation for why cultivating giant vegetables appears to thrive in mining – or, nowadays, former mining – communities. Beyond south Wales, raising monster onions and leeks has long been a favourite pastime around the old coalfields of north-east England. Joe Atherton, whose accent confirms that he comes originally from the north-east, is a former Nottinghamshire miner who lives on the edge of the disused pit at Mansfield Woodhouse. Gerald Treweek, another of those whom I have been shadowing as he tries to break the world onion record, is also an ex-miner. And growers in Cornwall, where there used to be tin mines, specialise in large pumpkins and cabbages. One theory is that men who spent their working lives underground relish a hobby that takes them outdoors. Another is that the mineral deposits in the soil of the mining areas stimulate the vegetables into rapid and excessive growth.

At 1.30, when the doors of the exhibition hall are due to open, Alan and Ray have still not finished the judging. The diehards, those who are not in the lower lounge waiting for the rugby to start, are clustered on the stairs, impatient to pay their 50p admission fee, buy their pint of XXXX from the bar (on special offer at £1.50) and marvel at the vegetarian freak show. It is close to two o'clock before they are admitted, and even then a few cards have still to be placed on the winning entries.

When they get in, the scene before them is not exactly pretty. Giant vegetables are, for the most part, ungainly and malformed. Swedes, beetroot and parsnips, far from being neat single globes or cones of sweet flesh, are usually made up of tangles of roots emerging from a misshapen central lump, like giant octopuses whose tentacles have somehow got out of kilter: it is the roots that usually make up the weight. Pumpkins and marrows are often lopsided, while runner beans are curly – unlike the disciplined sets of straight beans so much admired at conventional vegetable shows.

Kevin, Gareth, Kyle and Ian are among the first through the door, and they head towards their exhibits to see how they have fared. Good news! Ian has won two first prizes with his 29-lb beetroot and 34-lb swede, while the Forteys have triumphed with their 21-lb head of celery and a 17-lb cucumber, as well as producing the largest sunflower seed head – the only non-vegetable class in the schedule.

Their cucumber is a show-bench veteran. Two weeks ago it came third at the big Shepton Mallet contest – beaten by the 91-year-old Midlander Alf Cobb, who set a new world record – and last week it was second at Llanharry. Gareth is pleased with it, seeing that they had difficulty in getting their cucumbers and marrows to flower during the unkind summer, and this one did not set until late July – a week or two later than in a normal year. He is disappointed, though, that their long runner bean has come only third. It is an almost straight bean, nearly 30in long, and he is convinced it would have won but for the local rule about measuring along the contours. In the event, it was narrowly beaten by entries from Peter and Joe, both of which have significant kinks. Still, it is the longest the Forteys have grown, and they plan to keep the seed to see if they can better it next year.

Peter, Mary, Joe and Carmel have been having such a good time on the Brecon Beacons that they don't return until half an hour before the prize-giving. The results are good for them as well. Peter won not only with his long bean but also with his marrow (81 lb) and onion (11 lb 6 oz), as well as with a set of three parsnips he entered for the quality class. Joe's winners are the 'Rocky' carrot (even though it has lost a little weight since Llanharry, through dehydration), his new 14-lb radish, a 6-lb parsnip, a 10-lb 8-oz leek, a 2-lb 5-oz tomato and a potato that weighed 4 lb 4 oz. Both have covered the cost of their petrol, if not of the bed-and-breakfast where they will stay tonight before heading home.

As the Welsh rugby team sinks to defeat, by 32 points to 20, some of the disheartened enthusiasts drift upstairs to seek solace in the vegetables: at least they can be sure of a few Welsh victories here. Shortly before 3.30 the official guests arrive – the Chair of the Rhymney Community Council, which helps sponsor the show, and the Mayor and Lady Mayoress of Caerphilly, a few miles south, who present the prizes. Among the special awards, Joe picks up the Mike Fortey shield for the heaviest leek, given in memory of Kevin and Gareth's father, a pioneer of the Welsh giant vegetable scene, who died tragically young.

The Mayor declares that he is more impressed every year by the show and the work the exhibitors put into it. 'It really is a fine show and I wouldn't miss it for the world,' he says. The Mayoress, equally enthusiastic, says she has only one question 'How big a saucepan do you need to put that lot into?'

The growers laugh politely. It's not the first time they have heard jokes like that.

Chapter 2

The Big Story

Dramatic scenes like those in Abertysswg are repeated elsewhere every autumn. Cadres of obsessive vegetable gardeners travel to halls, marquees and social clubs around Britain, staggering under the weight of the distended products of a year's dedicated sowing, planting, feeding and pampering, customarily undertaken in near-secrecy – and with mounting excitement as the shortening summer days signal that show time nears.

The passion for gardening can take a variety of forms, driven by different motives. Many devotees are moved by watching a beautiful flower develop from a tiny seed, believing it puts them in touch both with nature and their own nurturing instinct. The more prosaic point out that, by growing their own food and controlling their use of fertilisers and pesticides, they both contribute to their family's well-being and help the environment by reducing the food miles involved in distributing commercially grown vegetables. When the competitive urge enters the mix, gardeners want to measure their achievements against those of other enthusiasts in local and national shows. And when that urge becomes dominant, some of the most driven cultivators readjust their sights and aim to produce not the best vegetables in the world (and certainly not the most beautiful) but the biggest.

When early horticultural shows began to proliferate in the first half of the nineteenth century, size was almost the only criterion for judging vegetables. With flowers, uniformity of shape and colour would be taken into account but, for vegetables, length, breadth and weight were decisive – and never mind if the largest specimens were often the ugliest and sometimes the least appetising.

The growing number of shows was fuelled by the formation of local horticultural societies that gathered pace in the 1830s; in December 1836 the *Gardeners' Magazine* reported that their number had nearly doubled in the previous six years. The magazine carried reports of their shows, and references to vegetable exhibits invariably stressed their size rather than their quality. For instance, a Yorkshire grower in 1835 claimed he had produced a head of broccoli measuring 1ft 11in across and 3ft 1in in circumference. One of the biggest shows was in Sheffield's newly created botanic gardens, and at the inaugural event in 1836 Mr Bolton from Manchester showed onions measuring between seven and eight inches across. In the same month a Scottish show was reporting 'four huge stalks of celery, of this year's growth, any one of which could have satisfied a dozen lovers of that delicious edible'.

The following year, a few weeks after Queen Victoria's accession, the Earl Spencer exhibited a gourd (we would call it a squash or a pumpkin today) weighing 60 lb at the Bawtry and Retford show. At Stirling a cabbage was shown that weighed 49 lb, despite many of its large outer leaves having been removed. Another 'monstrous' cabbage, grown by John Johnston, a bootmaker from Falkirk, measured 4ft in circumference.

Mr Johnston's and Mr Bolton's triumphs exemplified a significant sociological aspect of the shows: many of the best vegetable exhibits now came from individual hobby gardeners, or 'cottagers', while the trophies for flowers and fruit were still monopolised by the professionals from the great houses. Joseph Paxton, gardener to the Duke of Devonshire at Chatsworth, later designer of the Crystal Palace that housed the Great Exhibition of 1851, was regularly listed among the winners.

Some of the biggest shows – Sheffield, for instance – had separate classes for cottagers and for professional gardeners employed by the aristocracy. (This was welcomed by liberal newspapers such as the *Sheffield Mercury*, which felt that it 'cannot fail to give an increased taste for gardening among the working classes'.) In others they all competed together. This democratisation of horticulture, coming in the wake of the Reform Act of 1832, was noted by the December 1836 *Gardeners' Magazine*: 'The most remarkable feature of the horticultural societies of the present year is the increasing attention which has been paid throughout the country to the exhibitions of the poor. The produce of the cottagers' gardens has been generally admired.' And much of it, according to the magazine's show reports, merited the adjectives 'colossal', 'enormous' and 'gigantic'.

Only in the late nineteenth century, after the Royal Horticultural Society established a formal set of rules for determining quality in vegetables, did judges begin to take more account of their general appearance and taste. In 1924 A.J. Macself, in a guide for show competitors, wrote: 'The greatest misconception that formerly prevailed being that the object of competitive classes for vegetables was to applaud and reward the production of monster specimens, regardless of their utility.' And the current RHS guide for judges declares that size is meritorious only if accompanied by quality.

Most growers went along with that purist approach, but a minority of enthusiasts remained hooked on giant vegetables, in part because they are deeply rooted in popular culture and imagination. They play a pivotal role in two of our best-loved Christmas pantomimes – *Jack and the Beanstalk* and *Cinderella*, in which the pumpkin that turns into a coach has to be of a size that real-life growers are only now beginning to approach. More recently Roald Dahl wrote *James and the Giant Peach*, and the cartoon characters Wallace and Gromit featured in a full-length film, *The Curse of the Were-Rabbit*, whose plot hinged on the theft and sabotage of huge vegetables being raised for a local show.

There are, too, more tangible reasons why some gardeners prefer to grow for bulk rather than quality. The first is that size is an absolute, not subject to the aesthetic preferences and individual whims of judges: the scales and the tape measure are the only arbiters, brooking no argument and ruling out any suspicion of prejudice. The second is the sheer scale of the physical challenge. The production of swollen or extended vegetables is difficult and all-consuming, requiring high levels of expertise and ingenuity, a quantity of specialised equipment, plenty of growing space – much of it under cover – as well as constant vigilance and, above all, utter dedication. Growing a dozen unblemished tomatoes of uniform size, a feast for the eye and the palate, is indeed a triumph of horticultural skill. But to produce a carrot more than 18ft long – the height of three grown men – and get it to the show bench undamaged, requires a level of strategic planning comparable to that of the most sophisticated military operation.

So, while the main national and local shows moved towards encouraging the production of vegetables in which quality and uniformity took precedence over size, there remained a smattering of classes for the heaviest marrow or pumpkin, the longest parsnip, runner bean or cucumber, the biggest truss of tomatoes. And size gained international recognition at the Paris World's Fair of 1900, when a Canadian grower caused a sensation with a pumpkin weighing over 400 pounds: a tiddler compared with today's world record of 1,689 lb, roughly the size of a well-upholstered armchair.

Because pumpkins grow bigger than any other vegetable they have always taken pride of place among the giants. Every autumn, just before Hallowe'en, scores of pumpkin festivals take place across Britain and many other countries, notably the United States and Canada. In 1983 the World Pumpkin Confederation held its first annual weigh-off in Collins, New York State. In those early days the winners weighed about 600 lb, but the figure has risen dramatically year by year, and theoretically there seems no limit to how big they can be induced to grow, given a scientific approach to seed selection and nutrition.

Nonetheless, most serious growers of quality vegetables regard this kind of thing as a freak show, incidental to their principal objectives. Comparing the production of giant vegetables with the subtler skills needed to grow their smaller but better groomed counterparts is, they believe, like contrasting the brute force of sumo wrestling with the elegant thrust and parry of classical fencing.

All the same, in one corner of Britain giantism has remained dominant. The climate of north-east England is ideal for cultivating members of the onion family to their maximum size. Compared with most other parts of the country it is cooler in summer and autumn, so the vegetables take longer to run to seed. And the crucial extra minutes of daylight give them more time to develop – one of the reasons why, across the Atlantic, so many records are held by growers in Alaska and Canada. The passion for raising gargantuan onions and leeks seems to have originated in coal mining communities, with leeks reputedly introduced by the many Welshmen who came to work in English mines in the nineteenth century. Soon the growers began to compete in local shows, the most important today being the late September leek and onion show at Ashington, Northumberland, sponsored by a brewery.

If the pumpkin is the king of the heavy vegetables, the onion is the crown prince. A prize for the heaviest Kelsae onion – the variety that forms the largest bulb – was instituted in 1975 and won by a Scottish grower with a specimen weighing just under 5 lb. The competition then moved from one location to another until in 1983 it settled at the Northern Horticultural Society's Great Autumn Show in Harrogate, Yorkshire, where it has remained. The prize is £500 – one of the highest on the giant circuit – with an extra £1,000 if the winner breaks the world record. A measure of how far and how fast techniques have improved is that the winning onion in 2007 weighed 13 lb 5 oz – and that is more than 3 lb below the current world record.

The relationship between growers of conventional and monstrous vegetables remained distant in Britain until the early 1980s. One of the few specialist publications to acknowledge the increasing enthusiasm for giants, albeit still from a dedicated minority, was the weekly *Garden News*. It organised an annual competition with some 16 classes for the heaviest and longest vegetables and fruits, sponsored by the manufacturer of Phostrogen fertilisers. Contestants had to write in with the weights and measurements of their produce, and the winners would be verified: but this was not a show in the literal sense because the vegetables were not brought together in one place for the public to view.

One man who did more than anybody to bridge the gap, by bringing the giants closer to the mainstream, was Bernard Lavery from Llanharry in South Wales. A machine operator at an open-cast coal mine, he suffered a serious accident in 1975, resulting in a long hospital stay and subsequent convalescence. He had always been keen on growing vegetables, and while waiting to return to work he had much more time to devote to it. The first show he entered was in the nearby village of Llanharan: the organisers had told him they were short of entries in some of the vegetable classes, so he competed in a few and took second prize with his carrots. Then 'the next year I thought I'd grow for the shows, and started winning more'.

In the early days he grew his vegetables for quality rather than bulk, and became so good at it that he rose to become chairman of the Welsh branch of the National Vegetable Society. Then he and some fellow gardeners from Llanharry visited the Welsh Giant Vegetable Championship at Abertysswg, and they were so impressed that they decided to start a local show of their own, principally devoted to size. Bernard walked away with most of the prizes. 'Now and again you get a freak vegetable, and when this comes about you try to keep the seed,' he explained. 'Then you've taken the bait and you're hooked.'

Hooked he certainly was. He thought he had achieved virtually all he could in the field of quality vegetables and was excited by this new challenge. A forceful, outgoing man, with a flair for organisation, he also saw scope for increasing public interest in this then-neglected aspect of vegetable growing. 'It had always been the fun side of it,' he said. 'Nobody took it seriously.'

Very much the individualist, Bernard does not work well in committees and, after falling out with some of the other organisers of the Llanharry show, he broke away and won sponsorship for a show of his own at Cardiff, billing it as a national event. He was thus instrumental in transforming the cult of giantism from a novelty section at local shows to a national movement that attracted growers from many parts of the country. And they started to take it very seriously indeed. For a few years from 1983 the seed company Unwins sponsored a national pumpkin show with a prize of £100, increasing to £1,000 if the British record was broken and £10,000 for breaking the world record. In addition, the winner was flown off to the Half Moon Bay Pumpkin Festival near San Francisco, which then declared itself to be the World Pumpkin Championship.

At the same time a group of men from Cwmbran, near Newport, founded the grandly named British National Pumpkin Champion-ships, held in a local pub. Its founder was Mike Fortey, Kevin and Gareth's father, a foreman electrician with the South Wales Electricity Board and a passionate gardener. The idea arose much as that of the Abertysswg show had done. Mike and some friends were in the Mill Tavern discussing which of them could grow the largest pumpkin. To settle the matter they organised a contest in the pub itself, and so many growers wanted to compete that the following year it was transferred to the larger Cwmbran Working Men's Club.

It was also in the 1980s that the Government, as part of its strategy to regenerate the depressed areas of declining industrial regions, hit on the idea of promoting national garden festivals on sites reclaimed from abandoned factories or slag heaps. The aim was to attract visitors with a far broader range of interests than the knowledgeable gardening enthusiasts who usually went to flower and vegetable shows. They therefore included several classes for giant vegetables, for, while many visitors might not discern the inherent beauty of six flawless and identical King Edward potatoes, they could all marvel at the sheer bulk of a hundred-pound marrow. The first festival, at Liverpool in 1984, attracted 3.4 million people. Over the next decade it was followed by similar events at Stoke-on-Trent, Glasgow, Gateshead and Ebbw Vale. The flower and vegetable shows held in the last days of the festivals offered significant prizes for the most gigantic vegetables.

Lavery's and Fortey's shows soon merged as the National Giant Vegetables Championship, today held at Shepton Mallet in late August or early September. It is popular with growers because it offers cash prizes for the top seven or eight contenders in some classes – only small sums for the lower placings, but at least it helps with the cost of taking the exhibits to the site. In the middle of September come the two shows in South Wales, and there are classes for outsized produce at the important autumn shows at Malvern and Harrogate, as well as at smaller events across the country. In late September leek and onion growers head for Ashington, where there are top prizes of over £1,000, and in October they congregate at the Dewsbury Onion Fair. The season ends with pumpkin championships, two of the most important being at Soham in Cambridgeshire and at Southampton.

Lavery's show began to attract the attention of the national media when it was staged at Alton Towers in the late 1980s.

Photographers found the gargantuan specimens irresistible, and TV producers were quick to spot the potential both of the vegetables themselves and the dedicated men – and one or two women – who grew them. The gardening expert Peter Seabrook brought some of the growers and their prize specimens together on the BBC's lunchtime programme *Pebble Mill*, and they appeared too on *Record Breakers*, the BBC children's programme hosted by Roy Castle, in which the twins Ross and Norris McWhirter, the original compilers of the *Guinness Book of Records* (now *Guinness World Records*), were also involved. Norris and Bernard Lavery became friends. Lavery helped draw up the rules for inclusion in the Guinness book and established several records himself. He would be invited to the book's annual launch and sometimes mounted a display of some of his most spectacular successes. He put on similar displays at flower and farm shows across the country, sponsored by a fertiliser manufacturer.

By now he was experimenting with almost any vegetable that seemed suitable for growing to an indecent size – among them carrots, parsnips, radishes, cucumbers, pumpkins and especially cabbages. In 1989, at the Alton Towers show, he broke the world cabbage record with a specimen that measured 12ft by 13ft and weighed 124 lb, a record that still stands – although he claims he grew a bigger one the same year that disintegrated before it could be weighed.

Lavery's fame grew. He made more television appearances, lent his name to a range of seeds and was invited to write regularly for national gardening magazines. His world records for Brussels sprouts, cauliflowers and courgettes also still stand, as do two for growing tall flowers: petunias and chrysanthemums. For three days in 1989 he held the world pumpkin record with a 710-lb specimen, until a Canadian produced one of 730 lb.

Pumpkins grow best in a warm, damp climate, which is why the British record is usually held by growers from south and south-west England. This points up the regional divide in the giant vegetable community. The leek and onion growers from the northeast have traditionally kept their distance from the arrivistes from further south. They do not like transporting their bulky treasures across the country and declined to compete at Lavery's shows and those that sprang from them, even though at Ashington they tolerate the occasional bold interloper from other parts.

Southerners seldom win at the northern leek and onion shows, because the few degrees difference in temperature means that by late September their largest specimens are beginning to run to seed: that is why the northern shows are held a crucial week or two later than most of those in the south. In addition, the rules for presentation at Ashington are different. At other shows onions have to be weighed without any leaf and a defined length of neck; at Ashington they must have greenery still attached, which prevents growers showing those that have won prizes in earlier competitions. Where the rules allow it, vegetables that do not wilt or rot quickly – such as pumpkins, carrots and parsnips, as well as onions – can pick up two or three prizes on successive weekends before they begin to show their age.

So there are two distinct persuasions, operating under separate codes, like rugby union and rugby league. In both cases, the top prizes are invariably shared between a small group of dedicated growers who devote a large part of their lives to their demanding hobby. And they have to be dedicated, because giant vegetables need much more regular attention than ordinary-sized ones. From the sowing of the first onion seeds in late October to the last of the shows almost a year later, there is no let-up. If growers want a holiday, they can take it safely only in the two or three weeks between the end of one season and the start of the next – and even that window dwindles, as pressure grows to get the seeds and the leek offsets into their growing medium ever earlier, to try to get them to put on those crucial extra ounces.

Nor is there any profit in it. Even if one supreme cultivator were to walk away with nearly all the top prizes over a season, he could not make a living from his prowess. The seeds and seedlings need to be kept at a temperature of at least 10°C until the summer, and require hours of extra lighting. The prize money – hardly ever more than three figures and often less – will scarcely pay the fuel bill for the heated greenhouse. Then there are the costs of the special fertilisers and composts and of transport to the shows: a truck may need hiring to carry the biggest specimens. Even this does not take into account the capital cost of the pots, barrels, piping, outhouses, cold frames, polytunnels and other structures required to create perfect growing conditions.

Acquiring the seed or plant is the initial seasonal outlay, and this too can prove expensive, because not any seed will do. World record weights and measurements have been rising steadily over the years because of selective breeding. The most likely way of producing a Derby winner is to breed from a stallion who has won the race himself. As Scott Robb, a leading American grower, put it to me: 'You're not going to get a thoroughbred racehorse by starting with a Shetland pony.' So if you can acquire seed from a 1,500-lb pumpkin, or an offset (known as a 'pip' or 'grass' among enthusiasts) from a prize-winning leek, you stand a chance of growing one as big and maybe even bigger.

Prize-winners, then, can charge exorbitantly for such desirable genetic material. Alternatively, if their priority is to keep winning, they might refuse to supply it at all; and even if they know its particular strain or variety they will not disclose the secret. This forces rivals to undertake their own intensive research and perhaps to acquire the seed from other parts of the world.

The compulsion to come out on top can lead to passionate disputes between competitors. There have been cases of potential prize-winning vegetables being vandalised a few days before the show – although not as many as legend would have it, and it is seldom clear whether the culprits are rival growers or simply local mischief-makers who happened to hit on the critical garden or allotment. And bitterness can creep in even at a lower level than the national and international championships.

For some thirty years the neighbouring Hampshire villages of Milford-on-Sea and Everton held an annual pumpkin-growing competition, with proceeds going to charity. In 2005 Ian Paton, the proprietor of a local nursery, won for Milford with an 819-lb specimen, grown under cover. (He has since exceeded that with a pumpkin weighing over 1,000 lb.) Everton gardeners alleged that this was against the rules, and that all the pumpkins should have been grown outdoors. They claimed that Paton had further defied convention by using a variety known as Atlantic Giant, instead of the traditional but less gigantic Hundredweight. As a result of these irreconcilable differences the contest has been abandoned.

Many mainstream gardeners will try to grow just one or two supersized specimens of, say, a parsnip or a marrow, and enter them for their local shows. But the real stars of the giant vegetable fancy, the men and women who take most of the prizes at the national contests, number no more than a dozen or two and are scattered across the country, often in small local clusters. The strong group around Newport in South Wales includes Ian Neale and the Fortey brothers, Kevin and Gareth, who inherited the giant vegetable passion from their father and have started a website devoted to it. Near Newark in Nottinghamshire Peter Glazebrook, a retired surveyor for the county council, grows an immense quantity of outsize produce. Not far away lives Alfred Cobb, a spry 91-year-old, who has the world record for the heaviest cucumber (27 lb 5 oz) and in 2007 added the longest cucumber to his list of triumphs. Joe Atherton, who lives a few miles away near Mansfield, also competes vigorously and successfully, and usually travels to the shows with Peter, sometimes sharing the cost of transporting their exhibits.

At the other side of the country, Mark Baggs from Wareham in Dorset has, at 23, grown the world's biggest marrow, helped by his father Frank. Further north, Richard Hope from Wigan is king of the swedes and pumpkins, as well as holding the world record for the longest beetroot and parsnip. Four growers from Yorkshire – Jack Newbould, Vin Throup and Barbara and Michael Cook – vie with each other and with Peter to produce the biggest onions. For eleven years, between 1994 and 2005, that record was held by Mel Ednie from Anstruther in Fife, with a 15-lb 15-oz monster, until the late John Sifford of Halesowen grew one that weighed half a pound more.

Gerald Treweek from Chesterfield in Derbyshire is experimenting with growing onions in a sophisticated and expensive hydroponics system, in which the roots are suspended in water and absorb a fixed amount of nutrients when they need it. Trying it out for the first time in 2006 he encountered teething problems and achieved only an 11-lb onion, but he would try again in 2007 and was confident that he would beat the record before long. Most growers, though, stick to the traditional media of soil or soil-less compost.

All these dedicated people will feature in the following pages, but I shall devote most of my attention to just five of them (four, if you count the Forteys as a single unit). These are the men whose progress I monitored over the 2007 growing season, from the time of sowing the first seeds to their autumn triumphs and disasters at the big shows.

Approaching Peter and Mary Glazebrook's house in Halam, a scattered village near the small Nottinghamshire town of Southwell, the first thing you notice is the impressive 15-ft yew topiary, clipped to represent a peacock, that stands near the house at the end of the short drive. The second thing you notice is that, apart from two small, haphazardly planted flower borders, the peacock is the only decorative element in the half-acre garden. There is little else except structures: two glasshouses, seven polytunnels, a barn, two sheds, stacks of long pipes and, at the front, where the lawn used to be, a freshly dug raised bed for vegetables.

This is because, unlike most gardens, its principal function is neither to please the eye nor captivate the senses. Peter, a tall, lean and quietly spoken man in his sixties, dedicates much of his life to an aspect of horticulture that takes no account of beauty. He grows and shows the biggest and best vegetables he can, and has held four world records. Every part of his garden is given over to buildings and equipment that will help him produce these gigantic – some say gross – specimens.

He has lived in this comfortable red brick house all his life. His father worked here as a market gardener; so growing vegetables is in Peter's blood. He also benefited from a more tangible inheritance: a large brick-based greenhouse where he nurtures many prize-winning specimens. Until 2004 he was a buildings surveyor for Nottinghamshire County Council and devoted nearly all his spare time to gardening, concentrating on vegetables and, initially, dahlias. He began entering the flower and vegetable show in Southwell in the early 1980s, showing quality, standard-sized vegetables, and from the start his dedicated approach ensured that he figured prominently on the list of award winners. After scooping the overall trophy for the most points in vegetable classes for three years running he stopped entering that show and set his sights on the more important – and more competitive – regional and national contests.

His first serious foray into the giant-vegetable arena was at the Liverpool Garden Festival in 1984, when he did well in the competitions for the heaviest cabbage, swede and beetroot. That encouraged him to enter the Alton Towers and Spalding giant vegetable shows. There were usually about sixteen classes and he would try to compete in all of them, although he was never as successful there as he would have liked, or as he would become later. Those were the days when Bernard Lavery dominated the field and Peter, along with several other contestants, suspected that the competition categories were devised to concentrate on the vegetables that Lavery grew biggest and best.

In the early 1990s Peter gave up showing flowers so that he could throw himself more and more energetically into vegetables. He has never devoted himself entirely to growing for size and bulk, and continues to compete successfully in classes where quality is the criterion, although over the years the giants have come to dominate his repertoire. In one of his sheds is a stack of engraved silver cups and glass bowls awarded for his collections of vegetables at major shows, and a few of the most treasured are displayed in his living room. Yet when he shows you the four certificates he has received from *Guinness World Records*, for growing the longest or heaviest of a particular kind of vegetable, you sense it is the giants that get his juices running.

'I found that it was something I enjoyed doing,' he explained.

When I started growing vegetables for quality I found I could grow them bigger than most of the others at the show. I have the right conditions – the garden faces south – and I have the space, so we've got a lot going for us. It was something I found I could do and something I could win with.

Winning is very important to me. If I was coming fourth every year I'd give it up and do something different. I'm in it to win. If I get beaten I want to find out how the winner did it and how I can do it better next year. I don't do it for the money: I do well but I don't cover my costs, with electricity the price it is. But I

don't go to the pub and I don't drink. This is what I spend my
money on.

Some of his victories have been especially sweet. At the 2006
Dewsbury Onion Fair he was beaten fair and square in the class for
the single heaviest onion. But there was also a class for the
cumulative weight of three onions and in this he beat the individual
winner, Jack Newbould from Leeds, by less than two ounces.

'Jack was furious,' Peter chortled. 'He asked for the onions to
be reweighed three times, but I still won.' The rancour generated
by the incident has persisted, as I would discover later in the year.
It was, though, a good illustration of one of the tenets of successful
showing: it is important not to let your rivals know in advance the
size or weight of your best specimens. 'You have to be a bit quiet
about what you've got,' Peter confided. 'But of course you don't
really know what you've got, and how it compares with the others,
until you get there.'

Yet that particular grudge match is not typical in the world of
giant vegetables, where camaraderie is far more evident than fierce
rivalry. Because the number of enthusiasts is fairly small, they know
and respect each other. For instance, I mentioned to Peter that I
had been in touch with Richard Hope of Wigan, a former holder of
the long beetroot record, who told me that he might not be
competing this year because of a back and shoulder injury. 'That
would be a shame,' Peter responded immediately. 'He's been so
keen over the years – been doing it as long as I have.'

Sometimes when Peter gets beaten he has nobody to blame but
himself. He is still feeling the pain from a couple of years back when
his biggest onion was disqualified from the Harrogate show
because it was not sound: it had ripened too early and begun to go
soft. The rules state that the winners have to be in perfect condition, even in classes where weight is the deciding factor. Had he
shown instead a slightly smaller onion, but in acceptable condition,

he might have come out on top. Size matters; but getting the strategy right is almost as important.

In the 2007 edition of *Guinness World Records* was a picture of Ian Neale holding above his head the 51-lb 9-oz beetroot he grew in 2001, which has only recently been exceeded. Nobody would call it a pretty sight. 'Never mind how ugly it looks,' said Ian, 'so long as it's heavy.'

He owns a small and scarcely thriving plant nursery at Langstone, a village close to Newport in south Wales. From the picture window of his living room, in the house that he shares with his sisters, he looked out in early January over the large greenhouse and extensive polytunnels where he raises his monster produce alongside the conventional garden plants that he grows for sale. He revealed that his passion for giant vegetables first took hold in the early 1980s when he entered a charity contest in the nearby village of Llanwern to find the area's heaviest onion. (A local girl needed an operation on her eyes that could be carried out only in Russia, and the money from the show helped pay her way there.) Ian came close to winning: 'I grew the biggest one but it wasn't the heaviest,' he recalled. 'A friend of mine won it: his onion wasn't as big as mine but it was firmer, so it weighed more.'

Soon afterwards he entered the newly established Welsh Pumpkin Championship and graduated from there to the national shows that Bernard Lavery was organising at Alton Towers and Spalding.

Although I was a professional grower they asked me to come in because starting the new shows they didn't know how many exhibitors were going to turn up. That was why I did it. And I kept on because I like seeing the stuff grow.

He made friends with Mike Fortey, the initiator of the Cwmbran pumpkin show, and together they plotted how to grow ever larger onions, leeks, pumpkins, marrows and beetroot. To avoid duplication of effort, they would share the initial task of sowing and raising the seedlings and divide them later in the summer so that they would both be able to enter the maximum number of classes. Mike died from a heart attack in 1996, aged only 53, but his sons Gareth and Kevin are today rising stars in the giant vegetable firmament, and they continue to collaborate with Ian. 'I generally start the root vegetables off and they start off the melons and cucumbers,' he explained, but stressed: 'We only help each other by growing the seed. Once we've got the plants we're competitors.'

To succeed with giant vegetables you need to be dedicated and focused. Ian gets up at six every morning so that he can do what needs to be done to them before he starts work on the plants grown for the nursery. When the national show was held near Spalding, Ian used to leave home with his exhibits at 1.30 a.m. on the day they had to be staged. But being competitive does not rule out offering a helping hand to others: most gardeners are good-natured, and for some years Ken Dade, a leading grower from Norfolk, has stayed with Ian during the Shepton Mallet show. 'He brings his stuff in a trailer and comes to stay at my place on the Thursday night. We drive there in his car on the Friday and he follows me in his car on the Sunday, when the vegetables are cleared away.'

Like Bernard Lavery, Ian is convinced that the basic secret of success is to get the right seed. 'Until you can get hold of the proper seed it isn't worth doing,' he declared. 'Some people will give you seed from their prize-winners but some won't. Then you have to track down where they got it from in the first place.'

His beetroot odyssey began in 1992, when the world record was a mere 34 lb. He grew one to 37 lb 8 oz, but was beaten at a Spalding show by a 38-pounder. Then Mike Fortey suggested a better way of producing seed, by taking cuttings from the green stems of the beetroots, rather than letting them run to seed in the normal way. One of these cuttings survived to produce its own seed, and this allowed Ian to break the 40-lb barrier by 1994, gaining the world record. By taking more stem cuttings he increased the weight year by year until achieving the world record in 2001. And where is that champion beetroot now? Any root vegetable of that size would almost certainly be too fibrous to make good eating. 'I gave it to the farmer down the road to feed to his cows.'

He carried on trying to better that record while continuing to grow and show his other giant vegetables: unlike some of the other enthusiasts he never competes in quality classes. 'With the heavy stuff you can't go against the scales,' he pointed out, 'whether the judges like the look of it or not.' He holds the British record for a water melon – 162 lb 5 oz – and says he has grown a 13-lb 8-oz parsnip (3 lb heavier than the world record, set in 1980, that would only be beaten in 2007), but he did not enter it for competition, so it was not officially recorded. For the last few years he has been trying to break the swede record of 75 lb 12 oz, held by an American, but has not yet succeeded. He does not grow leeks or onions, which meant that his season would not start until after my New Year visit. The first seeds to be sown are celery, in mid-January.

Hitherto he had raised all his produce in the soil, in polytunnels. For 2007, though, he was planning to experiment for the first time with compost-filled barrels, in an attempt to beat the record for the heaviest radish – currently 68 lb 9 oz, achieved by a Japanese grower. He hoped to get sponsorship from a fertiliser company. Now he was approaching retirement age he wanted to sell his nursery to a property developer and use the money to buy a house of his own, with a large garden where he could devote himself full-time to his hobby and break even more records. 'I do get annoyed when somebody beats me,' he said. 'But a friend once said to me:

"Don't get annoyed – go out and beat somebody else." So that's how I look at it now.'

Gareth Fortey, who is 26, lives with his mother in the roomy suburban house in the post-war 'new town' of Cwmbran, a few miles from Newport, where he and his elder brother Kevin grew up and where their father Mike raised prize-winning giant vegetables in the sizeable garden at the back. Mike had always been a keen gardener and in the early years of his marriage had an allotment at Caerleon, site of an ancient Roman barracks and amphitheatre. Kevin first became interested in his father's hobby when he was taken to the allotment to help out. He remains more knowledgeable than Gareth – who is, however, commendably eager to learn.

When Mike died so young the two boys, both teenagers, decided to carry on with the giant vegetables, partly as a way of keeping his memory alive. They continued his complementary seed-sowing arrangement with Ian Neale and plunged in with gusto, despite the fact that they both have demanding full-time jobs – Kevin is a housing officer for Caerphilly Council, and the more earnest Gareth a solicitor in Bristol – as well as other time-consuming hobbies such as golf, football and mountain biking.

At the end of 2005 they launched a website, *giantveg.co.uk*, where they give tips on growing and showing, list the current world records and are trying to create a community of people who share their enthusiasm, encouraging them to write diaries documenting their season's efforts. There are many pictures of their own prize-winning vegetables, including a 34in cucumber that briefly held the world record. They are trying to establish an authoritative list of British as well as world records. Through the site they have made contact with growers in the United States and Canada.

Kevin now lives with his partner Sarah, a teacher, and their baby a few doors down the road; but when he has finished helping with the baby he spends many of his leisure hours in the garden of the old family house. The brothers acknowledge their debt to their father and are proud to show his trophies and certificates and press cuttings about his triumphs. 'We used to go to the shows with Dad and help him out,' Gareth recalled when I first visited him over the winter.

He taught us a lot about it. Kevin took more interest in the growing side and has more technical knowledge. I was happy to help with the watering and the practical jobs. Kevin's more technically minded and knows more about different types of flowers and where they should be grown and all that. I'm not as knowledgeable but nowadays where giant veg are concerned we both do everything.

Says Kevin: 'I learned it all from Dad. I used to like working with him in the garden and learned a lot of his skills. We continued, and did really well in the shows.' In 2006, for instance, they broke the British record with a 25-lb cantaloupe melon – though that's a long way short of the 64-lb 13-oz world record held by Scott Robb from Alaska. In the same year they invested in the large polytunnel, with controllable ventilation, that now dominates the garden. They grow everything under cover – in their two heated greenhouses or in polytunnels – except marrows, which do well outdoors. Their radishes and potatoes are raised in barrels filled with compost.

Although rather more than half the garden is taken up with the structures and outdoor beds, there is still space to expand if they want to dig up the lawn. 'Dad grassed it over when we were children so we would have somewhere to play,' Gareth recalled. 'We might dig it up if we need more space.' As well as competing in giant categories the brothers used to enter the quality classes in shows; for example the three best long carrots or three best parsnips.

> At the end of the day they're different skills . . . . We stopped doing it because we don't have the time really, with both of us working. It takes more time than giant veg, and we both have our other interests as well. Some of the other growers spend all their time on growing the vegetables.

Gerald Treweek, a retired coal miner, would devote 2007 to his attempt to grow the world's largest onion by beating John Sifford's 16 lb 8 oz, achieved in 2005. The ace up his sleeve was that he planned to do it hydroponically, by letting the roots trail in water regularly fed with nutrient. He first tried this method in 2006 after visiting a company named Aquaculture in Sheffield; he had heard that they sold a powerful mix of nutrients that night improve his show onions, then grown in soil in the traditional way. The company's owner Simon Spinks showed him their hydroponics equipment and wondered whether he would agree to try the method for growing giant onions; it had previously been used for other vegetables, especially tomatoes and lettuce, and is said to be favoured by cannabis-growers. Gerald did not think it had been tried for onions, although a grower that I met later in the year told me that he had experimented with the system a few years back.

Gerald's first year with hydroponics had been a disappointment. Although his biggest onion grew to a decent size, it was some six pounds short of the record. He quickly identified what he thought was the problem. He had used peat as the growing medium, and it had absorbed the nutrient so comprehensively that not enough reached the onions' roots: in consequence, they started 'tipping' – turning brown at the tips of the leaves. For 2007 he was planning to replace the peat with rockwool, which he believed would drain better; and he was confident of success. 'If I put my heart and soul into it, I won't just break this world record, I'll smash it.' He is a stubborn man who relishes defying convention, and using such a controversial growing method only added spice to the project:

> I want to do something different, you see. A lot of people are a little bit scared of hydroponics. They think it's dreadful – and that's what I thought when I first started doing it. But it isn't. It's simple. I can control everything – the medium and the nutrient.

Gerald lives with his wife Doreen in a substantial detached house at Brimington, on the outskirts of Chesterfield, just five miles from where he was born. Their half-acre garden looks north-east towards the foothills of the Pennines. When they went to live there in 1980 a tennis court occupied a large part of the garden, but Gerald soon removed it to give more space for flowers. He also put in some conifer trees, for privacy, and bought a greenhouse, later adding polytunnels for his exhibition vegetables.

It was when he retired from mining in 1993, at the age of 50, that he took up vegetable gardening seriously. He does nothing by halves. 'Miners always grew vegetables,' he said. 'I went to one or two local shows and thought: I can compete. And I've excelled since 1998' – by which time he was regularly winning prizes at local and national shows. 'I haven't had a holiday since.' He hates the idea of getting stuck in a rut. He likes to complete a project, then quickly move on to the next challenge.

> Everything I've tried to do, I've always achieved it. I wanted to win celery at the National, I wanted to win parsnips at the National, and I did it. Now I want to grow world record onions. ... My main motivation is to win, but when I've won it takes the edge off it, because I've done it.

Gerald has a large collection of photographs recording his successes, and videos of his television appearances. He keeps his cups and trophies on the landing and his rosettes in a garden shed.

I won the national title for long leeks in 2002 – three white, blanched leeks – but then I stopped leeks because they were too much trouble. All I wanted to do was win the title and I won it, so I stopped. The same with celery: I won that in 2000, then I stopped. I won the class for quality long carrots four times at the National Vegetable Society show and three times at Harrogate. . . . It's the buzz of it, the buzz that drives you forward.

After a while, though, that buzz started to get a little less insistent. He decided he had gone as far as he could with quality vegetables and in 2006 he determined to add giants to his repertoire, specifically to beat the world record for the heaviest onion.

However, he was not going to let the onion project dominate his life totally. He was also initiating a vegetable garden for Hasland Infants' School, the local primary attended by his two grandsons. He had the idea when the younger one, four-year-old Kyle, watched him digging up potatoes from his garden and was amazed, because he did not know they came from the ground. So Gerald went to the school and suggested to the headmistress that he should start a vegetable garden and teach the children the basics of food production. She said it was a great plan if they could find the money. Gerald used his contacts to get sponsorship from a garden equipment company; a firm of scaffolders donated some planks; a local builder contributed sand; and the council gave a small grant. The garden was built in five weekends by youths on community service: 'When I told them what it was for, they got stuck in.' It was agreed that Gerald would grow the vegetable seedlings and go to the school every week to show the children how to plant and care for them.

He also roped in James Martin, the TV chef who appeared with Gerald – and some of the other growers featured here – on BBC1's series *The Great British Village Show*, made in 2006. Gerald had been a judge of the vegetable classes – it was where Peter Glazebrook broke the longest carrot record – and James had been one of the presenters, involved principally with the cakes and jams. Gerald told him about the school project and James agreed to come to Chesterfield at the end of the summer term and show the children and their parents how the food they grew could be cooked. So the quest for the world's largest onion was to be one of two challenges facing Gerald in 2007, both making heavy calls on his time and energy.

Chapter 3

Winter

Winter is traditionally for armchair gardening. It is the dormant season for conventional vegetable gardens and those who tend them. With the bean poles and pea netting dismantled, the asparagus fronds cut back and the last of the root crops lifted and stored, several months stretch ahead when there is little to do but leaf through the seed catalogues, prune the soft fruit and complete the winter digging when the weather allows. For those who raise giants, though, there is no such let-up. No sooner has the last colossal pumpkin been trundled back from the last of the specialised shows than it is time to start thinking about next season. And decisions taken now can be crucial to the prospects of garnering next year's glittering prizes.

Leeks and onions are the first categories to consider. The question of exactly when to start these closely related vegetables on their journey towards the show bench is a delicate one. Superficially, you would think that the earlier you get them going, the better their chance of reaching their maximum potential. But all living things have a natural life span. If they peak before show time they will be going to seed, maybe rotting, and certainly losing weight, by the time they enter the fray. And since the showing season spans six weeks, calculations have to be made about which of the shows should be the prime target.

The ideal solution would be to start the leeks and onions off over a period of weeks, so that some are certain to be ready at the right time. But that would require larger artificially heated and lit areas, and more space in the polytunnel, than most growers have at their disposal. You cannot even think of growing those vegetables to supersize without generous quantities of heat and light during the cold, dark months. This pastime is not for those who feel guilty about using the world's scarce energy resources – nor those who can't face a daunting electricity bill in the spring.

It was December when I paid my first visit to Peter Glazebrook in Halam, so there wasn't a great deal of vegetation to see. Our first call was at the heated section of his greenhouse: a small area just 8ft square, partitioned from the rest of the greenhouse so as to minimise the use of electricity. Here he had around a hundred leek seedlings, planted some three weeks earlier. He had harvested these from his largest leeks as 'grass' or 'pips' – the offsets that, with the proper treatment, can be induced to form on the seed head, between the stalks that carry the seeds themselves.

If the flowers from the seed heads are cut off as soon as they appear, each leek ought to produce about thirty pips in the autumn. They are in effect clones that, unlike seeds, will reproduce the exact qualities of the parent. So, by garnering them from the heaviest leeks it should be possible, given careful growing, to equal or even exceed the weight of the previous year's prize-winners.

The temperature was kept at 10°C and a powerful electric light thrown on the leeks for eight hours every day, to reinforce the unreliable winter daylight. In the three weeks before my visit they had grown to between three and four inches high. As they filled out they would be transferred to ever larger pots until, in April, the two dozen or so most promising would be planted out in a cold frame and the rest given away or discarded. The timings of the sowings are crucial, determined by the dates of the shows and by Peter's many years of experience. 'If you sow too soon they'll come too soon,' he said. Then they would run to seed before there was time to get them to the show bench.

In the greenhouse was a heated propagator where a few days earlier Peter had sown his onion seeds. Onions are even more demanding than leeks. After germination, which takes about three weeks, they need to be in full artificial light and heat twenty-four hours a day for six weeks until they, too, are ready to be put into large pots and eventually planted into plastic barrels acquired from local farmers or food packagers. The barrels, most of them bright blue, were stored in one of his polytunnels, ready to be filled in late spring with the special composts Peter uses to grow onions, parsnips and other vegetables.

In his tallest barn we climbed steep steps to the space under the roof where he kept a dozen or so onions, roughly the size of bowling balls, some beginning to sprout at the top. These he would use for seed for the next crop but one. In a few weeks he would put them into large pots of compost, then in April plant them in the greenhouse, where they would flower in July and in August set seed that he would sow the following December. To be a successful grower you must plan many months ahead and, above all, you need infinite reserves of patience.

Finally we came to the current stars of his stable, the long carrots. Earlier his wife Mary, a farmer's daughter, had shown me what remained of the world-beating specimen that had once measured 17ft 3in. Allowed to dry out in the two months since it won the prize, it had shrunk spectacularly until it was only about a foot long from its shrivelled brown top to the end of its straggly root. Giant vegetables lose weight and volume extremely fast once they are deprived of water and nutrition, and this adds to the practical difficulties of getting them to the show bench at maximum size and optimum condition.

The most important pieces of equipment for growing long carrots are lengths of plastic drainpipe split from one end to the other. Some of these were leaning against the outside wall of Peter's tallest barn, others were supported on racks he had built inside a shed. They were empty, because carrot seed is not sown until the spring. The pipes are first packed with compost, then reassembled and the seed placed at the top end. As the carrots develop Peter monitors their progress and waters the compost through breaks in the pipe at regular intervals. Somewhat to his surprise, his world-beater was one of those raised outside by the barn, not in the shed.

The exact length of the carrot, and whether or not it is a contender for a prize, cannot be known for certain until it is removed from the pipe – a delicate process performed by unsealing the lengthwise joints that he made when he split it. After the first couple of inches, the carrot consists of no more than an elongated root, scarcely thicker than string. It is dangerously fragile: the end can easily snap off in one incautious movement, as happened at a crucial stage a few months earlier to Peter's friend and rival Joe Atherton. Opening up the pipe marks the peak of anticipation, but also the moment for steeling oneself against possible severe disappointment.

'In a bad year you can get nothing,' Peter observes ruefully. 'All in all it's a lot of hard work, and you've got to like it or you don't do it. There's no let-up at any time of the year.' As in other branches of horticulture, pessimism is a necessary defence mechanism against failure.

As spring approaches the pace of the work increases, and when I went back to Halam at the beginning of February there were already signs of substantial progress, at a time when ordinary gardeners like me had hardly started to think about the season's sowings. A few days earlier Peter had sown some beetroot in the heated propagator, although the seeds had not yet germinated. That morning he had been putting some of the leeks in larger pots.

To accommodate them, as well as the burgeoning onions, he took the partition out of his heated greenhouse, doubling the size of the heated area – and the heating cost.

He was spending more on lighting this year, too, with two lamps instead of one, switched on for around ten hours, mainly during the day, to bolster the pale natural light of winter. Every week he increased the lighting period by a quarter of an hour until he reached twelve hours.

> Sometimes I've given my long leeks twenty-four hours of light, but I haven't done that with any of them this year, because last year they were ready too early. They were peaking in August, and come September they were getting past it, so I decided I wouldn't give them twenty-four hours any more. They seem to be doing well enough without.

Every season he adjusts his techniques, even if only marginally, to try to achieve those crucial extra ounces.

Some of his onions were grown from seed and others from bulbils – miniature onion bulbs that are formed near the base of the plant. These are less reliable than the pips from leeks. 'I'm a bit dubious about the bulbils, really. There's always a danger of them running to seed.' He kept track of which was which by putting different coloured labels in the pots. Those from bulbils had brown labels. Yellow denoted the first sowings from seed, while those with green and purple labels were sown later, all from the largest onions that he grew the previous year. Those with red labels were sown from newly acquired Lamb's seed – a strain developed by the north-eastern grower Billy Lamb and a favourite with heavy onion growers.

I asked Peter what variety they were, but I soon learned that this is not a very useful question to address to giant vegetable growers. They are not interested in varieties, just results. Their aim is to acquire seed from vegetables that have proved their prowess in the previous season, whether their own or other people's. They do not generally ask questions about pedigree, although the word on the show bench is that Lamb's powerful seed could be a cross between a Kelsae – the most widely grown heavy onion – and an unusually bulky specimen of indeterminate variety, originating somewhere in Wales. (Later in the year I had the opportunity of asking Billy himself where the seed came from . . . but I ended up none the wiser.)

Peter initially gives 24-hour lighting to his onions grown from seed, but not those from bulbils. He has thought carefully about this, trying to work out how best to come to terms with their natural growth cycle while at the same time tricking them into developing faster and bigger than they would without his intervention.

Ideally the seeds should have 24-hour lighting from the day they germinate, so that when the first six weeks have gone by with constant light, they think it's all the one day. After that six weeks, when you take them off the twenty-four-hour light, it's the first night they will have recognised. But with the bulbils and the leek pips, they're little plants that have already lived through some nights, and I think twenty-four-hour light might make them run to seed. Anyway, you've got to try these things.

The ten leeks that he was growing for size and weight, as opposed to those destined for the quality classes, were clearly bigger than the others already, and had been moved into larger pots. The long exhibition leeks had been fitted with white tubes to ensure that they grew straight, all neatly regimented in their pots, while the onions had their foliage supported on spiral cages supported by canes.

He had sown his giant cabbages in early December and they appeared to be thriving as seedlings.

I don't always do very well with cabbages, although I won with one at Malvern. Before, I've sown them in October and let them grow a little before the winter. This year I sowed them at the same time as the onions and gave them twenty-four-hour lighting. Then I brought them into the unheated greenhouse . . . . Timing is the big problem. Sometimes they don't heart up, and just run to seed. You think as they're growing that they're bound to heart up, but they don't always.

Again, he could not tell me what variety of cabbage it was.

The seed was given me by a Cornish grower who won a giant competition. That's how it goes with giant vegetables – the seed gets passed on and its origin is lost. There are varieties you can buy, like Alaska Giant and Brunswick. They're decent, but these are better – at least they're better when they're grown in Cornwall. I'm growing ten, but five are for someone else. Eventually I'll plant the other five out in the garden.

Timing is something that Peter and his fellow growers spend a lot of time thinking about:

I worry about the late spring we had last year. It was too cold to plant anything out, so I had to keep them hanging about. I feel it's better if you keep things moving after you've started them off, so I haven't rushed this year. I'll probably start my carrots next week. I'm bothered that if I start them too soon the roots will start to touch the sides of the pots before they're planted out and you don't want that – you want to be able to get them into the bed before that happens, if you can.

In readiness for sowing the heavy carrots and parsnips he had prepared some ingenious receptacles, turning ordinary plastic flower pots upside down and cutting a large triangular hole in the base. Keeping the pots inverted, he stood them on trays, filled them with compost and sowed the seed within the triangle. When they were ready to be transferred into the barrels, where they would grow on to full size, he would simply lift the pots off without disturbing the roots and checking growth.

In most years giant squashes are the biggest vegetables Peter grows. They can get almost as large as pumpkins, their close relatives (the technical difference is that pumpkins have orange or yellow skins while squashes are green or grey). Hitherto he hadn't felt he had either the growing space or the transport capacity to grow both squashes and pumpkins, and, given the popularity and totemic nature of pumpkins, he finds the competition in the squash classes a little less fierce. However, he is always seeking to broaden his portfolio, and said he might try a pumpkin or two this year.

He had already started some of the squashes when I visited him, but these were not the ones he would be showing: he was simply running a test to see whether the seed, derived from two monsters that he grew in 2005, was still viable. Those from the bigger of the two had not germinated, but seeds from the smaller one had, and he planned to sow some in a few weeks' time to be ready for the September shows.

A lot of the best squash seeds originate in America, and the same goes for swedes. Peter had been trying to get some swede seed from an Alaskan grower but with no luck so far. 'I put some seeds in today but they aren't the right variety. They're just ordinary ones for eating, and I hope I'll be able to get some better seed later on.'

He had also sown some giant celery that day but was going to leave the main sowing of quality celery until a little later, although it was the same variety.

I have trouble germinating celery so we'll have to see what we get. Maybe I'll keep the two tallest for giant and see if the rest are good enough for quality, and if they are I'll put tubes over them to blanch them. You don't have to blanch the giants – they just have to be heavy.

Nor do they need to be perfect specimens, which means that growers can feed them with as much fertiliser as they like. Too much can induce heart-rot, which would disqualify celery from quality classes but is permissible to a limited extent in the giants.

As I was leaving, I asked Peter what had become of the shrunken world record carrot that Mary had shown me on my December visit. 'We got rid of it at Christmas,' he replied. 'Put it in the compost.' There is no room for sentiment in this business: but at least he had the coveted Guinness certificate to keep the memory of his triumph alive.

It takes about an hour to drive from Peter's house at Halam to Gerald Treweek's in Brimington, a mile or two outside Chesterfield. Gerald, a perfectionist, approached his world record bid with the precision of a brain surgeon. To succeed using his hydroponic method you need to combine the analytical skills of a scientist with a gardener's instinct for how plants grow and need to be nurtured. Gerald appears to have just this balance of practical know-how and intuition, which makes me believe his ambitious project has a chance of success.

He sowed the first seeds of his onions on 1 December in blocks of rockwool – an artificial, mineral-based growing medium widely used in hydroponic systems. A few weeks later he planted the bulbils. His aim was to grow three of each, in two separate tanks, and take the best of them to the Harrogate heavy onion championship in September, with the second best destined for the leek and onion show in Ashington a week later. 'You can't use the same onion for both,' he reminded me. 'At Harrogate you take the roots and leaves off but at Ashington you leave them on. So you've got to have two good onions to compete at both.'

The system he was using is known as 'flood and drain'. The onions were flooded regularly with water enriched with nutrient, then allowed to drain and dry out, allowing oxygen to reach the roots. After sowing he gave them twenty-four hours of light for six weeks, then reduced it to twelve hours, mainly supplementing daylight.

> If you give them too much light they'll bulb too soon, before they've thrown out enough leaves. You're actually tricking the plant with the twenty-four-hour light, so it will grow more foliage. It shouldn't start to bulb until mid-May and you want at least twenty-one leaves on it by then. I'm on schedule for that: I've got eleven and the twelfth is poking through, and it should put on one leaf every week.

To beat the world record of 16 lb 8 oz he would need to grow an onion with a circumference of some 36 inches.

> Peter [Glazebrook] had one last year of over 13 lb but I don't know how he can improve on that with the method he uses. He broke the world record in 1991 with 10 lb, and then again with one that weighed 12 lb. I think I can do better than him because with this method I can control the nutrients.

Like Peter, he supported the floppy leaves in an unsightly but effective structure of wires, sticks and string. 'Once they start to stand up the leaves will stiffen and I'll take the support away.' The rockwool blocks sat on wire mesh above a three-inch layer of clay balls inside the two six-inch deep tanks supplied by Aquaculture.

> The root comes out at the bottom of the block and finds it has nowhere to go, so it forks inside the block. The more roots it

forks into the better, because it makes for a stronger plant. So I pump water to the base of the blocks once a day, to tease the roots out of the system.

In one of the tanks he had added to the clay balls a product called Diahydro, made from dead plankton found on the coast of Australia. Once the roots hit the sides and bottom of the tank he started pumping three times a day for about two minutes at six-hour intervals, with nutrients contained in the water. The bed would flood, but after another two minutes would be virtually empty, although enough moisture and nutrient had soaked into the clay balls to sustain the onions until the next pumping.

The composition of the nutrient is a matter of great importance. Gerald had taken the advice of Aquaculture's Simon Spinks on the balance of nitrogen, phosphates and potash, but even at that early stage he wasn't convinced it was quite right. He had a meter to monitor the strength of the solution and could adjust it if it fell above or below the desired level. If it were too strong it could cause the leaves to go brown at the ends.

A heater ensured that the water stayed at a constant temperature of 21°C. He also had a humidifier.

All plants perspire, which means they have to take more water in to compensate. But again, if they take up too much moisture you get tipping on the leaves. The hardest thing is to keep them cool in summer. The ideal temperature is 21° but if it's hotter outside it will be hotter inside too.

If it's really hot they perspire more, so I put the humidity up, but that means they don't take up any moisture through the roots, so they don't get the feed. I don't quite know how I'll get around that. I can put some shading on, but if it gets up to 30° outside it will still be hot inside, and I really need some kind of cooling system.

To install air-conditioning in the greenhouse would increase the cost of an already expensive pursuit, even though the tank, the humidifier, the nutrients and an auto-timer for the pump, worth several hundred pounds, had been given or lent to him free of charge. He had to pay for the electricity and for the solid fuel to heat the greenhouse in winter, which cost several hundred pounds a year – and he would shortly need a new boiler, as well as a new greenhouse door.

He led me on a tour of the garden to show me the preparations for the quality vegetables he would be growing during the year. He had forty-five blue barrels to be used for leeks and root crops. The rhubarb was already looking good, and he was about to plant shallots and garlic. Surprisingly, he let slip that, despite all his artificial aids to perfection and the highly technical nature of his hydroponic system, there was a part of him that yearned to revert to earlier, simpler forms of vegetable growing, as practised in the great houses in the nineteenth century. 'It's always been my dream to have a walled garden to grow vegetables for the house.'

Soon, though, he reverted to the more down-to-earth business of growing for the shows. 'The next time you come all the beds will be ready in the polytunnels,' he assured me. That wouldn't be until April, but in mid-March I telephoned for a progress report. The giant onions were still on a record-breaking schedule, with the best of them sporting sixteen leaves. It was still early days, though.

In the Forteys' garden in Cwmbran in February we spotted a red admiral butterfly – proof of the mild winter South Wales had been enjoying so far. Kevin said it was a mixed blessing. 'It's good in saving heating costs but bad because diseases don't get killed off. And the ants live through it.' Whatever the weather, the dedicated gardener will always find something to complain about.

One of their two heated greenhouses was devoted to the giant vegetables, with tomatoes and cucumbers started in it already, and a few leeks, being grown on from pips, still looking spindly at this early stage. The brothers were expecting some leek seeds shortly from John Soulsby of Gateshead, a notable grower who won the heavy leek class in *The Great British Village Show*.

'He grows 20,000 leek pips,' Kevin assured me. 'It's best to have a whole leek bed but we don't have the space really. We'll only grow four or five.' Most of the other growers raise their leeks in barrels but the Forteys will have them in a bed in the new polytunnel. Their barrels will be for potatoes and radishes. 'Last year the radishes grew too quickly and only got to about 10 lb.'

Their own triumph at *The Great British Village Show* was with a 98-lb marrow: 'one of our own strain – we selected the seed.' At the regular shows they usually have to give best to Ian's friend Ken Dade, the acknowledged marrow king; but according to Kevin, nowadays he declines to appear on television. 'The thing that turned him off was when he took a giant marrow to *Blue Peter*, and in the end they didn't include him in the programme and didn't pay his expenses.'

Last year's biggest swedes and beetroot had been cut up to produce seed for next year, using the method pioneered by their father. 'The roots fork out and we take a bit from where the stalk joins the root,' Kevin explained. Already they were showing a healthy amount of leaf. Those not being grown on had been put into their large new compost area to rot down. 'You could eat them – they're quite sweet – but I wouldn't want to eat them now.'

It would be a few weeks before the pace began to hot up. 'The busiest times are March and April, when you're doing all the digging, and September, when you have the shows, and in between times you have to do a lot of watering,' said Gareth. 'When we first started we watered by hand, but now we have an automatic watering system . . . . We can get up in the morning, turn the tap on at ten, go and play golf for four hours, then come back and turn it off again.' Unlike some of the other growers, they insisted that their hobby had to fit in with other elements of their everyday life, not take it over completely.

They were making good use of this relatively slack period to improve their website. Through it they had made contact with Scott Robb of Alaska. Scott and his wife Mardie, whom I was to meet in Alaska later in the year, are recognised by *Guinness World Records* as the holders of five records for large vegetables, more than any other grower. Scott had been somewhat critical of the site's content, urging them to expand it with more technical tips and more news of fresh records. Gareth and Kevin accepted that an upgrade was called for; but it seemed unlikely that, with the time and resources at their disposal, they would be able to fulfil all of Scott's ambitions for it.

When I mentioned Scott Robb's name to Laura Hughes, who looks after giant fruit and vegetables for *Guinness World Records*, she responded immediately. 'Oh yes, he's one of our most consistent record-breakers. He takes it very seriously.' And she reeled off the list of the records he currently held: cantaloupe, celery, kohlrabi, swede and turnip.

The book, which automatically makes the best-seller lists as soon as it is published every September, is produced by a team of just thirty-five people in an anonymous, nondescript office in Drummond Street, near London's Euston Station – a street most notable for its array of Indian restaurants and spice shops, as well as a Chinese martial arts college. Inside, the office walls are adorned with often gruesome pictures of record holders, such as the world's hairiest man and the woman with the smallest waist, as well as a cabinet of curiosities containing such wonders as the world's smallest shoe.

Seven men and women divide the task of recording and validating the world of records, and giant vegetables are just one of Laura's responsibilities. In total, across all categories, Guinness gets about a thousand approaches a week from people who are planning to make a record attempt or think they might have already performed a feat worth including in the book. The initial approach has to be made via the book's website, and applicants who seem serious are sent a pack that includes the rigorous guidelines and rules for inclusion – rules so demanding that eighty per cent of applicants drop out at this point. Of those that persevere, only about half get to the stage of actually submitting their record for inclusion – and even then more are rejected than recognised, usually because they have failed to provide sufficient evidence to support their claim.

'A lot of people are put off when they see how demanding the guidelines are and when they look at the existing record,' said Laura. 'It's difficult – which is why a lot of the vegetable records are held by a small group of people, including Scott. Most of the people who get in are the professionals.'

There are some 40,000 records on the database. Each holder receives a certificate confirming the feat, but only between 5,000 and 6,000 every year are recorded in the book, which would otherwise be too bulky to fulfil its traditional role as a Christmas stocking-filler. That is why many records appear in the book only once every few years – but that does not mean that they are not still there to be broken. A fairly full list of heavy vegetables is published most years, but the records for length are included less often and more selectively.

The guidelines for the heavy and long vegetable categories were compiled some years ago with input from Bernard Lavery. They start off with a disclaimer: 'These guidelines in no way provide any kind of safety advice or can be construed as providing any comfort that the record is free from risk' – a defence, no doubt, against possible claims for backs being damaged in attempts to convey colossal pumpkins to the show bench. The first rule is that only fruit and vegetables grown primarily for human consumption can be considered for the record, with agricultural and fodder crops, such as sugar beet and mangolds, specifically excluded. This was to become the subject of some controversy over one record listed in the 2008 edition.

Priority is given to vegetables that have been measured or weighed at competitive shows, and those from Britain must be authenticated by qualified judges, as well as by two independent witnesses of some standing in the world of horticulture. 'It can't just be a neighbour or a friend,' said Laura. There are strict rules about the removal of foliage, roots and any dirt or stones before the weighing, which must be carried out on professional equipment. 'Weights registered on domestic kitchen or bathroom scales will not be accepted.' Finally: 'Measurement of length should be carried out by placing the specimen on a plain surface and by marking the exact position of each end . . . . A straight line should then be drawn between the two marks and this length measured exactly.'

Said Laura: 'We get a lot of suggestions for new categories, and we reject most of them. It's often suggested that we should have a record for the smallest vegetables, like the smallest cherry tomato. We don't do that because it doesn't take any skill to produce them small, but to grow the big ones is a real challenge.' Gerald, Peter, Ian, Kevin, Gareth and their fellow enthusiasts would go along with that. Growing a world champion is their principal motivation.

Chapter 4

April

For T.S. Eliot April may have been the cruellest month, but for giant vegetable growers it is the most optimistic. The leeks and onions have come through the winter, and most of the other crops have been or are about to be started into life. Any one of them could grow into a world-beater, warranting a mention in *Guinness World Records* and bestowing a kind of immortality on the dedicated man or woman who raises it. The inevitable cruel disappointments – disease, adverse weather or simple, unexplained failure – will not become evident until later in the season.

On a sunny morning early in the month I turned into Peter Glazebrook's driveway to find him at the top of a tall ladder leaning against the shed at the front of his garden. He was checking the long carrots and parsnips he had planted at the top of his 20-ft modified drainpipes about three weeks earlier. Peter is always experimenting, questioning, trying something new that might give his stuff the extra fillip needed to coax another inch or two on to the root, but he knew he had taken a risk here.

I started the seeds in the greenhouse in early March and transplanted them about four days later, as soon as they germinated. This is about a month earlier than last year. It should give them a better start – but, on the other hand, they might not like the colder weather. We're still getting frosts in spite of the sunshine, and the wind has been in the north. . . .

You have to transplant them just after germination, otherwise you might damage the roots. The carrots are probably about 12in long already under the casing – you can never tell – but they've only just got their first true leaves. You don't need to feed them, just give them a long enough growing season.

While with the long carrots the aim is to restrict growth to a single root, with carrots grown for their weight the opposite is true. The general rule is that the more the roots fork, the bulkier (and so heavier) the total carrot will be. They were in barrels in one of his seven polytunnels, their first thin leaves barely peeping above the compost. At that time there were three to a barrel but he would eventually cull the two weakest, leaving the whole barrel for the best one to expand in.

He made the barrels himself a few years ago, from Perspex sheets that he cut to size. They are covered with opaque polythene to keep the compost warm in cold weather and cool at the height of summer. This shows his attention to detail: the polythene is black on one side and white on the other, and at the time he had the black side facing outwards to keep the barrels as warm as possible. 'Later on I'll turn it round and put the white on the outside – a fiddly job but I think it's worth it.'

Decisions on timing are some of the most critical and difficult that growers have to face. Besides worrying about the frost getting to the long carrots, Peter was a little concerned that he might have put his cabbages out too soon, in mid-March. 'They're hardy but they won't put on growth in the cold weather. I thought they needed to go out because they were getting too big for their pots, and I thought they might spoil.'

In the greenhouse he had started some beetroot and had one of last year's radishes growing on for seed. He also had some heavy potatoes sprouting. Before planting them he would take off all the eyes except one, and later take off the shoots and plant those individually. The aim is to get only one or two potatoes on each plant, so that all its strength goes into a single tuber. After he plants them and they start producing tubers he will feel around the roots and take off any that he thinks are surplus to requirements, leaving just one or two. This is a fiddly job but his results seem to confirm its effectiveness: the heavy potato is a class he usually wins.

He had made the first sowing of tomatoes, just starting to show themselves above the compost.

The next thing to sow will be the cucumbers, then I'll start the marrows and squashes in about a month's time. And I want to get some heavy swedes away. I haven't done any for a number of years. I'll try two or three in a tunnel and the rest in the open. I haven't been very good at growing swedes so far, and I'm not sure I have the right seed. It's seed I've begged and borrowed, and I don't know if it's any good.

Peter's quality long leeks, about fifty of them in smart white collars, were still in the greenhouse, along with his pot leeks, but he would soon be selecting the most promising to put out into tunnels. The heavy leeks would go in the bed in front of the house, where he would give them protection. The previous night he had taken one of the pot leeks to a show organised by his local gardening club specifically for leeks at this early stage of their development. He did not win anything, but his friend Joe Atherton – whom I had arranged to visit later in the day – came second.

Joe is a better leek grower than me. He puts more effort into them. He heats his greenhouse to a higher level than I do, and he has hot water pipes around the walls and benches that provide constant heat. My heating only comes on when it's cold, then it goes off again. He also gives them more artificial light. I turned my lights off yesterday – I do it roughly when the days get to be as long as the nights. I think you have to wean them off the lights as soon as you can. I never give them more than twelve hours, but I think others do.

His heavy onions had been in their barrels for some three weeks already and appeared to be bulking up steadily, although the best had only ten leaves so far: Gerald Treweek, whom I would also be seeing later in the day, has told me his best has eighteen. 'I won't catch Gerald up, and he should get a bigger onion than mine,' Peter conceded. 'But I'm still not sure about his system. Mine are bigger than they were this time last year, and I'm quite happy with them for the time of year. They'll be all right unless they get some soil-borne disease – that's the only thing that can knock me back now.'

The sunny weather was forecast to last for a few more days, although the clear nights would bring the risk of frost. Long-range forecasts suggested that the summer would be warm, like in 2006, and Peter was not too pleased at the prospect.

You can cope with most weather conditions, but the worst is when it gets too hot for too long in the summer. Last year we had a very hot and dry July, but in August it got cloudy and cooler, and that saved things. If it had stayed hot in August the onions would have stopped growing. It's easier to heat than to cool.

As it turned out, though, neither he nor any of his rivals had any need to fear another hot summer.

The drive west from Halam takes you through a pleasant open landscape, past the northern edge of Sherwood Forest and then into the less appealing outskirts of Mansfield, a former mining town. I telephoned Joe Atherton just before leaving Peter's, and, because his house was hard to find, we met at Ma Hubbard's, a roadside restaurant in Mansfield Woodhouse. From there we drove in procession the few hundred yards to his house, across the road from what used to be Sherwood Colliery, where he worked underground until it closed in 1992. Today it is a housing estate.

Since 2000 Joe, a small, wiry man, had worked mornings only at a plant nursery outside Chesterfield. That gave him the afternoons to indulge his passion for growing giant vegetables, which first seized him some twenty years ago. Before that he mainly grew and showed quality leeks – up to a hundred every year. He gradually switched to giants and won his first prize, for the heaviest leek, at one of Bernard Lavery's shows in Spalding. Since then he has always been among the leading growers, as his impressive display of cups, shields and rosettes testifies.

His garden is at the front of the house. At about 130ft by 50ft it is a lot smaller than Peter's and, if anything, even more industrial-looking, with its greenhouse, polytunnels and eight long pipes for teasing out the string-like roots of carrots, beetroot and parsnips. Like many of his fellow growers, Joe is a dab hand at do-it-yourself and most of the structures are home-built.

Closer examination revealed that he was not growing his long stuff in drainpipes but in lengths of guttering, open at the front. The advantage was that he avoided Peter's problem of having to fill them with compost from the top and not knowing for certain whether it had completely filled the tube: he packs the compost in from the front. And, as he has no really tall buildings in his garden, he keeps the guttering at an angle of 45 degrees, less steep than Peter favours. This means he does not have to climb so high to water them.

'My carrots are more advanced than Peter's because I put them in earlier,' he told me. 'Of course if you do it too early there's a danger of them running to seed, but it's a chance you've got to take: you've got to be willing to take risks. I usually do well with carrots – the long ones, and the heavy ones too.'

With most of the other vegetables he was broadly in line with Peter's schedule. The tomato seeds had been sown a few days earlier, and he was about to take the leeks out from the tunnel and plant them in a bed he was preparing. He uses fewer barrels than Peter because he thinks they can get too warm at the height of summer. Most of the onions go into raised beds, about two feet above ground, protected in a polytunnel.

Like other growers, he has found it pays to start off the crops earlier, in autumn rather than winter. 'Years ago you wouldn't start leeks until December. With the shows ending in September you had a good two-month break. Not any more: I can't remember the last time I went on holiday.' His wife Carmel would take their children – now in their twenties – on short breaks when they were younger, while he stayed at home with the vegetables.

Today Carmel enjoys the shows almost as much as he does. They go to most of them with Peter and Mary Glazebrook. For the big show at Shepton Mallet they take both sets of entries in Joe's van ('It always smells of cabbage,' Mary told me later). They leave home at 5 a.m. on the day before the show opens and get there in time for lunch.

We have to have the exhibits benched by eight in the evening but we get there early. We give ourselves plenty of time. You don't want to be growing it for twelve months, then rushing to get it on the bench. When you take the vegetables in they're weighed, so you have some idea then whether you have a chance of winning. But you can never be sure because I've seen when someone comes in with a world record and within half an hour it's been broken.

Why does Joe do it?

I think it's the excitement. You can see a good carrot top growing but you've no idea what's underneath it until you come to lift it on the day of the show. Of course there can be disappointments as well. But that's part of the excitement too.

When I spoke to Gerald Treweek in mid-March he was full of confidence. His world record attempt was well on track, with the most advanced of his onions sporting sixteen leaves. Yet only three weeks later a cloud had appeared on the horizon.

'They've started tipping,' he told me dolefully, almost as soon as I entered the garden, 'and I think it could affect the result.' He meant that some of their leaves had begun to turn brown at the tips, as if they had been slightly scorched. This usually indicates a setback to growth. 'Three weeks ago I took a little video clip, and there was hardly any tipping, then all of a sudden it started to come.'

He put it down to the wrong balance of nutrients. 'I've been pumping too much.' As the onions grew he had increased his pumping rate to four minutes every four hours.

I think I should have been pumping every five hours for just one minute – that's just three minutes a day – and I've lifted the nutrient strength a little. Now I've had time to readjust and the leaves are looking stronger again. The centre of the plant is looking fine – and I've got my twenty leaves. Each leaf is a skin. I'll be taking them off as they die back but there will be other ones coming. I'll try to keep it at twenty leaves.

He now thought that the essential problem of the hydroponic system – and what cost him success the previous year – lay in the medium in which the onions were rooted. The roots are supposed to pass through the growing medium in order to pick up the nutrient. In 2006 he had used peat as the medium but concluded that it retained too much moisture, feeding the roots so that they did not need to reach out to the clay balls soaking in the nutrient solution below.

This year, on the advice of Aquaculture – the company that provided him with the tanks, the pump, the nutrient and other elements of the system – Gerald is using rockwool blocks instead of peat.

'Gareth at Aquaculture has been to university and studied it all,' he told me, in a tone of voice that left it unclear whether he was impressed by those credentials or slightly scornful. 'He says that rockwool is far better, but I still think it holds too much moisture.' As in the previous year, the roots were reluctant to venture out of the growing medium. He planned to address this the next time he changed the nutrient solution, by trying to flush the blocks out with plain water that had been standing in the greenhouse for a week to get rid of the chlorine.

'When people come and see all these cables and equipment they think it's complicated,' he declared. 'But it isn't.' Hydroponic methods have been used successfully to grow tomatoes, lettuce, beans and gourds, as well as cannabis, but Gerald pointed out that the onion has a markedly different leaf structure. 'It's like a pipe. If you get too much moisture in that pipe, it will just collapse on you – and that's what's happened.'

This year he had a fellow grower to measure his performance against. Medwyn Williams, one of the country's leading vegetable men and chairman of the National Vegetable Society, is known for the impeccable displays of quality produce he mounts at Hampton Court and other large flower shows. He writes a weekly column in *Garden News*, and at the beginning of April he told his readers he, too, was experimenting with growing onions hydroponically. He mentioned Gerald's efforts and the lessons he was drawing from them, reporting that the three onions Gerald had raised from seed were doing less well so far than those grown from bulbils, one of which had already grown to half the width of an adult hand:

> Gerald managed to stage an onion weighing more than 11 lb at the Harrogate heaviest onion competition last October after a late start. Having seen his onions this year I can understand why he is so confident of smashing the world record on his second attempt with hydroponics.

Medwyn's own onions were being raised in the greenhouses at Bangor University, which provided sixteen hours of light a day through the whole year. He was using the same system as Gerald but trying two growing media simultaneously, to see which was preferable. One was rockwool and the other a commercial product called Fleximix, made from lightly compacted fine bark. Those grown in Fleximix were performing better.

'Medwyn came here three weeks ago and took a picture,' Gerald told me.

> He's only pumping twice a day. His best one has only got thirteen leaves on – that was on Monday, when mine had twenty, although the three I grew from seed have only got twelve or thirteen leaves. The big ones might peak too early, but my theory is that if you've not got growth by the end of July you'll never get it.
>
> I've got them for the moment on 13½ hours of light – they come on at 6.30, supplementing the daylight, and I turn them off at eight. After another week I'll put them on fourteen hours. You'll see a lot of difference if you come up towards the end of May. My biggest onion has a girth of 11in now but it should be 18in by then. They really start to put on weight when they get fifteen or sixteen hours of daylight.

Gerald admitted that his work on the school vegetable garden had taken up more time than he had anticipated, and that as a result he was a little behind with his quality vegetables. Yet overall it was hard not to be infected by his optimism. While the tipping on the onion leaves was undeniably a setback, it remained to be seen whether his record bid could remain on track. He certainly believed it could.

Since my February visit the Forteys had completed most of their sowing. 'We basically share with Ian,' Kevin explained.

He grows some stuff for us, and we sow for him. We'll both start beetroot and swedes, so if ours fail we can use his, and vice versa. But we still compete against each other in the shows: they're the same seeds but it's a case of who grows them the best. You can have ten people in the same garden, all growing from the same seed or plant and all producing different results. It's a question of technique and experience.

The heavy leeks, pencil-thin on my last visit, had bulked out nicely. They stood on the bench in their pots, next to the newly sown parsnips. Heavy celery seedlings – one of the brothers' specialities – were peeping over the surface of large blue barrels. Kevin and Gareth had just started Ian's water melons in four-inch pots: new seeds from a friend who managed to get some from America. They are tough to germinate because the shell is so hard that it has to be scraped on concrete to break the protective casing. And they are labour-intensive – they would have to be moved into six-inch pots before being sent to Ian to plant out in his polytunnel. Ian had reciprocated by starting the boys' carrots and parsnips, which he would bring over during the next week to be planted in the new ventilated polytunnel.

'Dad used to co-operate with Ian, and they shared tips,' Kevin told me. 'Dad was king of the seed savers. He was expert in cross-pollinating and produced crosses that got bigger and bigger. Ian's problem is that he doesn't have much time because he's busy with the nursery in the summer.'

Shortage of time was why Ian did not try to grow long carrots, parsnips and beetroot. The boys do, but they conceded that they were at a disadvantage *vis-à-vis* Peter because they did not have any tall buildings to lean the pipes up against. The previous year they had placed them nearly horizontally, which goes against the roots' natural instinct to grow downwards, and they had no success. Gareth was building a structure this year that would allow the pipes to be placed at an angle of around 45 degrees. It was tucked away at the side of the house, because their mother wants their garden to look like a garden – not like the semi-industrial landscapes that the gardens of other giant growers have become over the years.

News from the *giantveg.co.uk* website was that about twenty growers had signed up to it so far, although they were generally reluctant to go into detail when it came to their growing secrets. Gareth planned to remedy this by introducing blogs and growers' diaries of the kind that had proved so popular on *bigpumpkins.com*.

Before I left for the short drive to Ian's nursery the boys brought out a file of press cuttings and other mementoes of their father's achievements. The earliest, from the *South Wales Argus* of September 1984, reported that Mike Fortey grew runner beans more than 2ft long, leeks longer than 6ft, and pumpkins that weighed more than 115 lb. There were also many certificates from the various shows at which he triumphed, as well as a picture of Kevin and Gareth as small boys, measuring themselves against one of their father's monster pumpkins.

This was the first time I had set foot in Ian's nursery. When I visited him in early January it had been closed, and we sat and talked in the warmth of his living room, looking out over the bleak, empty polytunnels that would later provide the stage for his record-beating efforts. This time I found him in the large, gloomy and rather chilly hut that serves as the shop and office, where his Saturday assistant, a teenager still at school, sat waiting at the till to deal with the trickle of customers.

The fertilisers, pesticides, compost and garden tools that he sells to support his plant business were stacked around the walls in a practical sequence that made no concessions to modern marketing and display techniques – no island shelving, no focal points or hotspots, no attempt to lure customers into impulse purchases. This was retailing at its most old-fashioned: people came in knowing what they wanted, asked for it, and it was produced for them.

However, the operation lies a few hundred yards off the A48 between Newport and Chepstow, and Ian was finding it ever harder to compete with nearby nurseries fronting onto a main road. Even more damaging was competition from the large garden centres selling a wide range of products related to outdoor living, often incorporating a café to encourage people to spend a large part of their day there. Ian could offer a more personal service, certainly, and better grown plants, but that was not enough to stem the gradual erosion of his customer base.

'Nowadays a nursery needs a restaurant under the same roof. You've got to be like a supermarket. People haven't got the money for shrubs and perennials, what with mortgages, council tax and electricity all going up in price. Everybody's short of money.' His hopes for the future lay in the possibility of being able to gain planning permission for housing and then sell the land to a developer. Already the nursery was exuding an air of gradual decline, anticipating its demise.

Outside, things were a bit more cheerful. Early bedding plants were on display on the open-air stands, with boxes of young seedlings spread over the floor of the principal polytunnel. Ian imposes a strict dividing line between his business and his hobby: the giant vegetables were firmly excluded from the large commercial tunnel and restricted to two smaller ones towards the back. In one of the tunnels he had an unwelcome visitor this year – a rabbit that raised her family there. If he had not got rid of them they could have played havoc with his young plants. Beyond the tunnels were some old outdoor beds where he once grew shrubs for sale. Given the diminishing trade, he no longer used them, because you do not have to pay business rates on ground that is not being cultivated. Behind these were the fields of the neighbouring farm.

Ian is a bachelor but far from a loner. A kind-hearted man, he likes to get involved in the community and to help people who find it hard to manage for themselves. He told me about an elderly lady who used to live nearby but has moved to Usk, some fifteen miles north. He takes her to get her pension ('I'm the only one she'll trust'), and last winter he shovelled the snow from her path. 'And the other day I took her down to Barry for fish and chips and a walk on the beach.'

He gets up at six every morning to minister to his giants before the nursery opens and, with the days lengthening, he could go back to them in the evening after it closes. He hadn't yet planted any of them out in the non-commercial tunnels because he was changing his fertiliser and was awaiting delivery, expected in the next few days. 'Then I'll make a start.' Before Christmas he had been through the tunnels with a Rotovator, mixing some volcanic rock dust into the soil to inject a fresh supply of minerals and to get the bacteria working. He would also be using pellets of chicken manure to produce nitrogen.

I don't change all the soil in the tunnel every year, only where the plants are actually going to grow. I take one-and-a-half-spit squares – that's fifteen to eighteen inches – and fill it with our special home-made compost, made from potting compost, vermiculite and some base fertiliser. Then I feed them with nutrients. I sometimes use last season's spent compost from the nursery if there's any left over: we always put a controlled release fertiliser into our pots.

I used to use a Dutch fertiliser made from pigs' droppings, but you could smell the pigs. And one year I used something called dinosaur fertiliser. Apparently they found a big pile of something on top of a moor in Yorkshire. When they analysed it they found a lot of nitrogen in it, and they called it dinosaur because they didn't really know what it was. It was on sale at £22 a bag but I got some from a friend and paid a lot less than that.

He puts the fertiliser into the beds a few days before he transplants the seedlings. 'I'm told the nitrogen in the fertiliser reaches its peak in twenty-one days, and if you put it in too early there's too much nitrogen for them. But if you time it right, the plants are big enough to absorb the fertiliser by the time it reaches its peak.'

His beetroot and swedes, thriving in their small pots, would be among the first to go in: he puts them out in the beds, rather than in barrels, because he agrees with Joe Atherton that barrels can get too hot and make things dry out too quickly. His heavy carrots and parsnips were still in the propagator. He had sown fifteen of each and would whittle them down to seven or eight by throwing away the weaker ones. The Forteys would take a few to plant out in their own tunnel. It had been an unusually warm spring so far, and he was a little worried by the dramatic difference between day and night temperatures, which he feared could cause some of the early-sown root crops to run to seed prematurely. He would not be sowing the water melons, cantaloupes, cucumbers and marrows until the beginning of May. 'The boys will grow the cantaloupes on for me because I don't have the time.'

Outside the tunnels Ian planned to grow marrows, and in the greenhouse behind his house he would plant potatoes in sacks – his first year of trying them – and radishes in barrels. He does not grow long carrots, parsnips or beetroot. 'I'm 64 now, and to do that as well as all this would be too much.' Nor does he do leeks or onions, because he has a root disease in the tunnels that he cannot eradicate. 'I only grow what I think I can win with.'

Chapter 5

May

'The weather's turned against us,' was Ian's greeting as I arrived at the nursery on a drizzly morning in the second week in May. 'We need more sunlight.' He was not talking just about the prospects for his giant vegetables but also for his business. When the weather is discouraging, people find better things to do than visit a nursery in search of bedding plants and hanging baskets.

In 2007 April and May reversed their traditional roles. April, supposedly the month of showers, was unusually sunny and quite warm. That led people to expect a second successive hot summer and fuelled fresh concerns about global warming. It also got Ian's trading season off to a deceptively good start – but, equally, it brought problems.

When it was hot I had to water all the nursery plants every night, which meant I had less time to look after the giant vegetables. I reckon to spend an hour and a half with them every night at this time of the year, but with the watering I could only spend half an hour. So in that sense I suppose the rain has come as a relief.

Later in the day the Forteys would be bringing over the cucumbers, cantaloupes and water melons that they had started for Ian, and he would exchange them for the root crops he had been growing for them. In the larger of his two vegetable tunnels he showed me the bed he had been preparing for the water melons. He had covered it with black plastic, to suppress weeds, and cut cross-shaped slits in this to accommodate the three plants that would occupy the whole of one side of the 60-ft tunnel. When I remarked that 20ft seemed a lot of space to give each plant, he assured me they would be crowding it out by the end of the summer. Water melons spread prodigiously. In the soil beneath each slit he had placed an empty 12-in pot, the size that the Forteys have used to grow the plants in. He was going to remove it when he planted them, ensuring that initially the roots had the space they needed to develop and prosper.

I confine them to one flower on each plant. Only the female flowers produce the fruit. I pollinate them by hand to make sure the job is done – that's at around the end of June. To get a female flower you need a temperature of 70°F [21°C]. It was up to 72° in here a few days ago, but when the rain started it dropped by about ten degrees. You need sunlight for water melons.

On the other side of the tunnel he planned to plant the heavy and long cucumbers, but he had not quite finished preparing their bed yet. 'I started doing it this morning and then some customers came. That's why I'd like to give up the nursery and do this full time.' He told me, too, that he had been having more trouble with his left leg. He damaged it in a car crash in 1980 and has had several operations on it since. 'I'm supposed to go in for another operation next month but I've asked them to bring it forward.'

In the other, shorter tunnel he had planted the swedes and beetroot that he sowed in the first week in March. The swedes, already measuring some 2ft 6in across the leaves, and the beetroot – about half that width – stood in neat rows on bare earth between the pierced hoses that irrigated them in warm weather. 'Actually I've been watering them by hand so far, so that I can control the amount of fertiliser they're getting. You don't want too much to start with. To me it's like feeding a baby: you make the feed weak until they're big enough to take more' – a surprising metaphor, I thought, for a lifelong bachelor.

'Everything was going well until the weather turned. You're geared up for the hot weather, then suddenly it changes and you've got to think again.' Although the panel at the back of the tunnel stayed open during the day to allow the air to circulate, he regularly closed it when the sun went down. Despite that, he had been having more trouble with marauding animals. Last month it was rabbits, and now he was complaining about some tears in the polythene at the bottom of one of the tunnel walls, the work possibly of a fox or a dog, but more likely a cat, to judge from the footprints in the earth.

His aim was to grow fifteen of each of the heavy carrots, parsnips, beetroot and swedes. This is three times as many as the Forteys can manage in their more restricted space, and of course it gave him a better chance of growing one or two exceptionally large ones. Even so, he would like room to grow more. Ideally he coveted a more modern tunnel like Kevin and Gareth's, to allow him to compete more successfully. 'I think Peter Glazebrook has more sophisticated equipment than I do. I'd like automatic ventilation and hydraulic watering. That means you can go out in the evening and don't have to worry about opening and closing windows.'

The rain over the last few days had been a setback for the Forteys as well. 'We got off to a good start in April,' Gareth told me, 'but I haven't been able to Rotovate the bed where we're going to plant the marrows yet, because it's been too wet.' The marrow seedlings, along with the cantaloupes, were still in the propagator, just pushing their heads above the soil. So they still had a bit of time –

but the weather forecast was suggesting that they would have to wait a while for another dry spell.

They were also worried about the effect of a long period of rain on their new polytunnel. Although it's impervious to rain, it stands over an old land drain that backs up and floods in wet weather. Kevin pointed out the dark patch in the tunnel's central gully that marked where this had happened. 'The trouble is, if the ground in the tunnel gets too wet, then we can't water – and it's in the watering that we give the plants their nutrients.' So far, though, the swedes, celery and beetroot in the tunnel appeared to be thriving and at this stage were at least as big as Ian's.

In the greenhouse, among a mass of bedding plants being raised for the front garden, were the three water melons, already growing out of their pots, that Kevin and Gareth would be taking to Ian later in the day: they do not have the space themselves to grow any on. Alongside them were the long and heavy cucumbers they sowed a week ago. 'We put them in on Saturday, and they were up by Monday,' said Gareth. 'We did well last year with long cucumbers and only narrowly missed getting the record. Somebody beat us by an inch.'

Their long carrot, parsnip and beetroot – only one of each – were in split drainpipes, 8ft long, laid horizontally on the floor of the tunnel for the time being. Gareth had had a setback with the rack he was building at the side of the house that would enable the pipes to be stored at a more suitable angle. 'One of the spars cracked in a high wind before I'd finished building it. The wind caught the polythene cover. The weather is conspiring against me – but I should have it finished in a week or so.'

Eight feet of pipe will not be nearly long enough to produce any record-breaking roots, but when he sees the ends poking out he will add another length of piping. 'The secret is not to feed them. By feeding you create a larger vegetable but what you're looking for here is the length of the root. For that you just need to water them.'

So determined were they to compete successfully in these particular classes that Gareth drove all the way to Evesham in Worcestershire to get a special compost – a very fine soil with sand in it – to fill the pipes; Medwyn Williams told them about it when they were competing in the televised *Great British Village Show*. They could not find any on the internet, and Evesham was the nearest place that stocked it. So the carrot, parsnip and beetroot would be getting luxury treatment – although growing only one of each left no margin for error.

The heavy leeks, by now about 18in high, would soon be ready to transplant into barrels or into the tunnel bed. Other plants destined for barrels were the heavy parsnips, potatoes and radishes – and for radishes, timing is all important. Ideally, they should go in a hundred days before the show.

Last year we sowed them too early and they were ready before Shepton Mallet. We try to time everything for Shepton [at the beginning of September], and quite a lot of the stuff we take to the Welsh shows later in the month is the same as the stuff we've shown there. The beetroot and swede will keep for three or four weeks if you put them back in soil. We're quite good at keeping things sound, as long as there are no holes in them or anything like that. The marrow we showed last year kept going for nearly six weeks, but it was on its last legs by Malvern.

At Shepton Mallet we'll go in for twelve of the classes of heaviest veg and all five of the longest. We won't win the overall prize because we're not entering enough classes: we don't have the time or the space that Peter Glazebrook has.

Their schedule for the day provided an illustration of the other calls on their time. After delivering the seedlings they had grown for Ian, and collecting those that he had grown for them, they would be driving north to Warrington, to stay the night before going on to Anfield to watch Liverpool's last league match of the season – and the legendary Robbie Fowler's farewell game. They are keen Liverpool fans, as was their father, who was once a player on the books of Newport County. For the energetic pair, life has more than giant vegetables to offer.

My May visit to Peter and Gerald came nearly two weeks after I went to Wales, and the weather in the Midlands had been holding up rather better. So much better that Peter had got ahead of himself, planting out some of his vegetables earlier than usual, including the cucumbers and tomatoes. 'Usually I plant them out when they're a bit bigger than this, but this year the weather was so good that I planted them out when they were quite tiny. I think they look stronger for being out earlier.'

But again there was the inevitable downside: the warm late spring might have done serious damage to his giant cabbages. He had planted six cabbages all told, two in cloches and the others in two separate areas of the garden. Two had already run to seed, and he wasn't sure about one of the others. What made this happen?

> They've had a check – too hot or too dry for them, probably. I sowed them in December and looked after them in the greenhouse, and they didn't have a check there. I planted them out fairly early when the weather turned good in April – but not too early – and I spent a couple of days putting supports round them. I don't know why they've gone to seed. You can never be certain of these things.

Only one of the six seemed to be truly thriving, with an impressive 4-ft leaf span already; but even that one had been suffering from the attentions of the pheasants who came in at night from the nearby woods and pecked holes in the tasty lower leaves. We watched one of them boldly stalking a neighbouring hay field, taking advantage of the close season for shooting.

Peter was also having trouble with his onions. He was growing the same variety for quality as for weight, and in both cases it is important that the neck should stretch to a good height above the bulb. 'I've been to see Gerald's onions, and his highest neck is higher than mine,' he admitted. Sometimes, though, the leaves get jammed up the neck and become distorted, seriously setting back growth. 'I've had it in the past but never as bad as this,' he said. 'Again I think it was to do with the weather.' He pointed at one of the sickly onions: 'I remember when you came last time I told you that would be the strongest, but the one next to it is bigger now.'

Peter is a natural worrier; but one of the secrets of his success is that he grows enough of each kind of vegetable, and places them in different parts of the garden, to increase the chance that some of them will come good every year. For example, he was not going to rely solely on the tomatoes that he planted out early, but was raising other batches that would mature later and stand him in good stead for the late September shows. In the past he had done well with heavy tomatoes and, despite his isolated disappointments and self-protective pessimism, there were plenty of positive signs at this stage that when show time came round he would enjoy at least his customary level of success in this and other classes. His heavy celery was looking good, in its row of sunken blue barrels, but he was worried that it might reach its peak before the Shepton Mallet show. 'I normally don't win on celery – Ian Neale usually beats me.'

The potatoes were already about a foot high, showing plenty of leaf and just starting to come into flower, which meant that the tubers would be beginning to develop. When they had swelled some more, in about a fortnight, he would start scraping carefully around the base of each plant, using a hosepipe to wash some of the dirt away. Then he would look and feel for the developing potatoes and remove all but the largest one or two, so that they would benefit from the plant's full vigour. It is a fiddly and painstaking process but he has found it repays the effort. And he had placed another batch in a different part of the garden, a little later than he planted these, to give him further options. 'Again, it's not having all your eggs in one basket.'

He had planted out one of his squashes and another was to follow it shortly. The marrows, too, were ready to take their chance outside, and the long runner beans had just been sown. The leeks were growing healthily in their pots, although the one he kept from last year, hoping that it would produce pips to plant for next season, was dying on him, and he was uncertain where next year's batch would come from: something else to worry about.

> It's always the special ones you lose. This year I bought the leek plants in, but the man who sold them to me has now sold his stock plants to John Soulsby in the north-east, so I don't know where I'm going to get them from next year. That's why I was hoping to get seeds from these. Soulsby does sell seed but other growers say they don't seem to get the best from him.

The swedes were looking good – at least as big as those I saw at Ian's earlier in the month – but he was cautious about their prospects because in previous years he had a problem trying to stop them going rotten before the shows. One of his heavy carrots was sending out plenty of side shoots: a good sign, because a winning carrot is nearly always one with multiple forks in the root. As for the long carrots, parsnips and beetroot, it was impossible to say how far their roots had reached down their pipes, but their tops were looking pleasingly healthy. As the current holder of the world record for the longest carrot – a feat that would shortly be revealed on television – Peter was entitled to feel confident of repeating his success; but we were still more than three months away from the first show, and his rivals would have plans of their own.

When I arrived at Gerald's house he had more potentially disturbing news, although it still had not dented his early-season confidence.

> I've had a slight problem. The onions I grew from bulbils . . . one of them split three skins. So I checked the nutrient and it seemed to be OK, but I thought there must be some reason – maybe they're getting too much food. So I went back to the hydroponics shop in Sheffield to check my conductivity meter, and it wasn't reading properly. It was reading 14 when the conductivity was in fact 18 – and I wanted 13 to 14. Last year I gave the onions 16 and they seemed to be going all right and then they just collapsed on me.

The literal meaning of conductivity is a rate at which electricity is conducted through a liquid. In hydroponics this is used as a measure of the strength of the nutrients in the water fed to the plants. The exact figure needed is a matter of dispute, still largely subject to trial and error. When onions begin to tip and rot, it is assumed they are suffering from an excess of nutrient they are unable to absorb, although this theory has not been tested scientifically. There is a parallel in human medication: the correct dose is beneficial, while an overdose can provoke an adverse reaction in the body or brain.

The onions grown from bulbils seemed to have suffered more than those grown from seed. The methodical Gerald had measured them just before I arrived and was impressed with the statistics.

> The biggest bulbil one is 19in in circumference – that's an inch

bigger than I said it would be when you last came up here. The biggest one from seed is just under that, but it had been 2½in behind the other one, so it's growing faster. To break the world record – and it's still possible this year – I need an onion that's 28in at the end of June and, at the rate I'm going, I'll get there.

When Mel Ednie from Fife broke the world record in 1994 with an onion that weighed just under 16 lb, he said that at the end of June it was 26in round and that you would need 28in by then to beat it.

Mine are putting on 1½in a week, so in six weeks I should be up to 28in. I'll tell you this – I'm optimistic. Last year I wasn't. Simon Spinks at Aquaculture was telling me to pump every two hours with a conductivity of 16. This year I'm doing it my way. I keep it between 14 and 12 and I pump just three times a day. It's never been done before with onions, so you've got to try something different.

He also switched off the heaters that kept the water at a constant 21°C, believing that the bulbs need to be cooler than that to stay healthy.

He was confident that he now had the balance of nutrients right. 'They're being mixed over at the hydroponics place. They have to add certain things, let them stand for half an hour, add something else and then mix them up. You've got to get it down to fine tuning. Onions need a lot of potash, or they go soft.'

He was working on his tactics for the big onion competitions at Ashington and Harrogate in September.

When it gets nearer the time I'll be ringing round and seeing who else has got big onions, and if I think someone else has got a bigger onion for Harrogate I'll take the biggest to Ashington. Harrogate has a £500 prize but an extra £1,000 if you break the world record. The prize at Ashington is £1,000. Word gets round. We knew two weeks before Harrogate two years ago that John Sifford was going to break the world record. He smashed it out of sight.

Peter Glazebrook and Joe Atherton had visited Gerald a week earlier, when Peter reported that his best onion had a circumference of only 13in.

But last year it was the same with Peter, and then his onions seemed to put this surge on, and he beat me. He had a 13-pounder; my biggest was 12 lb 3 oz, but it went soft so I couldn't show it.

Peter and Joe had brought him news of an allotment gardener from Wakefield, Walter Stringfellow, who had an onion with twenty-three leaves – but the suspicion was that he probably had two bulbs coming up instead of one, kept together by the outer skin, and that they would almost certainly separate before September.

Gerald was also continuing to compare notes with Medwyn Williams.

His onions are about on a par with mine but they only have seventeen leaves and have started to bulb up before they're throwing enough leaves. Mine have twenty-one leaves, so he's four leaves down and he won't catch up. I have to try to hold on to twenty-one leaves all the way through. His started to bulb early because he's on sixteen hours of light every day.

However, in his *Garden News* column, Medwyn remained optimistic. In May he told his readers that at the end of April his biggest onion measured twelve inches and was gaining girth at about half an inch a day.

Gerald took me through the garden to show me the onions in the greenhouse, stopping on the way to point out where robins and blackbirds were nesting in the bushes. He and Doreen enjoy their garden, and he ensures that the equipment he needs for his competitive growing does not become dominant, but is as unobtrusive as possible, mostly hidden away in the greenhouse. The onion leaves were flopping untidily over the side of the elaborate support structure he had built for them, and they all had ugly brown patches at the tips. 'But it's still throwing out leaves,' he said, pointing to the largest of the group. 'And it must have an extensive root system because, although it's on clay balls, I can't make it move.'

It measured some fifteen inches from the base to the cluster of leaves, and the cluster itself was some two inches across. He wanted that to bulk up to three inches – the maximum allowed at Harrogate. His experiment with Diahydro, the dead plankton from Australia, did not appear to have worked: the onions in the tank that he put it in were not doing as well as those in the tank containing the plain clay balls.

Before Gerald began experimenting with hydroponics, carrots were his speciality. He has been visited three times by television gardening programmes to talk about them, and he sells specialist carrot seed through advertisements in *Garden News* – 'It helps pay for the electricity and compost'. Being mentioned in Medwyn's column made him something of a celebrity among its readers, and that evening a man was coming to seek his advice on setting up a hydroponic system of his own – although he would be making too late a start to enable him to grow onions successfully in the current season. 'He asked me, if he started some onions now, would they grow in time, and I said no. Although they're long-day plants they have to have those short days when they start off.'

Gerald would be even better known in June, when *The Great British Village Show*, in which he was one of the vegetable judges, began its run on Sunday evenings on BBC1. He enjoyed the experience tremendously:

> They really make you feel important. I had a little girl – I think she was Kenyan – following me around everywhere with ice-cold water. There was a lot of travelling. I'd travel down on Saturdays to wherever it was being filmed, and they put us up in a really good hotel with a good meal in the evening with wine if you wanted it – although I don't drink wine. We filmed on the Sunday and we could have stayed over on the Sunday night, but I preferred to go back rather than face the Monday morning traffic.

However, he is not a man to let fame go to his head, and since the filming a lot of his time and energy had gone into the distinctly low-profile project of creating the vegetable garden at his grandson's primary school. The lads on community service did their digging work, the sponsors delivered their promised equipment, and most of his seedlings were in place and growing away – except the pumpkins, which would be planted later.

> It's all set out now, and they're going to have a lunchtime club to make sure it's watered regularly. James Martin's cookery demonstration is arranged for the end of term in a nearby park, because we couldn't have got his big lorry through the school gates. There's going to be an open day the week before, to let the sponsors and other people see the garden. Next year they want the children to set their own seed in the ground.

Chapter 6

June

When you're the proud grower of the biggest vegetable in the world, it's rarely very long before your record is broken by a rival. This was a theme played out in the BBC1 series *The Great British Village Show*, filmed late in the summer of 2006. As its name suggested, it was a version of the traditional local show, somewhat pared down because of the demands of the medium, with competitions for flowers and flower arranging, cakes, jams, knitting – and vegetables, some judged for quality and others for size.

The format was a series of regional heats culminating in a grand final in October at Highgrove, the Gloucestershire home of the Prince of Wales and the Duchess of Cornwall, who had undertaken to present the prizes. The first episode was broadcast on 3 June 2007, in the early Sunday evening slot customarily occupied by *The Antiques Road Show*, with the Highgrove final due to be aired at the end of July.

Gerald Treweek was the first of my new acquaintances to appear on screen. As a judge, he featured every week in the title sequence, enthusing over a choice display of quality shallots, along with other judges smacking their lips over pots of strawberry jam or tut-tutting over the consistency of a fruit cake. The first of the heats came from the Midlands region. The principal master of ceremonies was the jaunty Alan Titchmarsh, the ubiquitous gardener, novelist and TV presenter.

When the time came for the first giant vegetable segment, Alan introduced it:

> In the world of vegetable growing there's one moment of supreme satisfaction, and that's when you come to pull your vegetable, cook it and put it on your plate. But in the world of big vegetables, some of them quite simply wouldn't fit on your plate, and there are two men who know all about growing it large. Joe Atherton has spent the last ten years competing at the top level of the giant vegetable world, and knows that his heaviest leeks and longest carrots at *The Great British Village Show* have got to be the best. . . . But when you're a good heavyweight vegetable grower, coming first isn't always enough. The ultimate is to have the biggest vegetable in the world.

The camera turned to Joe, who went along with all that:

> It's not a hobby, it's an obsession. You want to win. Nobody remembers who came second, just who won . . . My aim, originally, was to try to break the world record for leeks. I equalled it one year and the following year I broke it, and the following year someone took it back off me, so I'm going to try to get it back again.'

He was also going for the prize for long carrots: 'I've had them 13ft long, and I want 14ft this year.'

Being television – and reality television at that – there had to be a rival waiting in the wings. Alan introduced him:

> Standing in the way of Joe becoming champion is a man who's already held the longest carrot world record – Peter Glazebrook, an expert giant vegetable grower, who currently holds the longest parsnip and cucumber world records. He's one of Britain's best.

But Peter's well aware that his place at the top could be under threat.

In a segment filmed earlier we saw Peter in his garden, filling his adapted drainpipes with compost and explaining how hard it was to get it compacted when you filled from the top. He went on to talk about his heavy leeks, which he was also entering for the show, but without much confidence: 'Last time I saw Joe he was a lot further on than me. His leeks were more than twice the size. But there's still a long time to go yet, and it's having them on the day, really.'

Joe was filmed on the eve of the first show breaking into his drainpipe to uncover his carrot in what Alan called 'the moment of truth'. Joe said that every time he opened a pipe he hoped to see a carrot a good two inches longer than the world record; but disappointment came quickly: 'A bit shorter than I'd been hoping for,' he declared, as he examined the straggly root, barely visible on screen. 'That carrot won't be long enough to win tomorrow.'

Responding to Alan's remark that growing giant vegetables is 'fiendishly difficult', even 'masochistic', Joe explained how he and Peter, although rivals, were friends: 'If we have a problem one year we sit down and discuss the problems we've had. He may try one method and I'll try another method, and we'll see which one wins.'

To sustain the tension during the programme's fifty minutes, viewers were not to be told who had won the various classes until the very end. Before that, Alan moved on to a category in which neither Joe nor Peter was competing: 'In the world of heavyweight vegetables there is one giant, one champion of champions, and that's the pumpkin. It can be anything up to 900 lb, the equivalent of four heavyweight boxers.' (This was a rare case of under-statement, given that the world record is now nearly double that.)

The format for the pumpkin section was different from the others. To avoid having to cart half a dozen of the monsters to a show each week, they were to be judged – measured, rather – at the growers' homes by the peripatetic Gerald Treweek, with the six heaviest to be taken to Highgrove for the final. The cameras did not follow Gerald on his visits to all the contestants, but four had been chosen as the likeliest to be among the winners, their progress monitored week by week. Three of the featured growers were in their teens: James O'Hanlon and Liam Culpit, who entered as a team and were holders of the current British record; and Joe Hallam, who comes from Glazebrook country, near Newark. Trevor Wilson, also a former record-holder, was another fancied contender. In front of the cameras all of them, especially the youngsters, were full of confidence that they could beat all comers.

At the end of the first programme came the results of the Midlands heat. Neither Peter nor Joe triumphed with their leeks, coming third and second respectively to Michael Poulteney, whose specimen weighed 11 lb 1½ oz. Peter, though, had produced the longest carrot, at 12ft 9in. 'I'm very pleased, yes,' he commented. 'It's been a long process but we got there.' For Joe, beaten in both classes, the bitter truth was that he would not qualify for the Highgrove final after all.

In the second episode we were introduced to Clive Bevan, a familiar figure on the giant circuit, whom I would meet when the 2007 show season began. He spent thirty years in the prison service, teaching prisoners how to grow conventional vegetables, and has since made a name for himself as a self-styled 'giant vegetable guru', selling specialist seed as well as a slim booklet of growing tips. Although his name seldom appears among the record-breakers he is a keen competitor, and he had high hopes of winning the heavy marrow class. More of a showman than many of his rivals, he knows how to construct quotes that find their way on to the screen after the final cut:

My confidence is riding high . . . I know when they see my marrow the other people will be as sick as parrots, because it will be something to behold . . . I'm confident, but I'm not going to jump over the moon. It never pays to be over-confident because one can land on one's bottom . . . When I see mine on the show bench, and it looks as if it's going to win, I feel like a dog with two tails, wagging himself to death, because I'm going to end up with a red card . . . because that's what it's all about. All I can say to the competition is: 'Bring it on, and may the best marrow win.'

When he arrived on the day, Clive roped in some Boy Scouts to carry his marrow to the show bench, underscoring its great weight. Of course, the best marrow did win – but sadly it wasn't his. His weighed 52 lb 8 oz, a good seven pounds lighter than the winner. Clive put on a brave face: 'When I eyed them up I suspected it was going to be pretty close. The best man has won. That's the name of the game. I've got the best strain of marrow in the world but unfortunately mine wasn't up to the job today.' And he concluded, somewhat opaquely: 'He who turns and runs away, he lives to fight another day.'

The third instalment of the show gave Kevin and Gareth Fortey – and their new polytunnel – their chance of national exposure, although Alan might have been overstating it in his intro: 'When it comes to giant vegetables, the Fortey brothers are practically royalty.' He was referring, I suppose, to the hereditary succession by which the brothers have taken over the mantle of giantism from their late father.

'It's fair to say that I think he [my father] would have been proud of us,' said Gareth, touchingly. Kevin added:

When we started we got a 60-lb marrow, but we got better seed and reselected every year, and we got bigger and better results. We have the Welsh record for the heaviest marrow which still stands at 109 lb. . . . Things have gone quite well overall. But when you go to the show with a marrow that

seems massive to us, someone can come along with one two
ounces heavier.

He need not have worried. Their marrow trounced the local
opposition and provided their passport to Highgrove.

Like many who share a minority interest, specialist vegetable
growers are a tightly knit community who like to get together from
time to time and compare notes. Peter is generous in letting people
visit his garden. Every year he opens it to a variety of interested
groups, and on 20 June 2007, the eve of the longest day, he
arranged an evening for members of the local branch of the
National Vegetable Society. He invited me to come along as well,
and we agreed that I should arrive an hour or so before the official
start time of 6 p.m., so we could have a short talk and tour before
the rest showed up.

It turned out that I was not the only one seeking that privilege.
In such highly motivated brotherhoods, enmities and jealousies can
arise. A couple phoned Peter asking if they could come an hour
before everyone else, because they knew there were going to be
people there they did not get on with and they wanted to have left
before they arrived. 'There's quite a lot of rivalry,' Peter explained
to me. Still, I managed to be the first there and, obeying the
instructions on a hand-written notice, parked on the newly cut
grass verge by the road outside the gate. Peter did not want visitors'
cars clogging up his drive.

The first thing we talked about was the weather, which had
taken a sharp turn for the worse since my last visit. It was now clear
that the forecasters had been wrong in predicting another warm
summer and that, failing a dramatic improvement in July, it was
going to be a difficult year for growers who wanted their crops at
their biggest and best for the September shows. In the past few

weeks there had been little sun and a lot of heavy rain – even a ground frost at the start of the month. At one point Peter thought he might have to cancel his open evening, or at least rethink the parking arrangements.

> In less than forty-eight hours we had three inches of rain, and one evening we had more than an inch in less than an hour. It was very dramatic – the main road was blocked for a time, and the water rushed down the lane and on to the verge where you parked and the lower part of the garden. And we had a bit of a thunderstorm last night as well. Everything I'm growing outside has put a spurt on, especially the marrows. It might not have done much harm but it would have been better if it was spread over a longer time.

That evening there were some dark clouds overhead; but also patches of blue sky, and no rain was forecast.

I was getting used to being given the bad news first. After the weather, Peter updated me on the cabbage debacle. Of the six he planted originally, only two remained in good health, and one of those was giving him cause for concern. The other four had all run to seed – and there was worse to come. 'Remember that celery you took a picture of last time that looked so good? It all went rotten and pulled away at ground level. It was probably because it was too wet, or maybe the slugs did some damage and a disease got in. It was my best one.'

He had also lost his best onion, along with two others. 'The leaves started to go yellow. I think it was white rot. It's a constant problem: it comes from the soil, and once in there it stays there. If it does get hot later I expect I'll lose some more, because the heat brings it on.' And one of his potatoes had succumbed to blackleg, a sudden and fatal blackening of the stem, possibly also caused by the wet weather.

We had not progressed far around the garden when the first visitors arrived: two couples from Worksop. The leading gardener among them was another former miner, who grows for both quality and size.

This will be my fifth year of showing, and last year I won three best-in-shows, so I'm getting there. I only go in for the local shows, not the nationals yet.

My soil is fifty per cent coal – I don't know why, there must have been a coal dump there or something. Gerald came round to see me and was amazed at the size of my Brussels sprout plants. He asked me what I did to them, and I said, 'Nothing special – it must be the coal.' It's my fourth year of growing the big stuff, and I'm just learning. In my second year I got an onion at 6 lb 11 oz, and last year I got that up to 9 lb 9 oz. This year they're 20in round already.

His friend was even newer at the game:

When I first left school I went to work on a farm, so I know a bit about gardening but I'd never done it seriously before. I thought I knew it all. But only since I've been coming to this club, where these lads know what they're doing, do you realise how poorly you're doing it.

He had an allotment alongside a camp for Polish workers, and suspected that occasionally they came and helped themselves. 'I've got quite an area of strawberries but I've not had any myself yet. And I put some fair-sized onions on the shed to dry and the best of them disappeared.'

The four visitors tagged along with Peter and me as we continued the garden tour. More drifted in, including Joe and Gerald. Some joined Peter's group and others took themselves around the greenhouses and tunnels, checking the details of his methods and making expert points. In contrast to the disasters that he had already revealed to me, everything else seemed to be doing reasonably well – the swedes, turnips, marrows, beetroot, all in varying stages of development thanks to his policy of successional sowing that allowed him to pick the best for each show as it came around.

Some of the beetroot measured about nine inches across – they would have to get up to at least a foot to stand a chance of a prize – but one or two had run to seed. The swedes that he was growing under cover were already a foot wide, and he thought he might have planted them too close together.

He had his doubts, too, about the heavy carrots, which he feared might be showing too much of themselves above the compost: 'It's not wrong but it might mean that the root hasn't gone down as deep as you'd like below the surface.' His onions perched on their barrels, supported by structures made of bamboo rods and rubber rings, the compost covered with white plastic to keep the warmth in. Although they lagged behind Gerald's in terms of girth, they looked healthier, with less tipping on the leaves. As for those being grown on for seed, they were in flower, and several bees had found their way into the tunnel, busily pollinating them for him.

Peter did not seem to be holding back on any details of his growing techniques, telling his guests the exact date that he sowed his onion seeds – 7 December – before he put them into their final positions in March. Unlike Gerald, he had not detected much difference in the progress of those grown from seed and those from bulbils. Someone asked him how he collected seeds from the onions that he grows on. Did he put a plastic bag over the seed head and shake them out? No. When the black seeds begin to appear in August a few might drop off, but most of them stay attached and when they seem ripe he shakes them into a bucket. He is careful not to get the seed mixed up. Each onion is clearly marked with the weight it achieved, and he keeps the seed from the heaviest for himself, giving some of the rest away. His heaviest last year reached 13 lb 8 oz.

The leeks in their polytunnel were already impressively thick, about the width of my forearm. 'A good inch bigger than at this time last year,' Peter commented. 'They're starting to split on the leaves, but that doesn't matter for the heavies. Some are supposed to be long leeks, not heavy ones, but they don't always grow true from seed.'

In the metal-framed greenhouse that he put up four years ago, to augment the larger one he inherited from his father, were a couple of water melons in peat-filled growing bags. The plants were not nearly as big as those I saw at Ian's nursery: 'I've not grown them before,' said Peter. 'I just felt that they might do all right in there and I'm trying to keep them damp. South Wales is warmer than here – that's why Ian grows them bigger than I can.'

One especially enthusiastic and persistent woman pressed him on where she could buy the equipment required to compete at his level at the shows. He recommended builders' or plumbers' merchants for the pipes she would need if she was going to challenge his long carrot record. What about the polytunnels – did he wash them down regularly? No need for that, he told her. She asked what fertilisers she should use, and was surprised when he said he seldom uses any on his crops while they are developing; he prefers to put all the necessary nutrients into the soil or compost before planting them out in it.

When we reached the bottom of the garden the visitors admired the huge pile of manure given to Peter by the farmer who leased the adjoining field. It was some 5ft high and 12ft across, and must have been an important factor in his success. The squashes, too, proved a talking point, their stems and leaves already creeping several feet along the ground from where they were planted. Not many of the visitors grew squashes, most pleading lack of space.

Peter said the plants should continue to spread rapidly throughout July and eventually, with luck, produce fruit as big as pumpkins (which he was also growing). He planted the pumpkins under cloches to give them a warm start, then took the covers off when the temperature began to rise – a method that he also used for his marrows.

By 6.30 about twenty people had arrived. Just then a curious incident occurred. Mary sought out Peter, caught his eye and held out a piece of paper bearing a single word: RADISHES. Peter immediately broke away from the group and strode quickly towards the back of the garden. My newsman's instinct demanded that I follow him, although he did not appear to welcome my presence.

'I hoped I could do this without anyone noticing,' he confided reluctantly, when he saw he was not going to shake me off; this was one secret he was not intending to share with the others. He walked to the barrels containing his giant radishes and started to put covers on, keeping out the light. He explained that radishes – unlike, say, pumpkins – thrive better on short days, so he ensures that they never get more than 12 hours of daylight, even at the height of summer. Every evening, at 6.30 precisely, he put the covers on, and at 6.30 the next morning he removed them.

He originally chose the times when he was still working, so he could do the job before leaving for the office. If he was late back Mary would put the covers on for him. When they go out together in the evening and get back late he still ensures that the radishes get their twelve hours of darkness by keeping the covers on until later the following morning.

When we rejoined the group we discovered that the star guest had arrived: Dave Thornton, the general secretary of the National Vegetable Society, who comes from Derbyshire and is one of the most respected growers in the country. By now, too, the sun had come out, and it was a perfect, almost idyllic summer evening.

Soon Mary brought out tea and cakes and served them at a table on a sheltered patio just outside one of the greenhouses.

Without exception, the visitors were full of praise for Peter's meticulous and knowledgeable approach to his vegetables. But then the talk, as so often among gardeners, turned to problems with diseases and pests and the ideal formula for fertilisers. 'Botrytis . . . white rot . . . nitrogen . . . potash' – the words drifted out from the buzz of conversation. Someone had spotted evidence of damage from a leaf miner on Peter's celery. Another bemoaned that his own greenhouse had been infested by red spider mite, but Peter said he had been free of it that year, probably because it had been so wet and humid. He did, though, spot greenfly in one of the tunnels. 'How can you get greenfly in a tunnel?' he asked rhetorically.

Gardening is a nerve-wracking business. Each morning these dedicated men and women head out in trepidation to inspect their tender charges, fearful that they will have succumbed to one or other of countless possible scourges. Gerald, for instance, told Dave Thornton – something of an expert in plant diseases – about the trouble he was having with his carrots. At first he thought it was alternaria, a fairly common fungal condition, but he was now convinced that it was a disease called sclerotinia, only recently recorded in carrots. The symptoms are rot at the base of the leaves and the appearance of a fluffy white mould containing large, dark bodies called sclerotia. It is hard to eliminate because it overwinters in the soil before attacking its targets in spring.

'I've had it since 2004, which is why I haven't been showing any long carrots,' said Gerald. 'Alternaria doesn't take hold until early July but sclerotinia comes earlier and totally collapses the plant.' The problem is that there is no spray available to home gardeners that will combat the condition, although there is a product obtainable by farmers and commercial growers, and Gerald hoped to be able to use his contacts to acquire some. He expected to have to pay about £40 for a litre but was prepared to invest that if it would bring his carrots back to health.

Joe, too, was discussing his horticultural ailments. He had lost three potentially prize-winning cabbages that stopped growing when the leaves started to turn red. He thought it was some kind of virus. I congratulated him on his appearance in the first instalment of *The Great British Village Show* and sympathised with him for not qualifying for the final at Highgrove. It turned out, though, that he did get to Highgrove after all, not as a participant but as a spectator – a member of Peter's party. Peter had won two classes in the Midlands regional heat, for his long carrot and sunflower, and was allowed two passes to the final for each class; so he and Mary took Joe and Carmel with them.

All in all, Joe had found the experience disappointing. 'Have you ever been to Highgrove? Save your money. I wasn't impressed with the garden and we weren't allowed in the house.'

There was still a knot of enthusiasts enjoying the evening sunshine when I left for the long drive back to London. A week later I telephoned Peter to ask how he thought the evening had gone and how many people had been there. 'We counted the dirty teacups and there were thirty – which means there were more than thirty people, because not all of them had tea. The following evening we had twenty from the local rotary club, and next Tuesday we have a visit from some children from a special school in Derbyshire that does gardening.'

But in the week since my visit the weather had turned bad again. 'We had heavy rain on Sunday night, and the lane and the end of the garden were flooded.' The school bus had been stranded on the road to the village when the stream overflowed its banks, and four houses were damaged by the water.

The marrows probably liked it but I think it might be too wet for the potatoes, which don't like being waterlogged. One of the leeks in the covered trenches rotted away because the water got inside it, between the leaves. I keep records of the weather and I've been comparing this June to last year. This time last year we were getting temperatures of 31°C – now it's cold and wet. We've had ten inches of rain this June so far, compared with a quarter of an inch for the whole of June last year.

Yet he remained philosophical about his chances of winning prizes at the September shows. 'It's the same for everybody, and coping with the variations from year to year is part of the interest and the challenge.'

A little further west the weather had been even worse, and flooding extensive. On the Tuesday of that week I had been going to Chesterfield to see the garden Gerald had created at his grandson's primary school and watch the cookery demonstration James Martin was to stage for the pupils and staff. I had planned to go by train from St Pancras, but the line north of Derby was flooded, and when I asked Gerald whether it would be a good idea to drive he told me that the approach roads to Chesterfield were in chaos; so I stayed at home.

Later he told me that, despite the weather, James Martin and his truck had turned up, and his demonstration had been a great success. With other VIP visitors, James had admired the school garden and the vegetables that came from it. It all looked so good that word quickly spread, and Gerald was asked to plant one at another local school next year.

Kevin and Gareth, too, had been hit by appalling June weather. 'We're not quite on top of things,' said an apologetic Gareth, as I arrived at his house on a comparatively calm day between the storms.

> We've had a lot of rain, so it's been hard to get out into the garden just to do the weeding. And we had a small landslip in the tunnel due to the water backing up and whooshing down the middle of the path. Nothing flooded, but the tunnel was quite wet. It's been none too warm, either.

I could see an indentation in the soil down the centre of the tunnel, like a dry rivulet, indicating where the water had rushed through.

> So much water came in that the water table rose and swelled the soil. It doesn't seem to have done the vegetables much harm, though. Rainwater is supposed to be good for them, and they only get tap water through the hoses.

The main downpour had come as an early evening cloudburst. Kevin was home from work but Gareth was still on his way back. 'It was literally torrential,' said Kevin,

> and it played havoc with the polytunnel. I texted Gareth about it, and then when I came down the road from my house it was horrendous, like a river running along the road and over the kerb. At my house we had about eight inches of water, and it almost came up to the door. It lasted for about an hour, with a lot of thunder and lightning.

Out in the garden, I saw that there had been some collateral damage to one of the marrows. The main stem split in the high wind, and Gareth had done a neat repair job, binding the wound with four lengths of a new soft green plastic material developed specifically for gardeners. The plant was a direct descendant of the

98-lb marrow that won its heat of *The Great British Village Show*, but Gareth had his doubts about its prospects, because the seed was removed a little late.

> The Highgrove final wasn't until October, and to get the seed out of it at its best we should ideally have cut it two or three weeks earlier – four weeks after we originally harvested it. It had plenty of seed, but some of it seemed to have gone over, and some didn't germinate too well. But the two that we have grown on seem fine.

They had also successfully germinated one seed from the marrow they grew the previous year; the parent of the prize-winner.

The *Village Show* had already raised the brothers' media profile. The previous week they had been to *Gardeners' World Live*, an indoor event in Birmingham organised by the BBC and the Royal Horticultural Society, and were asked if next year they would organise a display there about giant vegetable growing. They had not yet made up their minds, because there were two main difficulties. The first was that it would commit them for a week, eating into their precious holiday entitlements. And because the event is in June, they would not be able to take along any of their vegetables at their final weight and maturity: they would be no more than works in progress. However, they said they would consider it if they could attract a sponsor.

The brothers quizzed me in some detail about how Peter's vegetables were looking compared with theirs. They seemed to have some larger beetroot than he did, with a leaf span of some 3ft already, and there was little to choose between them when it came to swedes, celery and rhubarb. With rhubarb, the heaviest single stick wins the prize: the trick is to take off most of the sticks (they can be used in the kitchen) to keep the plant producing until show time. 'Actually about a third of the stuff we grow here is for us to eat,' said Gareth.

He reported that when he last saw Ian's swedes they were 'fantastic . . . massive' – and substantially more advanced than theirs. I told them that Peter's leeks were looking thicker than theirs, which had some white mottling on the leaves caused by thrips – microscopic insects that suck sap from the plants they infest. 'I've sprayed them, and it's not as bad as it was,' said Kevin. 'They're the best leeks we've had for a while. We grew some last year, but they weren't the right strain and we only got to 8 lb. This year we sourced them from John Soulsby. We gave him some marrows, and he gave us some leek pips. We'll save our own seed from them this time and hopefully we'll push on.'

Their four heavy and three long cucumbers were dutifully climbing up the strings that would support the fruit when it developed. 'They're doing all right, but they'd appreciate a week of nice weather,' Kevin observed. 'That would do the world of good and dry everything out.' They would be pollinated in the middle of July, with only the largest on each plant allowed to grow to maturity.

The tunnel also contained their tomatoes and cantaloupes. Their technique with tomatoes is to strip off all the fruit except two, let both grow for a while and then take one off.

> The plant gets used to feeding two, then when you take one off it puts all its energy into feeding the one that's left. Cantaloupes do really well here too if you put fleece on them; but you have to be careful of ants. They make mounds under the roots, so there's no firm structure for the roots to hold on to. That's why we try to get rid of the ants before we plant the cantaloupes out.

Gareth had repaired the damage to the rack that he built for the pipes where the long carrot, parsnip and beetroot were growing. It was a makeshift structure but it seemed to be working all right, although one couldn't tell how far the roots of the vegetables had reached down the pipes. He was worried that, because the pipes were resting at an angle of 45 degrees, not all the water that he put in at the top might get down to the base of the root, where it was most needed.

Back in the house, Gareth was anxious to show me the new logo that a friend, a graphic designer, had created for the *giantveg.co.uk* website. The old logo was a nondescript jumble of large vegetables, some quite hard to distinguish. This one features simply a giant carrot against the background of a blazing sun. 'We're trying to give the site an identity,' he explained. 'Kind of new-age and aspirational.'

Although Ian's nursery is only a fifteen-minute drive from Cwmbran, he had suffered less than the Forteys from the June downpours. 'We did have rain, but not all that much,' he told me. 'But we do need more sun.' He had been troubled less by the weather than by natural predators: 'Mice, rabbits, ants, moles . . . I keep them down with guns, traps, poisons and the cat from next door.' When I told him that Kevin and Gareth also had ant trouble, he said it was because they were reluctant to spend money on keeping pests at bay.

With the complaints out of the way, Ian admitted that he was quite pleased with the performance of his potential giants so far. 'They're all doing well at the moment. A bit of weed but I don't mind a bit of weed as long as you stop it seeding – that's the main thing.' He had spread black biodegradable polythene across the ground to keep the weeds down around some of his plants; others he weeded by hand, down on his knees. 'At this time of year I can spend half a day weeding,' he told me.

He was especially hopeful for his swedes. The plants were about 3ft tall already, and he parted the leaves to reveal a root the size of a football. The beetroot were looking good as well, and the parsnips and celery seemed more advanced than Peter's when I looked at them earlier in the week. 'You can't tell whether they're as good as last year because you can't be putting a tape measure round them at every stage,' Ian pointed out.

His three water melons had put on a tremendous amount of leaf since my last visit, filling a whole side of their polytunnel; but he had located only a few female flowers so far, probably because of the shortage of sunshine. When he does find them he hand-pollinates them with a brush. 'This one is the biggest I've ever had at this time of the year,' he declared, indicating a fruit about a foot long.

While he went off to deal with a customer I looked around the other tunnels. The big one that had been filled with bedding plants last time was now almost empty. It was getting towards the end of the season for planting them out, and he was selling what was left at three for the price of two. Several boxes past their sell-by date had already been thrown on to a pile towards the back of the nursery, to go on the compost heap. All that remained in the tunnel were a few petunias, marigolds and hanging baskets.

Ian rejoined me there.

Some garden centres carry on with bedding plants all summer, but I dump those I have left at the end of June. Everyone is doing badly with plants at the moment. Business is bad because people are taking three or four holidays a year and spending less time in the garden – and if they're on holiday there's nobody to look after the tubs.

I'm a hundred hanging baskets down on last year, and last year was a hundred down on the year before. I'll have sold between 600 and 700 this year. The weather is a factor too: if they're going to have a barbecue they'll come and buy two or three pots to add a bit of colour, but nobody's going to have a barbecue in the kind of weather we've been having.

And looking ahead? 'Next time you come I'll have cleared out the big tunnel for the Christmas chrysanthemums.' That is his second sales peak in the year. He grows the chrysanthemums to be ready in December for sale as cut flowers – cut to order. People put them on loved ones' graves, as a seasonal tribute. 'I make more money out of the dead than the living,' he joked. 'But people don't buy them as much as they used to. One local grower has already gone out of business.'

His bid to get planning permission for housing, so that he could sell the nursery to a developer, was moving slowly, partly because some of his neighbours were also involved in the project. He insisted, though, that if he did sell up he would want to continue raising his giant vegetables; and he would have a lot more time to devote to the quest for glory.

Chapter 7

July

By late July – just six weeks before the big Harrogate show – Gerald was forced to concede that his onions were not going to break any world records. The second year of his hydroponics experiment had not been a total fiasco, but a series of setbacks and miscalculations meant that in the available time his one remaining large onion had no chance of gaining enough weight to become a contender. He was confident, though, that the lessons he had learned could be put to good use in a third, and possibly final, attempt on the record in 2008.

'My best one stopped growing at 24½in,' he reported.

It got stuck there for about two weeks, so I changed the feed to give it more potash, and now it's up to 26½. It needs to be about 30in to win at Harrogate, and I hope it will get there if the weather stays warm and light. As long as it's still growing leaves it will get bigger. Peter's was 23½in when we saw it last month – he's very good at timing.

He believed that the reason for the failure was the problem that had been nagging at him all season.

The balance in the nutrients hasn't been right. I'm having a meeting with the biochemist at Aquaculture in November so that

I can tell him what I want next year: I want five per cent nitrogen and ten per cent potash. But that isn't the only problem. In that really hot weather we had in mid-May the temperature in the greenhouse went up to about 39°C. What Simon [Simon Spinks of Aquaculture] wants to do is to give me a big humidifier next year that will cool the air.

On the day of my visit the sun was shining for almost the first time after two months of unremittingly dismal weather. It was hard to recall the golden days of April, when we were complaining about too much sun and naively assuming that we were in for another summer of hosepipe bans and dire predictions of global warming. 'The sun was what we wanted in June,' Gerald observed, 'and all we had was rain.'

He had identified a third probable reason for his failure, as well:

I've been pumping too often. I increased it from three to four times a day, but now I think it only needed twice a day. That's ample. Even if I pumped only once a day they'd be getting enough nutrient, because the clay balls hold it. They need some water, because they lose moisture, but with too much flooding you get too much water into the bulb itself, and that tends to soften the roots – and if you haven't got a good root system you aren't going to get a good onion.

He started with six onions, three grown from seed and three from bulbils. 'The ones from bulbils started off really fast, then they went soft because the nutrient was too high in nitrogen – higher than I'd asked for. So I threw those three out.' Two of the remaining three were over 26in, but one had stopped growing. Only one was still sporting healthy green leaves; on the others they were brown and shrivelled.

Gerald could console himself with the knowledge that his was not the only hydroponics record bid to have failed. The formidable Medwyn Williams, undertaking a parallel and almost identical experiment sponsored by the same company, was about to reveal to his readers in *Garden News* that his efforts had been equally fruitless. 'My second attempt to beat the world record for the heaviest onion has come to a grinding halt,' he wrote. His biggest specimen began to struggle when it reached 24in. 'The onion has now finished growing at 25½in in circumference, and I shall remove it from the tank.' A second onion had a slower start but stopped growing at about the same size.

His diagnosis was much the same as Gerald's:

I have a feeling I was pushing the conductivity levels too high, with the cell walls within each onion already having sufficient nutrients in them. My feeling is that I need to run the conductivity levels much lower, possibly at 10. The big question I have to ask myself is when and to what level do I drop the conductivity reading. I'm sure it's possible to grow some very large, quality onions using this system. . . . Watch this space next year.

Those who did watch that space learned the following April that Medwyn had decided to 'give hydroponics a miss this year'. Yet he was still bullish about the long-term effectiveness of the system. 'I'm still convinced that it's possible to beat the world record for the heaviest onion growing hydroponically (top grower Gerald Treweek won't be far away from it this year on his third attempt at the record), but I'm sticking to containers.' In the containers he had planted some very large bulbils that Gerald had raised from his 2006 crop, grown from Billy Lamb seed.

Gerald at least had one onion worthy of showing – but, with

just the one, he had to rethink his strategy for the two key competitions. He had to decide whether to take it to Harrogate, where the top prize was £500 (unless you break the world record), or to Ashington, where it could earn double that. He thought he would plump for Harrogate, where he would in any case also be exhibiting quality onions and carrots – classes that do not exist at Ashington.

But he recognised that there was no realistic chance of his single remaining giant onion carrying off the spoils, and he was already planning for 2008 a strategy that would give him the best possible chance of beating the world record. He intended to grow ten giants in the polytunnel – in conventional compost – and six in the greenhouse: hydroponically, but with his new formulation of nutrients and a more conservative pumping regime. The horizon had been extended, but hope lived on.

Every weekly episode of *The Great British Village Show* had an update on the pumpkin contest, described by Alan Titchmarsh as 'a world of bitter rivalries and secret ingredients'. Gerald was shown visiting contestants' gardens with his tape measure. He had developed a technique for letting down lightly those who were not going to make it to Highgrove: 'borderline' was his tactful way of putting it when their pumpkins did not measure up.

The final from Highgrove, which had taken place the previous October, was broadcast on 29 July in a specially extended episode. The pumpkin segment was one of the highlights. First we saw Gerald on the telephone, telling contestants whether their prized and cosseted monsters had been sufficiently monstrous to be admitted to the royal presence.

'When I make these phone calls I could be making somebody's dream come true, or breaking somebody's heart,' he said, and his observation was borne out as we heard snatches of his conversations with those who had made it (*'Yes!!!'*) and those who had not, who bore the news with a momentary silence followed by stoical resignation.

Cut to a picture of some Welsh Guardsmen, brought in to add pomp to the proceedings but who found themselves being dragooned into carrying the giant pumpkins to the show bench. Young James and Liam had qualified for the final, and so had Joe Hallam, although all reported that their pumpkins were smaller than the best they had grown in previous years.

When it came to the weigh-in, though, the prize went to Richard Hope from Wigan: not one of the four whose progress the programme had followed, but a veteran of the giant vegetable scene nonetheless. He struck gold with a pumpkin weighing 892 lb 13 oz. This was not far short of the then British record of 912 lb although substantially below the then world record of 1,502 lb, set by an American, Ron Wallace, in 2006. But Richard revealed it was the biggest one he had ever grown, and, like a true enthusiast, he immediately turned his mind to how it could help him do even better next year. 'I'm not going to take it home,' he told viewers, 'but I've just cut it up here now to get the seeds out. If you wait too long the seeds will be no good.' (Gerald told me later that he had wanted to disqualify Richard's pumpkin because it had a hole at the stalk end, but the producers wanted it for the programme because it was so big.)

Kevin and Gareth picked up a prize for their 98-lb marrow. It was the same one they had won the regional heat with, and it was touch and go whether it would last until Highgrove. It did – and turned out to be some 40 lb heavier than its nearest competitor. The heaviest leek (11 lb 7 oz) was grown by another well-known figure on the show circuit: John Soulsby from Gateshead, who usually concentrates on quality leeks and onions rather than heavy ones. 'Now that I've grown a heavy one I've been bitten by the bug and want to try to break the world record,' he said. He still has a long way to go to achieve that, though: the record is 17 lb 2 oz, set by Fred Charlton in 2002.

We were kept waiting until the last few minutes to be told of the only world record broken at *The Great British Village Show*. When the time came to measure the longest carrot we saw the judges scurrying around, whispering conspiratorially and consulting their record books. Then it was announced that Peter's 17-ft 3-in specimen was indeed a new record.

'Breaking the longest carrot record at Highgrove – that is special,' said Peter. But that whole segment of the programme was rushed through rather quickly, in an oddly low-key fashion. Given the level of hype that had been apparent throughout the series, and that this was the only world record broken, it was surprising that the producers did not think to mark the great occasion with a special ceremony.

Why did they not place the carrot on a platter and have the Welsh Guards march through the Highgrove garden with it, while a military band played triumphant music? I suspect it was because the carrot was a sickly looking object: just 17ft of skinny, string-like root, impossible to display impressively on a small oblong screen. More time had been allotted to Richard's giant pumpkin. Even if it had not broken a record, it was much more televisual than the long carrot – with its bright amber skin and a shape faintly reminiscent of a fat lady's bottom on a saucy seaside postcard.

Peter's victory gave him the chance to engage in a dialogue with the Prince of Wales, who was sporting enough to express great enthusiasm, even though he must have known that the techniques used to produce these horticultural freaks are the very antithesis of the organic, natural methods he espouses in his Highgrove garden.

'Do you grow them in special pipes?' the Prince inquired. 'Yes,' Peter replied, 'up the side of the house.' 'So presumably,' Charles quipped, 'if you win the record you've got to get a bigger house!' And the Prince wound up the show with a comment on 'the trouble taken by all these characters, the techniques, the black magic that goes into this. They're all terrified somebody else is going to pick it up.' The heir to the throne has spent a lifetime observing people and their quirks, and it hadn't taken him long to gauge the depth of passion that consumes the giant vegetable fraternity.

Later Gerald told me of a dramatic incident at the Highgrove filming that confirmed how seriously everyone takes it: 'Peter had just laid his carrot out on the table when a cameraman knocked the whole table over. Peter went ballistic – I think he knew he had a record. He's usually a quiet-spoken man and I've never seen him so angry.' Luckily for the cameraman, the carrot – and the world record – survived unscathed.

The final of *The Great British Village Show* was screened the weekend before I visited Peter in late July, and we agreed that his achievement was not given as much fanfare as it deserved, squeezed as it was into the last few minutes of the programme. He was not resentful, though. He has the perfect temperament for a vegetable grower, calm and stoical, accepting the inevitable setbacks with a resigned shrug and, even when confident of success, not letting himself be carried away, conscious that pride too often comes before a fall.

A few days before my visit he had been to see Gerald again and inspected the one remaining viable hydroponic onion. While it was clear that Peter thought he would have the beating of him at Harrogate, he was too canny to deliver a hostage to fortune by saying so specifically. He went no further than: 'I don't think Gerald's has the look of a champion.'

He was still talking up the chances of Walter Stringfellow, the Wakefield grower he told Gerald about, whose biggest onion had measured 28½ inches when he saw it ten days previously. Peter thought Walter's secret weapon was his traditional greenhouse with a solid fuel boiler and heated pipes running through the beds – a luxury few of his rivals enjoyed. 'I think he might get the world record this year. But he's had a setback because he grows his stuff on his allotment and had a bit of vandalism there. They pulled up four of his onions, but luckily none of the very big ones. He's very proud of his stuff, and he took it very badly. He refuses to show anyone round any more.'

Peter's own problems had been less dramatic, dominated by the continuing poor weather – dismal enough to try the patience of even the most phlegmatic gardener. (Figures later showed that in May, June and July 2007 Britain's rainfall was the highest since records began in 1766.) 'Soon after you were here last time I looked out of the window and saw ground water from the field behind us running along the lane. The traffic couldn't get through, and I tried to walk to the village but I couldn't even do that. The houses that had only just dried out from the last time got flooded again. And only last week the road was under water for a time.'

Most of the vegetables had suffered from the conditions, some more than others.

The marrows and melons are hopeless. I haven't had any female flowers at all on the cantaloupes – I'll be lucky if I've got one to take. Usually you have to tie in the side shoots and stop them every day, but this year they haven't made any. They might come now that the sun is out, but it's a bit late.

And only one of the water melons has set so far. They started off well, but then we had all those dark and rainy days, and they didn't put on any more growth. I shan't be beating Ian this year: I'm looking for third place. The marrows are as bad. The fruits start coming but then they turn yellow and drop off, because it's too cold and dark.

There was still just time, though, if he could get one to set in the next few days. The first giant show, at Shepton Mallet, was four weeks away – and that could be enough time for a marrow to develop, so long as it stayed healthy.

The tomatoes were also behind their usual schedule, and the rain had rotted a few of the leeks and potatoes. Peter did not think the weather would have affected the length of his long carrots, beetroot and turnips, although there was no way of telling until he removed them – ever so carefully – from their pipes on the eve of the show.

Some of his quality and heavy carrots had been afflicted with alternaria.

Every week I've been cutting diseased leaves off. I spray with what I can buy commercially, but it doesn't stop it – the sprays are a waste of money, really. The effective ones are only sold to professional growers: I don't know what the hobby gardener is supposed to do. The trouble is that there are too many carrots grown round here – acres and acres of them.

In spite of the disease, he thinks he probably has a competitive heavy carrot. And his long runner beans look promising, given that there is still a month to go. With the beans, timing is crucial. 'I take most of them off until a few weeks before the show. I don't let them grow too early because I always think the first trusses are the best ones. The later ones get a bit curly.'

He was still having trouble with those of his cabbages that had not mysteriously gone to seed early in the season. The two survivors were growing at opposite ends of the garden, and something was eating the leaves of the one at the lower end. 'I've looked hard and I can't find anything. I keep spraying it but it doesn't seem to have any effect.' Peter thought it might be an infestation of rape beetle, but – since they generally feed on pollen, not leaves – I doubted his diagnosis. The damage would not disqualify him from the heavy cabbage classes, although of course it would reduce the weight. In any case he had higher hopes for the cabbage at the top of the garden, which so far had not been attacked. 'It has thicker foliage: it looks a different cabbage – but it came from the same batch of seed.'

He held out scant hope for his heavy and long cucumbers, although they looked buxom enough to me. His 91-year-old friend Alf Cobb, who also lives in the Newark area, specialises in giant cucumbers. Peter had been to inspect them a few days earlier and was sure they were bigger than his own, which he feared might have been weakened by a virus attack. Ian and the Forteys grow their heavy cucumbers up strings and support them in bags of fine netting when they get to this size; but Peter had built a more robust frame and had not needed to give them any extra support yet.

He was unsure about his squashes, two growing in tunnels and one outside. The outdoor one, like the marrows and melons, had been reluctant to produce female flowers, but one had set in each of the tunnels. 'They took their time, and they aren't as big as I'd like at this stage, but if I can get one up to 200 lb it should have a chance. And there's a pumpkin growing at the back. It flowered yesterday and I pollinated it, but whether it's taken I don't know.' His giant cauliflowers, too, suffered from a late start, but he had an extra week for those: there was no class for them at Shepton Mallet, only at the later Welsh shows.

But now that the sun had finally broken through, that was causing Peter problems as well. The quality vegetable show season had already begun, and he needed to get his stuff together for a show at Bakewell in Derbyshire the following day. It would take him an hour and a half to get there, so he would need to gather and prepare his entries that afternoon. The trouble was that they would deteriorate rapidly in the hot weather – and once they got to the venue they would start wilting very quickly in the marquee – so he had to delay digging and gathering for as long as he could. He was entering four main classes and was also considering taking along a large beetroot that looked a bit like an elephant, to enter in the class for the most unusual looking vegetable: last year he had come second with a long radish.

His first important quality show of the season had taken place the previous week at Leek in Staffordshire – mainly devoted to leeks, as you might expect. Peter won the class for long leeks, and his stick of celery took the prize in the class for any other vegetable. That should have put him in good heart for what to him are the really important contests, in particular that vital first clash of the giants at Shepton Mallet, now just four tense weeks away.

The weather had turned the corner in Wales as well. It was a warm, sunny morning when I visited the Forteys at the end of July, but Gareth feared that the improvement had come too late. 'It's been the worst weather I've ever known, raining on and off since May: I don't think we've had two consecutive days of nice weather, really. It's either been dull or raining, and in the last month especially it's been raining so heavily that we couldn't do anything outside.'

While we waited for Kevin – still at home feeding baby son Jamie, now nearly a year old – Gareth told me they had found a short-term solution to the problem of the water rushing down the centre of the new polytunnel. A plank in front of it diverted the deluge – although it did not address the more serious problem of the rise in the water table at the bottom end, due to the old blocked drain. 'The ground simply can't cope with the water,' said Gareth.

The lack of sunlight had been at least as serious as the excess of rain:

Pollination has been low because the pollinating insects don't come out when it's damp and there's no sun. You need sunlight during the crucial time when the male and female flowers are on the plants. It's affected the melons [cantaloupes] and marrows, especially the melons. We've tried several times to pollinate them but they go yellow and die.

We think we may have succeeded with two – one in the tunnel and one in the cold frame. We won with melons at Shepton Mallet last year, but, with only five weeks to go, we probably won't win this year: you usually try to pollinate six or seven weeks before the show. Of course everyone else might have the same problem.

Root crops such as beetroot and swedes were in danger of rotting in the damp soil, and the rain also ruled out watering. That might look like a benefit, saving time and trouble – until you realise that the only way to feed many plants is to add nutrients to the water: so no water means no fertiliser.

Still waiting for Kevin, we conducted a post mortem on *The Great British Village Show*. There was talk of a second series, but the brothers had not been approached about it so far, which meant it would not be filmed until 2008 at the earliest. 'I'm not even sure we'd enter if they did it again,' said Gareth. 'The exposure's fine but it takes up a lot of time. They came here three times to film, apart from us having to go to the shows themselves and stay there from nine to six, at their beck and call.'

Kevin arrived, his paternal duties fulfilled, and we went into the garden to inspect the produce. The first thing we saw was a marrow, about a foot long and seemingly on track to become a contender at Shepton Mallet. But appearances are deceptive, and Kevin pointed out that it was hollow, with a hole in the flower end, which meant it would not grow any bigger. The second largest was healthy and thriving, but it was touch and go whether it would be heavy enough to show in five weeks. Taking that uncertainty into account, the brothers had already worked out their tactics.

We'll just let the biggest on each plant grow on for the next few weeks. Then, if there's one that's getting very big and still growing by the time of the Shepton Mallet show, we'll leave it to get bigger and take a smaller one to the show. We'll leave the biggest one to grow and take it to Malvern [four weeks later]. You can tell by the shape if it's going to grow really heavy.

Kevin added that they nearly always do better with marrows than Ian, because their garden is better protected against wind and cold than his exposed nursery.

The soil in the polytunnel was still looking soggy from the blocked drain overflow, and Gareth pointed out another, unrelated problem in there – yellowing leaves on the swedes. He put this down to magnesium deficiency. 'It won't kill them but it checks growth' – just what you don't want when you are aiming for maximum weight. He applied the recommended remedy – Epsom salts – and it had visibly worked, because the swedes were sprouting new healthy green leaves and were still growing. But the biggest of them measured only thirteen inches across (it would need to get up to twenty to be a winner). And the change in the weather might not help: 'If you have a warm spell after a cold one there's a danger they'll split,' Kevin said. All in all, then, the swedes were unlikely to earn the Forteys any prizes this year.

Other plants were looking more hopeful. One tomato remained on each stem and, although these too were a little later than usual, the boys had won with them before and thought they could do so again. They were their own strain, selected over the years from the biggest they have grown.

Some of the cucumbers were already more than a foot long. 'You can tell when they're small if they're going to be the right shape, and, if not, you take them off.' To my untutored eye it was hard to discern the difference between the long and the heavy ones, but Kevin explained that it was to do with the length of the stem that joined them to the vine: the long ones had the longer stem. The heavies had to reach twenty pounds to be in with a chance of a prize, and so far they were all some way short of that.

The Forteys' technique with runner beans is different from Peter's. Whereas he takes off the early blossoms, attempting to time the first beans to coincide with the Shepton Mallet show, they let several beans form throughout the season and often find that the later ones are the longest. They already had one that stretched from the tip of Gareth's finger to his elbow. 'They were smashed to smithereens by the wind and rain when they were small,' he said. 'But with the better weather they've suddenly come to life.'

Finally we looked at the long carrot, parsnip and beetroot in the newly built frame near the house. Because they grow them in open half-drainpipes – rather than fully covered as Peter does – they could monitor progress by examining the white tips of the roots as they showed above the surface of the compost. They then put in dated plant labels to indicate the rate of progress. The beetroot was doing the best of the three, at around 10ft, but the brothers knew it would have to be something like double that to have a chance of winning.

They thought it might reach 14ft by the time of the show but, as this was the first year they had had the frame and made a serious attempt at the long stuff, they were reasonably happy. They had not started them until May, which they knew was several weeks later than Peter. Next year, with an earlier start and using the experience they had gained, they hoped to do a lot better.

Back indoors, Gareth showed me the new computer he had constructed from parts he ordered from the internet. He is proud of his technical wizardry and assured me that his new set-up is 'future-proof for a few years'. Given the time he had spent on that project, and the fact that he had recently been working quite late at the office, it is not surprising that he had fallen behind on his plans to upgrade the *giantveg.co.uk* website. Scott Robb had been sending more indignant emails from Alaska, complaining about it.

At Newport Ian took me to the back of the nursery and pointed over the hedge to the neighbouring farmer's field of maize.

> It should be 6ft to 8ft tall by now, but it's only 3ft. You shouldn't be able to see the bare earth underneath it. It just hasn't developed in the usual way. It won't ripen without sun. The fertiliser companies have got to find out what sunlight does for a plant and put it in a bottle. The only way round it is to go for lights, but that's unfair on the other growers, the amateurs. I know I'm a professional nurseryman but I like to grow things in an amateur way. I don't use lights at all.

All the bedding plants had gone from the nursery display tables by now, the unsold ones being discarded on the compost heap. The big polytunnel would soon be filled with his Christmas chrysanthemums, bought as unrooted plants for growing on. But with the first of the shows only a month away, the giant vegetables were taking up more and more of his time.

He had visited the Forteys recently and was able to compare his progress with theirs. Like them, he had trouble pollinating his cantaloupes and marrows. The marrows, in particular, were a disaster: so far he had not managed to produce a single one. 'They've been lying in water. I had a female flower there the other day, but it was too wet for me to get out and pollinate it. By the time I did get out the flower had closed up. It could be that a pollen beetle did it for me, but I won't know for a couple of days.'

His heavy cucumbers were being supported by bright red string bags hanging from supports by the vine. 'They're nowhere near heavy enough to win yet, but should get there with five weeks to go.' He had lost one overnight: 'I don't know why. Maybe the roots get too wet with the rain getting into the soil, and they rot.'

Ian's swedes were bigger than the Forteys', partly because he had fed them well enough to prevent any magnesium deficiency.

I think they're a bit smaller than last year, but I don't go running a tape measure around them, because there's nothing you can do to make them any bigger. I'm growing seven, but the two by the door are small because they get the wind, and that keeps them cool and keeps their size down: so I've got five good ones. I'll take two to the shows, and with luck I could win first and second prizes.

He thought his celery was level pegging with Kevin and Gareth's, but it was hard to tell. Like theirs, it was about 3ft high, but the decisive weight comes at the base of the plant. When I put my hands down to feel the bulk he warned me off: celery burn is a familiar hazard to vegetable growers. 'You get nasty blisters on the hands. I've had it and so has Gareth and we both had to go to the doctor. You'll see several people at the show with scars on their hands.' The blisters are caused by excessive contact with a substance in the leaves that provokes an allergic reaction.

Ian was still being plagued by natural predators, including mice, rabbits, ants and cats. There were more rabbits about than usual, he said, judging by the holes in people's lawns. More seriously, the mice and the ants appeared to have joined forces to threaten the water melons, normally among his most successful crops. Clear bite marks showed where the mice had been gnawing away at the melons' flesh. The marks would not disqualify the melon from the competition but would clearly affect its weight. The ants, meanwhile, had been feasting on the leaves and stems of the plants, which was likely to harm their vigour. Yet so far none of the damage was terminal, and Ian still tended the plants carefully, feeding them twice a week and throwing water over the leaves as much as three times a day, to keep them moist and cool.

> I've won with water melons the last three years. The world record is 268 lb, held by an American, and these are probably 80 to 100. I've had one about 163 lb. If the ants and the mice left them alone I don't see why I shouldn't grow one big enough to beat the record. We need the right seed, though, and nobody in America will give us the right seed.

The soil temperature within the tunnel was also a factor. 'It should be 70° or 72°F [21–22°C], but it's down to 68° today, and some days it's been as low as 60°. The Americans like it in the eighties.'

We crossed to the greenhouses behind his house, erected by his mother and father when they lived there. That is where he was growing potatoes in sacks and radishes in blue barrels. The radishes could scarcely have benefited from the attentions of local cats, who had climbed into the greenhouse and used the barrels as toilets. It was the first time he had tried radishes for four or five years, and he did not think he had any really big ones, although he would not know for certain until he dug them up before the shows.

Maybe he had not given them the attention they deserved. 'It's finding the time, really,' he sighed. 'With your job and your age, you get to the point where you can't do it all. Five years ago I'd stay out here until nine or ten at night, but not now.'

We talked about the practical details of getting ready for the shows. Shepton Mallet opens to the public on a Friday, and the vegetables have to be staged during Thursday afternoon and evening. Ian digs, harvests and cleans his stuff on the Wednesday, ready to take to Shepton – a drive of about an hour and a half – the following day. He starts digging in the morning with the heavy carrots and parsnips. He is growing fifteen of each and will dig up as many as half of them initially, hoping to find two really big ones, leaving the others in the ground for later shows. Then he will get through his other crops as the day goes on.

He agreed that I should come and watch him do this. My plan then would be to drive north to stay with friends who live between Brecon and Builth Wells, then head for Cwmbran early on the Thursday to see Kevin and Gareth harvest their produce. After that, we would all make our way to Shepton Mallet, to watch the heavy vegetables being weighed as the exhibitors unloaded them. But, before all that, I had to go to Alaska.

Chapter 8

Alaska

It can be illuminating to see ourselves as others see us. Charles Elliott, an American garden writer living in London, observed in 1996 that you only had to visit a British country show to discover 'a whole class of expert gardeners devoted to – indeed obsessed by – deliberately growing giant vegetables: virtually everything from leeks to cabbages, from pumpkins to parsnips'. And he thought he had worked out why. 'It's almost as if the nation's gardeners are trying to make up for the fact that Great Britain isn't very great any more.'

An ingenious – if patronising – explanation, but mistaken, not least because giant vegetables are big in America, too. In the 2008 edition of *Guinness World Records,* twelve of the thirty-nine heavy vegetable records are attributed to American growers, only one fewer than the British tally. Arkansas has its water melon championships, while several states in the north-east and New England, notably Rhode Island, foster mammoth pumpkins. But nowhere has the cult taken hold more strongly than in the most northerly state of the union, Alaska.

Scott Robb had reacted warily when I first emailed him in the spring, and understandably so. To be contacted out of the blue by someone claiming to be writing a book about giant vegetables is not a routine occurrence. Suspecting, perhaps, that it was part of some elaborate internet scam, he replied politely but noncommittally: he was unsure of his movements during the summer – family weddings and all that – but I was welcome to get in touch when my plans were more concrete.

He was not the only person to signal surprise, bafflement almost, when told about the project. To fund the Alaska trip I had secured a commission to write an article on the state fair for the *Sunday Times Magazine*. And, having worked as a newspaper correspondent in the United States some years ago, I knew that anyone proposing to work as a journalist there should obtain an 'I' visa – 'I' standing for information media. That involved filling in a lot of forms and joining a long queue for security checks at the US embassy in London, before being granted a face-to-face interview.

'Tell me, Mr Leapman,' asked the bemused official, cutting to the quick, 'why would the readers of the *Sunday Times* be interested in the Alaska State Fair?' A reasonable question that deserved a proper answer. 'It's the giant vegetables,' I began to explain. 'They grow bigger there than almost anywhere, because of the long summer days.' I saw his eyes narrow. Did he really want to pursue this? He was a busy man with a lot of cases to deal with that morning. I might be mad, but the chances were that I was neither bad nor dangerous to know. Sometimes in his job you had to follow your instincts. It took him no more than five seconds to sigh, stamp my form and declare: 'You're approved.'

The quickest way from Europe to Anchorage, Alaska's largest city, is over the North Pole. In summer 2007 the only passenger flights on that route were flown by Condor, a German charter company operating out of Frankfurt. The plane was full of Alaskans returning from European vacations and Germans flying out to join cruise ships or begin activity holidays – sea and river fishing, climbing, bear-watching or exploring glaciers.

In the taxi from the airport, I told the driver that I had come for the state fair. 'Wouldn't miss it,' he replied. 'Fun among the giants, huh?' He was quoting the slogan of that year's fair. The giant vegetable contest, and in particular the public cabbage weigh-off, are two of its unique features, and the organisers marketed the 2007 fair around the theme, with posters showing a young woman peering at a swollen cabbage and pumpkin.

The Anchorage visitors' bureau had booked me into an elegant bed-and-breakfast on the fringe of the downtown area. It was Saturday afternoon, and there was a small farmers' market on a patch of ground just across the road. Walking through it on my way to the centre, I saw immediately that the vegetables were at least half as big again as you find in British markets. It was like seeing the cabbages, cauliflowers, broccoli, kohlrabi and everything else through a magnifying glass. But this was just the regular vegetables grown commercially for cooking and eating – nobody had been fussing over these individually, cosseting them with artificial lights and heat to induce them to add the crucial extra inches and ounces that could get them among the prize-winners.

And the vegetable theme was maintained even in the ornamental roadside beds downtown, planted and carefully tended by the Anchorage Parks and Recreation Department. Large ornamental kale and cabbages, red as well as green, were mixed in appealingly with the summer flowers. Here were a city and a state that took their vegetables seriously.

Alaska is the smallest state of the union by population, with just 650,000 people, but at 50,374 square miles it is by far the largest in area, easily beating Texas. Alaskans boast that, if you sliced their state in half, Texas would drop to third place – the same streak of chauvinism that leads them to refer dismissively to the other continental states of the USA as the Lower 48.

Much of northern Alaska is too cold and rugged to be inhabitable. Anchorage, in the less forbidding southern region, is much the largest city and has nearly half the population. I spent two days in Anchorage before moving to Palmer, about an hour's drive north-east in the fertile Mat-Su Valley, which, for reasons rooted in Alaska's history, is the permanent home of the state fair. The Americans bought the vast, almost empty territory of Alaska from the Russians in 1867, but for more than sixty years made no formal attempt to colonise it; the first American incomers were principally adventurers seeking their fortunes from gold mining or trading for furs with the Eskimos. In the mid-twentieth century, though, after the Depression and the New Deal, the Government launched a scheme to settle impoverished farmers on previously undeveloped land, and Palmer was the place chosen to take 203 hopeful families from Wisconsin, Minnesota and Michigan. Each was granted between forty and eighty acres of land, including a house and outbuildings, along with a $3,000 loan to be paid back over thirty years. A few people in the town still remember coming as children in May 1935 and living that first summer in a tented camp with primitive amenities. Things improved when their proper houses were finished, but Alaskan winters are fierce, and there were many families who found the life and climate too hard and headed back south.

A year after the colony was established, those farmers who had stuck it out decided to start an annual show where they could exhibit their livestock and their produce, and to make it part of a fair celebrating the establishment of the colony. The first fair, in 1936, ran for four days and included boxing matches, horse races and a baby show; a few hundred people turned up and had a whale of a time. Then the farmers discovered something odd about the vegetables they were growing: they were reaching sizes unheard of in most other parts of America, especially cabbages and pumpkins.

The principal reason was not hard to fathom, once they thought about it. Alaska's spring comes later than elsewhere but changes swiftly into summer, and, with only four hours of darkness in late

June, the vegetables are flooded with natural light at their critical growing period – and they revel in it. Add to this the valley's mineral-rich volcanic soil, and you have the perfect conditions for growing big.

So the farmers decided to stage competitions at the fair not just for the best vegetables but also for the largest – and they persuaded the manager of the Alaska Railroad to offer a prize of $25 for the heaviest cabbage. The first weigh-off, in 1941, was won with a specimen reaching just 23 lb. By selective breeding over the years the growers have produced larger and larger cabbages, and the prize fund has swollen dramatically, to $2,000 for the winner, with $1,000 for the runner-up and another $2,000 shared between the also-rans, down to twentieth place.

The present state record is 105 lb, achieved in 2000 by Barb Everingham, a fabric cutter at the local Wal-Mart supermarket who had never tried growing giant vegetables before and retired from the fray the following year. The dedicated group of Alaskan growers, who compete at the fair year after year with their cabbages and other enlarged vegetables, and who had been straining to exceed the elusive 100-lb mark, were naturally mortified to be beaten by this comparative amateur. The most dedicated of all of them is Scott Robb, and he was determined to claim the record one day . . . maybe even in 2007.

When I emailed Scott for the second time, a couple of weeks before my departure from London, he responded with the courtesy and generosity that I would soon learn are characteristic of him. Like the visa official at the embassy, he had decided to give my unlikely intentions the benefit of the doubt, although I later learned that he had first emailed Kevin and Gareth Fortey to check: 'Do you know this guy Michael?' He suggested I should visit him on Wednesday, the day before the fair opened, when I could look at his garden and

▲ Peter Glazebrook needs a head for heights to inspect the top growth of his long carrots.

▲ Ian Neale has dug up a seriously heavy parsnip.

► Gareth Fortey shows off his most promising runner bean.

◄ Kevin Fortey and Kyle Phillips release the Forteys' long beetroot from its drainpipe.

◀ Scott Robb and his prize-winning kale behind the fence that keeps the Alaskan moose at bay.

▼ Scott struggles to load the unruly kale on to his truck.

~ NEW ~
WORLD RECORD
(Tentative - certification pending)
Kale 105.9 lb
Scott Robb - Palmer

▲ Mission accomplished: the world record is confirmed.

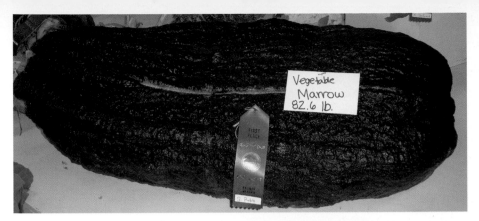

▲ A blue ribbon adorns Scott's prize-winning marrow.

▶ Scott takes the marrow to the bench.

◀ A feast of giants at the Alaska State Fair.

◀ Shepton Mallet: Joe Atherton and his champion parsnip.
(Bristol News and Media)

▶ Long carrots on display.

◀ Mark Baggs *(right)* needs help to unload his pumpkin.
(Bristol News and Media)

▶ David Thomas's six-year-old daughter, Madeleine, proudly guards his cabbages.

▲ Ashington: visitors cast their expert eyes over the leeks.

▲ Getting the measure of the runner beans at Abertysswg.

▶ At Ashington the onions are weighed with foliage attached ...

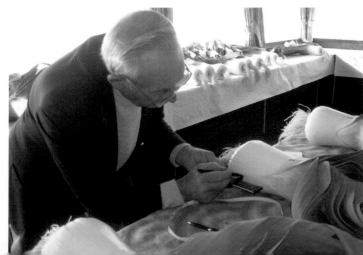

◀ ... while Robert Bell assesses the leeks.

◄ John Evans displays his Guinness certificate for growing the heaviest carrot in the world.

▼ Alf Cobb with his record-breaking cucumber. *(Left)* Alf and Peter Glazebrook open up the cucumber to retrieve next year's seed.

► Peter's system for keeping track of the weight of the onions that will produce seed for future years.

► Weighing one of Ian and Stuart Paton's giant pumpkins at their Lymington nursery. (Ian and Stuart Paton)

◄ Peter with one of his winning onions at Dewsbury.

► Ian and Stuart with two of their monsters. (Ian and Stuart Paton)

▲ Bernard Lavery, father of the giant vegetable cult, with a massive carrot. (Stephen Daniels)

▲ Ian Neale celebrates his record-breaking beetroot. (Nigel Andrews)

▼ Gerald Treweek checks the progress of his hydroponic onions.

Apart from those credited, all photographs are reproduced courtesy the author.

talk, and later maybe accompany him and his wife Mardie to the fairground for the staging of the giant vegetables.

The Robbs live about a mile out of town, on a narrow street off the main road to Anchorage, right opposite the permanent fairground. Their spacious house, modelled on a Swiss chalet, stands on top of a fairly steep slope, above the greenhouse and polytunnels of the nursery where they operate a thriving business for three months of the year, starting when the snow melts in the spring. 'We bought the house for the view,' said Scott, pointing to Lazy Mountain in one direction, Pioneer Peak in the other.

He is from Ohio and has been in Alaska since 1975, when, like so many, he came to work in the oil fields as an engineer. Soon he met and married Mardie, whose father was in the same line of business, and they had three daughters. As the family grew, Scott found it increasingly irksome that his job took him away from home for up to two weeks at a time. 'When your daughters get to be teenagers you need two parents to handle the situations.' After they moved to Palmer in 1990 he resolved to start the nursery business, even though his only relevant experience had been helping out at an Ohio nursery for three summers during his school holidays – and he hadn't enjoyed that much. 'Life's kind of full circle,' he observed.

If you're exposed to certain things when you're younger, you might think at that time 'I hate this; I don't want to get dirty,' or whatever – but later on in life you come back to it. And when I was very young my grandfather had a really green thumb – he grew anything and everything.

When we moved to this spot we started to fall in love with gardening. At the beginning we mostly grew ordinary vegetables for eating and preserving, but we started growing the giant cabbage straight away, because that was what Alaska was known for. I bought Bernard Lavery's book, and that gave me a lot of hints. It was a great help. I'd like to meet the guy some day. He was at the forefront of getting everybody excited and interested.

I also got to know John Evans, who came here from Ireland. He was the one who started to try to break world records here. I couldn't figure out how he did it until it dawned on me that he was using special seed. When growers are equal in ability, the varieties and the genetics become very important. When I found out that these other guys were using special seeds, that's when things started happening, when I started doing things. I didn't get any world records to begin with, but my personal best jumped considerably.

John Evans, whom I was to meet later in the year, effectively quit the giant vegetable scene a few years ago when he developed a soil additive called Compostea that he markets as an aid to healthy and prolific growth.

Scott was impressed to discover that some growers were so dedicated that they drove from Fairbanks, 450 miles away, to exhibit their produce at the fair.

And there are Gene and Don Dinkel, two brothers who have been beating everyone in the giant cabbage department for years. Their parents came up here in 1936 and they picked up homestead land from people in the original 1935 Mat-Su colony. It's on a slope by the Cook Inlet where the weather's milder, and they can start stuff and put it outside a month earlier than most of us.

They've never really got anything other than giant cabbages. But sadly Gene is ill now, and one of his grandsons, Seth, has taken over. Don used to be Professor of Horticulture at the University of Alaska. He still grows the cabbages, but his grand-daughter Brenna shows them. The first time she showed she was six and won with a 90-pounder.

I was not destined to meet any of the legendary Dinkel clan. The state fair runs for two weeks, ending on Labor Day at the beginning of September. There are separate giant vegetable competitions for each week, and the cabbage weigh-off comes in the second week, by which time I had to be back in England for the Shepton Mallet show. The Dinkels customarily bring their cabbages only in that second week. Like John Evans, they bred their own seed, based on a hybrid called an O/S cross – Oriental crossed with Super. 'I used to complain that it was unfair on the rest of us to create their own variety, but if you're going to compete that's what you've got to do,' says Scott.

Over the years I've made six, seven, eight crosses myself, and now I've got one that I call Giant Jac (I called it after the initials of my three girls: Jaesah, Amanda and Chelsea). The ones that the Dinkels bring usually have dense heads, but mine are big, leafy cabbages that don't head up much: the weight is in the leaves. It's a kind of challenge because they're self-incompatible, so you have to have another one for pollination. I've spent such a lot of time and money developing the crosses that as long as I'm competing I'm not going to give out any of the details.

The problem with hybrids is that they're too uniform. As a giant-vegetable grower, that's the last thing you want: uniformity. Over the years the O/S cross has got to that uniformity stage where it's just no good for giants: if I can grow 60-pounders, so can everybody else.

Scott sows his cabbages around 15 April – a good four months later than Peter and other British growers. He starts them off in 3½-in pots in heat, in his commercial greenhouse at the bottom of the hill. Five weeks later he transfers them into the garden in large pots or drums.

It's five-star accommodation for them – it's well drained, and the soil stays warm. But the drawback is that they sometimes get badly damaged by the wind at that time of year.

Cabbage is what I've been growing most of for the longest time, and it's something I'm fascinated with; but I've never even come close to Bernard's record [124 lb]. I can't even imagine a cabbage that big. I don't know if we'll ever be able to do it, because we can't sow stuff in the autumn and let the roots develop over the winter like you can in Britain. What you guys do in eight months, we do in four. Early spring for us is June 1st. And the cabbages react differently – so you can take a variety that may not be listed in any of the seed books as a giant, but you bring it up here, with our long days, and it might grow bigger.

At the height of summer we get 19½ hours of daylight, and the rest is twilight – it never really gets dark. In the latter part of April we get 16 or 17 hours of daylight, and that's valuable sunlight. Before 1st April we might get 10 or 12 hours, but there's no real intensity to it, because the sun's not high enough in the sky to do much good. So from April on, those are the important months to really get stuff going and establish them with a nice root system, so when you do put them out they take off.

Timing is critical here because, unlike in England, where the shows run all through September, in Alaska everything has to be perfect for the single show at the end of August. 'That's what's so challenging. We couldn't hold our show any later, because in September it starts to freeze at night; when we're still getting fourteen hours of daylight there can be frost at night.' And within a few weeks the ground has frozen totally. 'We tried to keep carrots in the ground one winter, and I put straw all over them. I came down at Christmas time to pull them, and cleared away two feet of snow, but the ground was frozen under the straw. I couldn't get anything out.'

Scott works hard at mastering the theory as well as the practice of growing vegetables to their greatest potential.

I've got three greenhouses, one is east–west and the other two north–south, and they have different microclimates. In the garden you try to create some sort of a microclimate if you can – but it doesn't always work out, because you can only control so much. Everyone has their ways and means. I read Bernard's book about the cantaloupe. He says the same thing about growing giant marrows as cantaloupes – that you have to keep the vine pruned. With the cantaloupe I tried that for a number of years, pinching off the secondaries, but it's just a lot of work, and I never could grow anything over 30 lb. So I decided to let the vine grow, and that year I grew a 60-lb cantaloupe – a world record – and I had one vine with two 50-pounders on it.

So I'm discovering that what might have worked well for him doesn't necessarily work for me. You read the book, you get a lot of good ideas from it, but you know he's not telling you the entire story. Giant-pumpkin growers train their vines to a certain pattern – mostly so that they can make it manageable, so they can get around and spray underneath the leaves – but I don't know that they prune the vine itself.

Scott's cantaloupe world record of 64 lb 13 oz has stood since 2004, although he was not growing either cantaloupes or water melons in 2007, because he was refurbishing the greenhouse where they do best. They can be grown outdoors in an Alaskan summer, but the really big ones have to stay indoors to allow them to build a vine substantial enough to support fruits that will grow immensely quickly in the sixty days between pollination and harvest.

My world record cantaloupe was grown in a 25-gallon pot. I went down twice a day to water them and feed them with a small amount of feed. Every time they got watered they would get fertilised. It's like you and me. If you gorge when you eat it's not healthy, but if you eat three square meals a day you're going to be better off. They're like humans – they require a certain amount of food at certain times of day, consistently.

You have to give space for the roots to grow, but really it's more about nutritional needs and providing the plants with enough food. You can stymie some things by putting them in too small a pot. I put some marigolds in little pots and some in big pots, and the ones in the little pots are going to flower first, because the others will continue growing leaves when they have more root space to expand into. It's the same with giant vegetables. If you crowd them they aren't going to get as big, because they need the root space, like a tree.

I'm quite proud of the fact that I could grow that cantaloupe up here, even though it was in the greenhouse and in a soilless compost. In effect I was doing it hydroponically because I was in full control. I hand-pollinated them, because the placement of the fruit on the vine is very important.'

He got out his scrapbook and showed me pictures of his world records.

There's the cantaloupe. One of ordinary market size on the left and mine on the right. It was beautiful.

. . . And that's my world record celery. I'm not growing celery this year. Once I achieve something I move on, because I only have so much space. As you can see that's in a 25-gallon pot. I started them in the greenhouse early and then I cut the bottom out of the pot and put them in the garden. And that's my beautiful turnip. I started those in little pots just like cabbages and put them in the garden when they were four weeks old.

The biggest water melon he has achieved is 115 lb, a long way from the world record 268 lb 12 oz set in 2005 by Lloyd Bright from Bill Clinton's birthplace – Hope, Arkansas, which has held an annual water melon festival since 1926. 'Lloyd has a field that he grows them in – acres of water melon plants as far as you can see: they're massive.'

The longest-standing record that Scott still holds is for a 75-lb 12-oz rutabaga (in Britain we call them swedes) that he grew in 1999.

It was a beaut. A lot of time you'll see that these rutabagas have these huge extended necks, and that adds to the weight, but I cut them all off. I saved it, wintered it over, and the next year it produced seeds. I sent some of the seeds to Keith Foster [a leading English dealer in giant seeds], and he got seeds from Ian Neale and sent them to me, and I think that's why Ian Neale is creeping up on me because Keith traded him some of those rutabaga seeds. Once you've made a name for yourself you have real marketing power, and you can start swapping seeds.

The marrow I have in the garden is from Bernard Lavery seeds. I sent him some from my record rutabaga and cantaloupe. What I love about you guys over there is that you're so diverse. You've got guys doing so many different things. It's one thing to concentrate on the pumpkins and grow one big pumpkin, but I think it's much more challenging to take on so many things. One day I'm going to come over and you're going to have to show me these guys in action.

It was time to go into the garden to see what Scott was – and, just as significantly, what he was not – going to take to the showground. But before that Mardie, who plays an active role in the enterprise and who had been sitting in on much of our conversation, came in with lunch – a delicious wrap, filled to bursting with fresh vegetables and much else.

The whole garden extends to three-and-a-half acres, and the main vegetable plot is 100ft by 60ft, just a little bigger than a standard British allotment. It has a sign on it, with black lettering on a yellow background, reading

ENTERING THE LAND OF GIANTS. LOOK BUT PLEASE DO NOT TOUCH

A white electric fence stretches right round the plot, to keep the moose at bay. Scott does not have a problem with vandals or other human intruders. 'Nobody's interested except me and the moose. They've been here twice that I know of, because I've seen the footprints.' He has never had a visit from a bear – although they do roam the hills not far from the town – but he has spotted a red fox and a couple of wolves. And one year he and Mardie came back from the cabbage weigh-off at the state fair to discover that a neighbour's pigs and cows had escaped and eaten all their cabbages except the two they took to the show.

The current stars of the garden were a pair of tall kale plants standing just inside the electric fence. For the last few years Scott had been vying with Dave Iles from North Pole, near Fairbanks, for the world kale record. Dave, a pipe fitter by trade, is a really serious grower, using both hydroponic and aeroponic (a modified form of hydroponic) methods. In a magazine article in 2005 he wrote that his greenhouses covered 11,000 sq. ft, and he had invested $150,000 in them.

Scott claimed the kale record in 2001 with a plant that weighed in at 42 lb 6 oz, but Dave beat it in 2006 with 58 lb 9 oz. Scott was confident that both those in his garden would exceed that by a significant margin. His first record-breaker had been a plant that he originally thought was a cabbage.

The seeds and plants got mixed up, and I thought I was planting a giant cabbage, so I put it in with my cabbages. After about five weeks I noticed it was growing straight up. It was huge, it was tall and it wasn't going to form a head. It looked like a big walking-stick cabbage; but it was a kale.

There's different types of kale – you have the smooth-leaved and the curly, and this is the smooth. This one is a pretty good size. Unless my calculations are way out, it should easily break the world record. The other one seems not quite as tall but has a different structure and a broader leaf and sits lower in the garden.

He believed both kales would beat Dave Iles's record and had worked out his tactics for the fortnight. He would dig up the smaller of the two that day and take it to the fair, saving the second for the second week's competition. He had done this with other record-breaking vegetables in the past.

Last year I grew four kohlrabi and all four broke the previous world record. I took my two smaller ones the first Wednesday, because I didn't know which was heavier. The first one on the scale beat the previous world record by about a pound and a half, and the second one was heavier, so I was happy.

He did not have to worry so much about the competition this year, because Dave had told him that he was not going to compete. He was on a long-term assignment at a gold mine in Nome, in the far north-west of the state. He had been working there all summer and so had to abandon his vegetables for the time being.

I was looking forward to seeing how Scott and Mardie would get the colossal kale out of the ground without breaking off too many leaves – but before that we had to look at the rest of the garden. Our next stop was at the cabbages. He was growing two sorts: the Giant Jac and another cross whose secrets he is not giving away. 'This Giant Jac has a lot of leaves but two small heads. It's not about pretty, it's about weight. I think it will be up there but I won't know for nine days, when I take it up and weigh it.'

He uses sophisticated equipment to keep his cabbages in the best possible shape.

We have really hard water in the greenhouse, and a fluoride problem. I've had to install a thousand-gallon water tank to capture or bring in rainwater, because when fluoride gets up to a certain level it's not good for the plants. They don't like it.

He has 600ft of hose in the cabbage bed to take the water where it is needed, controlled by a timer that comes on at night and waters for the number of hours that he sets.

I'm hand fertilising now but earlier in the year I was feeding them every time I watered. I have three hoses I can hook up to the tap – two for the vegetable garden and one for the flowers. You put the fertiliser in the top and mix it up and it's ready to go.

To double check the fertiliser injector he has a salt meter.

I always check my solution. Every time I fertilise I know that I'm within a certain range. I put the fertiliser in the top so I know it's the right strength and is giving them a steady diet to help them keep going at a steady pace. You can bump up the dose when you see that things are starting to accelerate. Every plant has certain nutritional needs. You've got to know what they are.

Scott had built frames to keep the cabbage leaves off the ground and put plastic on the soil to warm it in April and May, when it was still extremely cold. And he had installed two fans, one at each end, to keep the air circulating underneath them.

That's my system. It's something I've been messing with for a number of years and I've finally settled on this. One day I'll do what Bernard did – grow them in 25-gallon drums with the wire stretched out on some posts to hold the leaves up. I believe the lower leaves die because the bigger upper leaves overtake them and shade them from the light.

He leaves nothing to chance. Slugs can do devastating damage to cabbages, and Scott invented a vacuum device to suck them off the plants or the ground. 'When the slugs were bad I'd suck up 500 a night. They're messy things – I have to run water through to stop the mechanism getting clogged up.'
What about weeds?

We get a lot of liverwort moss, which has been introduced from somewhere else. We get a lot of chickweed and snake grass. The older we get the harder it is to bend and get it out. John Evans thought when he got into this Compostea thing that it was the silver bullet, the answer to it all, from healthy soil food, to nutrients, to fungicide, to pesticide. I think he thought it was going to do everything for him – but it won't.
    John started falling off when he got into that. He quit using all the tools in his tool box. He became organic. Organics are a key component to what I do – there's a lot of good organic material in my garden – but I've got to be ready to kill the root maggots and caterpillars. You can't just let them run rampant.

We moved on to inspect his marrows.

I put four out this year. One vine was 15ft long, and the wind came and destroyed it. But once they decide to take off and grow, they're scary. I haven't pruned any of them, I just let them grow. One went yellow too early, but I thought it was pretty, so I left it. This is only my third attempt at growing marrows, and I've got a lot to learn.

As with the kale, he was going to take the smaller of his two best marrows to the show that day, leaving the bigger one for the following week. He thought the smaller would weigh from 80 to 90 lb, with the other possibly reaching 120 lb. 'Sometimes with marrows you think it's stopped growing, but the stem end starts to grow. You can feel that this one is still viable and still growing. I just hope I've given it enough time.'

Scott is an outgoing man who enjoys communicating with other giant vegetable growers, wherever they might be. A while ago he had contacted Mark Baggs in Dorset and asked for the measurements of his 136-lb 9-oz marrow, holder of the world record.

He said that at the widest part it was 54in in circumference, by 42in long. This one is probably going to be 51 or 51½in round by next week, but it's only 34in long. So it's not going to beat Mark's record but it should beat the state fair record: I'm hoping for over 100 lb, although it has slowed down. At one time it was growing seven-eighths of an inch a day but now it's down to three-sixteenths. In sixteen days it's gone up seven and a half inches.

Normally I hand pollinate everything. This year I came down to look at the marrows and found on each plant four that had already pollinated themselves, so I left them. Two of them didn't pan out – one cracked, and the other one just quit growing, so I had two left. I had to redirect the vine on this one to make it grow in the right direction: you can't do that safely with a pumpkin but these guys are stronger. This marrow's what I'm most excited about this year. I've never grown one that big, but whether or not it weighs heavy I just don't know.

He had a niggling doubt about it. 'Normally I put them on blue Styrofoam board but this time I didn't get the board under it and I hope it hasn't gone rotten or something eaten it underneath.' Some small slugs were visible on the fringes, but probably too small to make any serious inroads into the monster.

The afternoon was ebbing away and it was time to tackle the task of digging up the kale to take to the show. 'The test is whether we can get it out of the ground without destroying it,' said Scott. 'Any part that's not attached when you get it to the fair can't be weighed. You just can't bring a plant in that's been dismembered.'

He walked over to his garage to bring out the canvas carrier he keeps for transporting large marrows and water melons. He uses it only once a year, and when he found it he discovered that squirrels had been nibbling at the tough cotton cloth, though the damage was not serious.

The first thing to do was remove the white electrified wires, and the posts supporting them, from the end of the plot where the kale was growing. Then he and Mardie took a rope and began to bind the plant to keep the leaves tied in. There was a loud crack as an outer leaf snapped off. Mardie looked apprehensive, but Scott told her not to worry: it was inevitable a few leaves should be lost. What they had to do was bind the plant as loosely as possible, to minimise the breaks.

It was a complicated, laborious business, underlining that the long process of growing giant vegetables is actually only a part of the battle. Getting them to the showground intact can be just as tricky, requiring a high level of ingenuity. Having loosened the earth around the roots, Scott and Mardie decided that the best way to proceed was to use their Bobcat loader to help excavate the giant from the bed and deposit it on their flatbed truck. 'It's the first time I've had to use the Bobcat to get anything out of the garden,' Scott told me.

Mardie's job was to keep the plant upright, since it would certainly lose a lot of leaves if it tumbled over. Once or twice she squealed, thinking she was going to lose control of it. Eventually, when it was loaded on to the truck, Scott announced: 'We've lost just three leaves so far. That's pretty good.'

Now they turned their minds to transporting the kale and the second biggest marrow to the fairground. If the kale was allowed to rest on its side on the back of the truck, it would bounce up and down on the rougher parts of the journey – the side road to Scott's house and the grass on the showground itself – and lose more leaves. So Scott decided that he would ride on the back of the truck holding the kale upright. Mardie meantime would move the marrow in the family car. So who would drive the truck? Scott slapped me on the back: 'You've got a driver's licence, haven't you, Michael?'

I have, but driving a bog-standard Citroen hatchback to and from my allotment is scarcely adequate preparation for taking charge of a truck with such a precious cargo on an unfamiliar foreign road. Still, it would have been discourteous to refuse. Even climbing into the cab was an effort, although I did my best to look nonchalant. The idea was that Mardie would drive ahead. I would follow her, and when we got to the main road we would drive slowly, with our hazard lights flashing, along the track at the side of the carriageway – the rough (in both senses) equivalent to the hard shoulder on a British motorway.

It was only a mile or so to the fairground entrance, but the journey seemed to take an eternity. I followed Mardie's car to the large green shed, the size of an aircraft hangar, labelled 'Livestock Pavilion and Valley Harvest Exhibits'. As I climbed down from the cab, Mardie congratulated me on my driving. 'I'd have been happier,' I replied, 'if the steering wheel had been on the other side.' 'I know,' she said. 'I'd forgotten all about that until I looked in my mirror and saw you fumbling for the controls.'

Not many other entries had turned up by the time we arrived. On hand to greet us was Kathy Liska, who for the last fifteen years has been superintendent of the crops section of the fair, making sure everything is above board and that the records are properly kept. 'They get bigger every year,' she assured me. The weighing and measuring was to be carried out by no less a figure than Don Campbell, Chief Weights and Measures Inspector for the State of Alaska.

Don, tall and laconic, comes from Georgia and has been in Alaska for twenty years. This was his seventh year officiating at the fair. He and Kathy went out to inspect the kale on Scott's truck. Before it could be unloaded, though, Kathy was called away and told us not to do anything until she got back. Scott showed signs of frustration at this unanticipated delay to one of the pivotal moments in his year of dedicated effort. He paced nervously outside the shed until she returned.

When she did, Scott recruited some helpers to unload the kale. Next he climbed into the truck's cab and backed it up as close as he could to the entrance to the shed. Then, before taking the kale off the truck, he sawed through the thick stem to remove the roots, which do not count as part of the official weight.

Don had prepared the industrial hanging scales to receive their burden. I asked him how he made sure the weight was accurate, given the volume of leaves hanging down over the side. 'I'm a trained professional,' he assured me. 'I've been weighing stuff for years.'

Meanwhile Kathy had been rounding up other exhibitors and officials to watch what she assured them was going to be an historic weighing. They cheered and gasped as Scott and his helpers placed the mass of dark green foliage on the scales, under Don's close supervision.

Kathy has a keen sense of the melodramatic, and with bated breath she reminded the onlookers of Dave Iles's record-breaking feat the previous year. 'The record stands at 58.6 lb,' she announced. Don added to the tension by adjusting the weights for several seconds before officially endorsing the verdict. 'It's 84.7 lb,' Kathy finally shouted, to wild applause. '84.7 is memorable,' Don observed. Scott smiled and relaxed. He had known it was a big one, but it was good to have confirmation of just how big.

A hand-operated fork lift was brought in to take the kale off the scale and manoeuvre it towards a large dustbin filled with water, where it would stand to be admired by visitors during the first week of the fair. Several leaves were lost during the transfer but that no longer mattered – provided they are attached when the plant is weighed, that is all that counts. The separated leaves were stuffed into the bin alongside what was left of the kale.

Kathy was still making the most of the occasion. 'We already have a world record,' she announced to anyone within earshot, before settling down to write the news on the label that would be placed on the ungainly vegetable while it was on display. A trickle of new exhibitors arrived with their cabbages, zucchini, cucumbers and the rest, while Scott, with yet another world record under his belt, placed his marrow on the scales and then on the display bench, before going home to cut his second biggest cabbage to take down to the fairground later on, when he would be able to size up the competition.

Our image of a state fair is of an archetypal American knees-up. Women in swirling skirts and horny-handed men in cowboy outfits cavort in boisterous hoedowns – at least when they are not trying to stay seated on excitable steers or bucking broncos. Salesmen in broad-brimmed hats shout the virtues of snake-oil, while children scream as the rollercoaster makes its stomach-churning descent.

But over the years state fairs in the Lower 48 have lost their distinctive flavour. At breakfast the day after the Alaska fair opened, a fellow guest at my lodging house (like Don Campbell, he was from Georgia) told me how state fairs today are as often as not hijacked by agribusiness as a showcase for sophisticated, gas-guzzling farm machinery. Passive steers, probably fed on genetically modified corn, wait peacefully to be sold on, and nobody tries to ride them. The dominant figures are not the cowboys but the smart-suited salesmen doing deals with clean-fingernailed farming executives.

Alaska, though, is the exception. For two weeks at the end of August, the fairground at Palmer puts on a show bursting with bucking broncos, country singers, lumberjacks, hillbilly fiddlers – and, of course, the giant vegetables. 'That fair,' drawled the man from Georgia, as we tucked into our landlady's scrumptious blueberry muffins, 'is like state fairs used to be.' It attracts nearly 300,000 people – close to half the population of the state.

Although the vegetables are only a part of the fair, they are still one of the most popular and distinctive parts. Families flock to marvel at the ugly swedes bigger than footballs, pumpkins that could feed a battalion, the huge misshapen parsnips and carrots, the cucumbers you could mistake for marrows, and leeks as thick as your arm. They absorb this horticultural freak show, and chat with the proud growers, to the strains of hillbilly music from one of the fair's six performance stages just outside the shed.

Among the many other attractions are a Demolition Derby, Fred Scheer's Lumberjack Show and the Great Alaska Racing Pigs. For many visitors, the fair's chief attraction is the food. They stroll along the avenues tucking into traditional local specialities. Seafood is the highlight of the Alaskan table, and the crab cakes are a particular favourite. Salmon, smoked or grilled, is everywhere, and halibut, the principal white fish of the region, is delicately fried to order and served with chips to be eaten al fresco at one of the picnic tables scattered over the grassy site. Other regional offerings include reindeer sausages (only for the truly adventurous).

Back at the giant vegetable stand, on the first Saturday of the fair, food was also on people's minds. Mardie had a microphone and was fielding questions from a crowd of fascinated onlookers about whether the unsightly monsters are edible. Three days after it was dug the kale was clearly drooping, but Mardie insisted it would be good to eat. 'You just have to have a big crowd in when you cook it,' she joked.

A questioner pressed her. Would she and her family be eating this one when they got it home? 'No, we'll grow it on for the seed to keep the genetics going.' She added that the cabbages and the marrow would both be good to eat but the root vegetables, such as parsnips and rutabagas, would be too tough to get your teeth into.

The winning vegetables in the first week's competition had by now all been labelled with their weights and the names of the successful growers. Scott's green cabbage had been edged out of first place by a 56-lb specimen grown by Steve Hubacek, a local dentist – an augury of things to come – but Scott's red cabbage, at just over 29 lb, was a winner. And a second state record had been set – a 5-lb 4-oz parsnip entered by Ron Castor, a 77-year-old retired postman.

'I might have a bigger parsnip under the ground at home,' Ron told me as I congratulated him.

'What do you do when you don't grow giant vegetables,' I asked.

'I think about it,' he replied.

By now Mardie, with her microphone, was well into her stride. 'Make sure you have plenty of room in your garden before you plant any of these,' she advised the knot of fascinated onlookers gathered around her, before going into detail about why some cabbages were shown with their outer leaves still attached, while others were stripped down to the heart.

> To be a giant, a cabbage has to be over 50 lb. If they exceed that they can be exhibited with their outer leaves on, but if they're under that the outer leaves are stripped off to save space, and only the hearts are displayed. Red cabbages never make 50 lb, but they are always shown with outer leaves attached.

She told a story about an exploding water melon and then, in response to a question, had to explain what a marrow is. They are seldom grown in the USA – stuffed marrow is a distinctively British dish – although Americans do grow and eat zucchini (what we call courgettes), and if you leave those on the plant they will grow into medium-sized marrows. The technical difference is that zucchini grow on a bush, while marrows are carried on a vine that trails along the ground – and the variety most commonly grown for its size is usually ridged, where zucchini have smooth skins.

Mardie invited the visitors to return for the ceremonial cabbage weigh-off the following week, but announced that there would be no pumpkin weigh-off this year. The previous year's largest pumpkin had weighed over 1,000 lb – still a long way short of the then world record of 1,469 lb – but there would be no such massive beast this year because the man who grew it had lost it when it was only up to 325 lb. 'How can you lose a 325-lb pumpkin?' shouted a joker in the crowd, and Mardie gave him a serious answer: 'Pumpkins need to take up a lot of water but this one took up too much and started to go rotten from the inside at the blossom end.'

By early evening people had begun to drift towards the main outdoor stage to hear the Charlie Daniels Band ('Fiddle your way through folk, southern boogie, country and rock') or Thirty Years of Alaska Music, with Matt Hammer, Doc Schultz, Mr Whitekeys and other local heroes. Darkness fell shortly before 10 p.m., when proceedings ended with a spectacular fireworks display. Nobody minded the time it took for traffic to leave the grounds: the children were mostly fast asleep in the back seat anyway, reliving the day's thrills in their dreams.

As for me, I had a few things to wrap up in Alaska before heading home – touristy things, such as a trip to a nearby glacier on an air-boat, visits to a musk-ox farm and an old gold mine, a ride on a trailer pulled by racing huskies. Then it was back to the airport for the flight to Frankfurt and, before long, Shepton Mallet.

Two weeks later I telephoned Scott to see how he had fared in the giant cabbage weigh-off. He was miffed: he had been pipped for the $2,000 first prize by the dentist Steve Hubacek, whose cabbage tipped the scale at 87 lb 12 oz – a crucial twelve ounces heavier than Scott's. Seth Dinkel was third with just under 80 lb. Scott was also disappointed by the marrow on which he had pinned such high hopes. When he lifted it from the ground he found it had a concave bottom and weighed only 82 lb 9 oz – a paltry 1 lb 9 oz heavier than the one he had taken the previous week, although it still won first prize in its class.

On the plus side, Scott picked up the $1,000 second-place cabbage prize and, as he had predicted, his larger kale broke the world record again, smashing through the 100-lb barrier at 105 lb 15 oz. He assured me he was still determined to beat Bernard Lavery's long-standing cabbage record. 'I didn't do it this year but I'll do it some time. I'm very determined. If you want to do this thing well you've got to be passionate and focused.' I didn't doubt it for one moment.

Chapter 9

Shepton Mallet

For the growers, the moment of truth was approaching. I arrived back from Alaska on 27 August, the late summer bank holiday, with less than forty-eight hours to adjust not just to the ten-hour time difference but also to the more muted rhythms of the British giant vegetable season. The three-day National Amateur Gardening Show at Shepton Mallet, which includes the national giant vegetable championships, would open on the Friday. I had arranged with Ian Neale for me and my wife Olga to visit him on Wednesday to watch him dig up his produce and share the apprehensive moments when he discovered whether he had any world-beaters this year. Then on Thursday we would do the same at the Forteys' before driving to the showground to see the selected vegetables unloaded, weighed and staged.

We arrived at Ian's place by half past ten on a dullish morning, and he was waiting for us, keen to get on with things. It was a quiet time at the nursery: he was selling mainly alpines, but not very many of them. Some wallflowers were growing in the large polytunnel, ready to be sold in the autumn, and the Christmas chrysanthemums were thriving, except for one row nibbled by rabbits. Two weeks ago, he told us, he had an operation on the leg that had been giving him trouble all summer – indeed ever since he was involved in that motor accident twenty-seven years ago – but the surgeon said he ought not to give up any of his normal activities.

I am not sure whether medical science classifies it as 'normal' to dig up and manhandle a lot of heavy root vegetables.

Ian had also had a bad blow on the domestic front: his beloved if decidedly haughty cat had developed a kidney problem and had had to be put down.

> I've never been so upset about a cat as this one, even though my pocket is better off since she died. I'm not going to get another. I've had two dogs die . . . never replaced them; one woman hurt me . . . never replaced her; and I'm not going to replace the cat.
>
> Instead of keeping pets I want to do more for wildlife. There was a programme on Channel 4 about an old barn that was falling down, but they put up a new building alongside it and left little pockets for the little birds to go in, then higher up they left bigger pockets for the small owls and, higher still, a bigger pocket for the tawny owl that lived in this old barn, hoping it would move across to this new building so they could pull the old barn down. And they left the roof space for bats. I thought what a wonderful idea – you can go on holiday and they can look after themselves.
>
> But cats and plants can't. I don't really have holidays. Up till ten years ago I enjoyed what I was doing with the nursery, but since then it's been diabolical, with trade and profits going downhill. This year I had to chuck more tubs and hanging baskets away than in the last four or five years put together.

However, it was time to put such troubles aside for the moment and get down to the job at hand. Ian was going to start with the carrots and parsnips, to get them out of the way.

> I'm going to dig up two carrots and three or four parsnips. I don't weigh them when I've dug them out – it can't make any difference when you get them to the show. If there's one really big carrot, I

can take it to four of the shows, because I dig them back into the ground when I bring them home. They'll lose a bit of weight, but not too much.

It is hard to judge how big carrots are just by looking at what shows above the surface: mostly foliage, and not very prolific foliage at that. But Ian had identified one he thought could be a potential champion. He dug around it, loosening the compost carefully to avoid snapping off any part of the root. He drew out the carrot, shaking off the remnants of the soil, and immediately sliced most of the green foliage from the top.

I always like to do that straight away, because I think the foliage draws some of the goodness out of the carrot. But I don't take it right down to the top of the carrot because some judges let you get away with a bit of green stalk. Bernard Lavery always made you cut right back, but Ray Davey [the judge at Shepton Mallet] might let that go. You can always cut it off but you can't put it back on. It's only ounces, but it might make a difference.

With swedes, which are among the vegetables he grows best, he once had to intercede with the judges to get the rules modified.

Bernard would insist on cutting every bit of root off, but I had a photograph of the world record, and they allowed an inch or so of thick root. I spoke to the judge about six years ago and showed him the photograph and told him that if we don't match them we'll never beat them. I'm not expecting to beat the record this year, mind.

As soon as he had lifted the first carrot he could see that it was not nearly as big as he had hoped. 'That one's disappointing. Maybe it could have done with more water – but if they get too wet they can rot. I really need one of those probes that tell you how much water there is down there.'

That first carrot came from the north side of the tunnel, so Ian decided to try one from the south side. This was even worse. It looked handsome enough, at least compared with the first, but that was because the roots had not forked out – and it is the roots, ugly though they are, that make the weight that makes a winner. 'That one's too small. You can eat that one for breakfast.' So it wasn't going to be a bumper year for Ian's carrots.

On to the parsnips, where he planned to dig two on the south side and two on the north. Again, he could not tell their size from the foliage. Before digging them he plunged his hand into the compost and gently felt around the roots, trying to ascertain how far they stretched from the main plant. He told me he once grew a parsnip of over 13 lb – nearly 3 lb more than the present world record – but at that time he did not know how to register it with Guinness. There would be no such record this year, although the best of those he dug up looked as though it could be competitive at the show, measuring more than 2ft from the top to the end of the longest root. He had to wash the dirt from the crevices before he could estimate the weight with any accuracy.

The two dug from the north side of the tunnel were not as big as those from the south. Ian shrugged his shoulders. 'I can make wine out of them,' he remarked. 'You make parsnip wine?' I inquired.

I'm not a wine drinker but I gave a fellow half of one of my water melons one year, and he brought me back twelve bottles of wine that he'd made from it. I thought I'd better drink it, and, you know, it was like champagne – very strong. I drank eight bottles.

By now, appropriately, we were in the water melon tunnel and it looked as if these were going to be Ian's most successful crop once again. They had certainly put on weight since I last saw them a month earlier. He cut the biggest three from their rambling vines and had difficulty picking up the largest and putting it on the two-wheeled trolley that carried them to be stacked on a pile of gro-bags near the shop. It was a strain: the surgeon who operated on his leg would not have approved.

'I think it's the biggest water melon I've ever grown,' he said, breathing heavily after the exertion. One of the smaller ones, though, was starting to go rotten at one end. 'I'll take that one with me and on the Sunday, at the end of the show, I'll cut it up and give it to members of the public, just to show them that some giant vegetables are good to eat.'

Next he turned his attention to swedes and beetroot, his other specialities. He dug up the two best-looking swedes, removed the leaves and roots, sized them up and didn't think there was much to choose between them. Neither was quite what he had hoped.

Some of them seem to have made weight lopsidedly. One side spreads, and the other is a bit pinched. I'm a bit disappointed; but, there again, that's the year it's been. In the tunnel you can control the weather – but not the light. We've done the best we can but we aren't going to break any world records this year.

To Olga and me they looked massive, albeit, as Olga remarked, overpoweringly ugly, with prominent and unsightly protuberances. 'Never mind how ugly they are so long as they weigh heavy,' Ian responded.

At one show I saw a lady admiring my swede and I said to her: 'Look at that, she's well blessed.' 'Just like my daughter,' she said. So I said: 'You haven't got a bra I could put on it, have you?'

He chuckled, paused and added thoughtfully: 'But you've got to pick the right person to have that sort of joke with, haven't you?'

He found one good beetroot, but again not a record-breaker, then got out the hose and washed it down along with the swedes. He put them all under damp sacks, to keep them fresh and avoid weight loss and the risk of bruising, ready to load on to his van later in the day. 'I can take the same swedes and beetroots to all the shows. There's no rule against it, although the people who go to all the shows tend to recognise them.'

Time for a break. We offered to take Ian to lunch at a nearby pub but no, he had ordered pies from a local shop. We sat in his back store and munched them, while he made us all a cup of tea. Afterwards we went over to the small greenhouses in his back garden, beside the nursery, to inspect the potatoes and radishes. Olga plunged her hand into the barrels to help him ease the radishes out without damage: they were the white variety, sometimes called Chinese, favoured by nearly all giant vegetable growers. They looked impressive to us, but Ian was pessimistic about their chances of picking up a prize.

He was uncertain, too, about the potatoes. There were some sizeable bulges in the side of the six sacks where he planted them, but we couldn't tell whether there were any really big tubers until the sacks were cut open. 'We'll either have a couple of nice big ones or we'll have plenty for dinner.' As he cut into each successive sack, it became clearer that the latter was more likely. There were just three potatoes that would make a hefty meal if baked, but even they did not look like prize-winners. 'They're going to be quite average by the look of it. They'll last me all winter, living on my own.'

He had planted one potato in each sack and left two eyes on each. Next time he would experiment with different varieties. He conceded that it might have been better to grow them in barrels or in the ground. 'But putting them in the ground takes a lot more time. And you have to prepare the beds and do the planting at my busiest time of year with the bedding plants. When I retire I'll try putting them in the ground.'

We went back over to the nursery to assess the cucumbers in the greenhouse. In this poor year for setting cucumbers he had only one long one, but he had cut it a week ago because it was starting to go rotten. He had a few heavy ones but did not think much of their chances.

> I think I should sow them earlier. They always seem to start ripening and stop growing on 15 August, whenever I sow them. So if I sow them earlier they might grow bigger before they ripen. My theory is that when they turn yellow they start dehydrating and going backwards. The boys start off my cucumbers for me. Kevin rang me this morning and told me that his are still growing. The seeds all start the same size, but then some grow bigger than others.

A few years ago Ian briefly held the world record for the heaviest cucumber. He grew it from seed that he had swapped for some beetroot seed with his friend and rival Ken Dade from Norfolk, who regularly stays with him during the Shepton Mallet show.

> I grew one up to 20 lb, but it had no seed in it. Only the smaller ones had any seed. I kept persevering until I broke the world record – but I've done no good ever since. But Ken took some seed back from me and started to beat me again.

The last crop he dug was the celery, first putting on a pair of gloves to reduce the chance of celery burn. He found a plant of a respectable size. 'I think it's about 40 lb,' he said (when weighed at Shepton Mallet, it turned out to be a little less). He was careful not to snap off any of the leaves but said that the judges at the British shows – in contrast to those in Alaska – will usually allow detached leaves to go on to the scale with the rest of the plant. 'Nobody's said anything yet,' he assured me.

He washed the roots and placed damp sacking over the plant to prevent it wilting. As we watched him we were joined by Marilyn, his weekday helper in the shop and office, who looked faintly bemused: she had seen it all before. It was now mid-afternoon and, as Ian began to load the stuff into the van in readiness for tomorrow, Olga and I headed north to stay with our friends near Builth Wells, before driving to Cwmbran next morning to see what Gareth and Kevin, after their difficult summer, were going to be able to take to the show.

When we arrived at the Forteys' house Kevin was under the apple tree, choosing the best apples to enter in his mother's name in the quality section of the Shepton Mallet show. 'It's a good old tree,' he told us. 'We enter every year, and we often do quite well. We've got some good blackberries too, and we usually take those along.'

Before getting down to the business of the morning, he and Gareth were keen to hear about my visit to Scott in Alaska. They correspond with him frequently by email and via their website, but have never met him. I passed on Scott's cordial greetings, as he had asked me to do, and told them about his world record kale – naturally boasting of my own role in conveying it to the showground – and about his hopes for his second marrow. I gave them as much detail as I could remember about his set-up, in particular his sophisticated systems for watering, fertilising and keeping his plants warm.

The boys had said they would start digging as soon as Olga and I got there, but there was a complication: Kevin had an imminent doctor's appointment, and most of the work would have to wait until he got back. This meant they were unlikely to be able to set out for Shepton Mallet by midday, as intended, and Gareth was slightly peeved.

They just had time to sort out a marrow and a cantaloupe before Kevin's appointment. On my last visit they had told me that if their best marrow was still growing at the end of August they might hold it back for the later shows, and this is what they had decided to do. They had despaired of getting a cantaloupe to set, but one finally did. It had grown no bigger than a tennis ball, but they decided to take it along all the same, assuming that others would have had the same setting problems, so they might pick up some place money if there were not many entries.

Their young friend Kyle Phillips, a tall, talkative 19-year-old from across the street, was there to help. He acts as a third member of the Fortey team and has done some work on their giant vegetable website. While we waited for Kevin to return, Kyle regaled us with tales of previous shows, talking up the virtues of Abertysswg: the snooker table at the Working Men's Club and the ace fish and chip shop. 'It has the best atmosphere of any show,' he insisted.

I left him talking to Olga while I went out to inspect the garden. Over the fence I saw a neighbour working on his plot, where he had good-looking beans, onions, potatoes and other produce. He returned my greeting and I quickly discovered that he did not approve of the Forteys' horticultural aims or methods. 'They put a lot of fertiliser in and they just grow for show,' he grumbled. 'You can't eat their stuff. All mine I grow to eat.' This criticism is often made by gardeners outside the charmed circle of giant growers, but in the case of Kevin and Gareth it is particularly unfair, because they do grow for the kitchen and the flower garden as well.

It was past noon by the time Kevin returned, and it was now certain that they would not be able to set out for Shepton Mallet nearly as early as they had hoped. The trio immediately got down to work, starting with the radishes. Kevin scooped the compost out of the barrels carefully – but not carefully enough to prevent an early setback when a piece of root snapped off one of the bigger specimens. He warned Kyle, who was trying to ease one out of another barrel: 'Don't rock it: they're really brittle.' He estimated the biggest radish as '10 lb, give or take' – a respectable size, but probably not big enough to beat the likes of Peter and Joe.

The Forteys usually beat Ian with their cucumbers and celery and, judging by appearances, would be doing so again this year, despite the problems they had had with drainage in the new polytunnel. Their beetroot and swedes, though, looked smaller than his, and again this accorded with tradition. They thought they had a good chance of a prize with their longest runner bean, which had grown by a few inches since I last saw it, but were disappointed with their heavy leeks.

They left the long carrot, beetroot and parsnip until last, scraping away the soil in Gareth's home-built structure to see how far the roots stretched. There was another dispute between Kyle and Kevin, this time on the best way to remove them without breaking bits off the end of the thin root. When they were uncovered the results were unimpressive: less than 7ft for the carrot and about 10ft for the beetroot – some way from the likely winning lengths. All the same, this was their first serious stab at these highly specialised classes, and they had learned lessons that should ensure they did better next year. They decided not to take the carrot along, but coiled the roots of the other two in a shallow box to protect them on the way to the show.

Olga and I had to hurry off because I had an appointment at Shepton Mallet with the show's press officer. We arranged to meet Kevin and Gareth and Kyle at the weigh-in later on.

It is drizzling when we finally reach the Bath and West Showground – late, because of traffic jams on the way. Shepton Mallet itself is an attractive town, fringed by the Somerset hills, but the showground, to the south, is a large, flat, open expanse dotted haphazardly with sheds and other permanent structures put up to accommodate the agricultural and other shows held there throughout the year. Driving through the main gate, I am directed to the press office. 'You're in luck,' the press officer tells me excitedly as she hands me my pass. 'I hear that three world records may have been broken already.'

The giant vegetable display area is at one end of a large shed that also houses the quality vegetable exhibits and most of the floral classes. Exhibitors have to bring their entries in by 4 p.m., and with little more than an hour to go most have already arrived and had their produce weighed and measured. As soon as we enter the shed we spot the familiar faces of Ian, Peter, Mary, Carmel and Joe. Three world records do indeed appear to have been broken – two of them by Joe.

Less than a year after Peter set his record for the longest carrot at Highgrove, Joe has surpassed it by a considerable margin. His carrot, already taking up nearly the whole length of the bench allotted to this class, has been measured at 19ft 2in – nearly 2ft longer than Peter's previous record, and 3ft longer than the best Peter has brought this year. Joe has also managed to grow the world's heaviest parsnip, at 10 lb 14 oz – a marginal but critical six ounces more than the previous record, set as long ago as 1980 by another British grower, Colin Moore.

The third record has been achieved by a man who has not been able to get to the show. The 2008 edition of *Guinness World Records* has a picture of the 91-year-old Alf Cobb, Peter's friend from Newark, brandishing the 35.1-in cucumber that was declared the longest in the world at this show last year. Now Alf has just beaten it, if only by a bit less than half an inch. He is usually driven here by his son, who this year is laid low with a bad back. Peter brought Alf's vegetables here for him and says he hopes Alf might be able to get here tomorrow, to bask in his glory – but it was not to be.

With three potential world records achieved, you might expect some stirring of excitement, some of the drama Kathy Liska managed to whip up in Palmer last week over Scott's kale. We do things differently here, though. Showmanship is not a quality bred into our vegetable growers. They are not by nature demonstrative – and it is, to be fair, hard to get over-excited by gazing at an unlovely straggly root stretched out on the bench, even if it is the length of three tall men. At least Scott's kale, although just as unsightly, was clearly of formidable bulk: it had the look of a giant.

Growing a world record vegetable is not the same as running a world record 100-metre dash. There is no digital clock ticking away to deliver instant news of the achievement to spectators and to millions watching on television. Gardening is not primarily a spectator sport. So, although Joe is clearly pleased with his double success, and is being dutifully congratulated by friends and rivals, there is no triumphalism, no exultant punching of the air with clenched fists – just the quiet satisfaction of knowing that, in his chosen field, he has done something better than anyone else.

For Peter this is not to be a record-setting year; but he can claim a legitimate connection with all three of the new world champions. As well as bringing along Alf's cucumbers, he drove to Shepton Mallet in company with Joe. He and Mary had left home at 4.30 a.m. and, as usual when going to shows in the west, met Joe and Carmel for breakfast at a motorway service station. Both couples are staying at a local bed-and-breakfast establishment and hope to have time for some sightseeing together.

It comes as a surprise to the assembled growers that three records have been broken in what is generally agreed to have been a dismal year for vegetables. One of the first I speak to is Ken Dade, from near King's Lynn in Norfolk. He is a successful grower and seems to have done well with his marrows, but he says that nearly everything here is down on last year: both the number of entries and their weights. His biggest marrow, at 100 lb, is about 20 lb lighter than his biggest of 2006 – though still big enough to take the first prize, beating Peter's by 11 lb.

Ken tells me he has grown vegetables for some forty years, and started going in for giants when Bernard Lavery organised the early national shows at Spalding, not far from where he lives. 'If it wasn't for Bernard, there wouldn't be a national championship,' he avers. 'Bernard is a great fixer – he has the gift of the gab.' When I ask Ken why he now concentrates on growing for size rather than quality, his answer is the one I hear from so many growers: 'I can't put up with the judges' whims in the quality classes. I like it when the scales are the arbiter.'

Although Bernard Lavery neither competes any more nor comes to the shows, his influence is still pervasive, and his name tends to crop up when I ask growers how they first became addicted to giantism. One such is Ray Davey, now chief judge of the giant classes here, as well as at some of the other shows on the circuit – although, since the only true judges are the tape measure and scales, perhaps he should be better termed an arbitrator: deciding on fine points, such as how much stalk and root are permitted on the vegetables, and whether they are sound, as the rules demand. Now a qualified National Vegetable Society judge, Ray tells me he used to grow a few giants himself, and once held the British record for the longest runner bean. He has been judging here for ten years, since the national championships moved from Spalding, and his manner is one of calm authority. 'It was Bernard who codified the rules,' he says. 'And they're still the rules we go by.'

Ian, though, is not sure that the rules are being followed to the letter in respect of the swedes. Although his two are the biggest to have been weighed so far, he notes that some of his competitors have not trimmed the roots and stalks back as much as he has. 'Every one should be trimmed the same,' he says, and goes off to have a word with Ray.

Clive Bevan, the 'giant vegetable guru' of *The Great British*

Village Show, is helping Ray to weigh and measure the entries as they come in. He tells me that if two of them seem quite close in weight, or if one looks like a potential record-breaker, Ray will insist that they are uniformly trimmed. Where that is not the case he is prepared to allow a certain amount of latitude.

Clive, an outgoing Welshman, has brought a few exhibits of his own along, but is pessimistic about his chances. 'I've not had a very good year,' he confesses. However, he is not here just as a competitor. When the show opens tomorrow he will be stationed at a table at the edge of the hall, discreetly selling his range of giant vegetable seeds and an instructional leaflet on how to grow them. Meantime, as other hopefuls continue to arrive with their produce, he hurries off to help Ray organise the unloading, weighing and measuring.

Several growers have told me that among the principal pleasures of the show circuit is meeting their fellow enthusiasts and catching up with their news. They exchange complaints about the weather, gossip about mutual acquaintances and details of new techniques tried this year – although they take care not to give too much away to potential rivals.

Suddenly the buzz of friendly conversation comes to a halt as a large station wagon backs up as close as possible to the door of the shed and an impressive pumpkin comes into view. Regulars can guess that this means the father-and-son team of Frank and Mark Baggs have arrived from Wareham in Dorset. Frank, a farmer, specialises in growing large specimens of the cucurbit family, especially marrows and pumpkins. He is the principal grower but always enters shows in Mark's name, and they have a place in *Guinness World Records* on the strength of a 136 lb 9 oz marrow they grew and showed here in 2005.

This year they have not brought a marrow, just the pumpkin – which is a lot bigger than any that have arrived so far. They unload it from the car, using a large sheet as a sling, and carry it to the industrial scales where Ray and his helpers set about determining its weight. At 443 lb it is more than twice as heavy as any other pumpkin on the bench, and more than three times as heavy as Peter's best effort this year. However, it is smaller than the biggest they grew last year, and a long way short of the world-record 1,502 lb achieved in 2006 by Ron Wallace of Rhode Island, USA – which would itself be beaten later in 2007 by Joe Jutras, also of Rhode Island, with a monster of 1,689 lb.

Frank tells me he grows his pumpkins outdoors. He started this year with five viable specimens but two split, making them ineligible for the competition. Splitting, one of the most frequent hazards with very big pumpkins, has been especially prevalent during this wet summer. Given that, he is quite pleased with this, his biggest one this year.

Hard on the heels of the Baggs pumpkin comes an even more colossal cucurbit – David Thomas's squash. It is so big that he cannot unload it single-handed. Several other growers, including Frank and Joe, willingly volunteer to help him carry it in the sling to the scales, where it registers 463 lb – almost twice as heavy as Peter's largest squash, which it relegates to second place.

David, tall and muscular, comes from near Hayle in Cornwall, where he works for a vegetable farm specialising in cauliflowers. As well as the squash, he has brought two mightily impressive cabbages, the larger of which looks to me about the same size as the biggest that Scott was growing in Alaska. This is confirmed when it reaches the scales and registers 95 lb. The smaller of the two makes 81 lb 7 oz – big enough to win second prize in the class. David has brought along his six-year-old daughter Madeleine, who happily climbs on to the show bench and poses by the two cabbages for the press photographers.

The sight of Madeleine dwarfed by the two colossal vegetables prompts the thought that, of all the giants, the cabbage is among the most responsive to growers' efforts at selective breeding. It is derived, after all, from the skimpy wild cabbage that you see occasionally growing close to the seashore. The Romans are said to have introduced it to northern Europe, and it was they who began seriously to cultivate it and increase its size. They not only liked the taste, they also saw it as a cure for a variety of ailments, including constipation and deafness, as well as an antidote to an excess of alcohol: a kind of green Alka-Seltzer. According to *The Cambridge World History of Food*, from about 100 BC it became a highly fashionable vegetable, and Romans were 'lavishing such attention on it and cultivating it to such a size that the poor of Rome could not afford to buy it'.

The irony is that the cabbages on view here today have been cultivated to such an immense size that neither the poor nor the rich of Rome, or anywhere else, would want to buy them. For I am about to learn that this particular variety is derived from 'cow cabbage' – originally used, as the name indicates, for feeding cattle. One of the key figures in its development is George Rogers, a friend and close neighbour of David's. George, who is also competing here and has come third in the cabbage class with one of just over 60 lb, was the first to identify and deliberately reproduce the strain from which nearly all today's entries have been grown.

Now retired, he used to be a cattle farmer in Cornwall, where every year a neighbouring farmer, Mr Hawtrey, would grow a field of large cow cabbage. 'They were a cheap cattle feed in those days,' George recalls. Conditions in Cornwall are ideal for cabbages. The most famous feature of its climate may be the lack of extreme cold in winter, due to the proximity of the Gulf Stream, but for cabbages the key factor is that summers are usually cooler than elsewhere in the country – and cabbages do not thrive in excessive summer heat.

Mr Hawtrey used to exhibit at local shows. However, the increasing labour cost of tending and harvesting the cabbages made them uneconomic as livestock feed, so when the farmer retired, his son did not want to carry on growing them. Instead he handed over all the seed to George, who began to win prizes with it. 'I'd started gardening when I was four. My father was a keen vegetable grower. He gave all his children a corner of one of his fields, and every year he'd give us a bigger corner. That was how my interested started.'

With the reputation of his cabbages established, other growers came to George for the seed, which he started to sell and give away. He has been improving the strain for some thirty years, although once or twice its survival has been in doubt.

> One year I'd let the usual number stay in the ground and run to seed but, the day before I was going to take the seed off, my neighbour's cows came over the hedge and ate them. I only had a few left. Another year I grew them in pots, and they dried out; but luckily I'd kept a few in the bed.

One of the growers he gave the seed to was David Thomas, who started to grow cabbages bigger than his. He puts this down to David having a larger garden and roomier cold frames, although in other respects their growing conditions are the same. 'I did beat him at Malvern one year,' he recalls. 'I want to beat him again.'

Being in a farming area, George and David have access to almost unlimited quantities of manure, which they use copiously. David also feeds the cabbages with a small amount of nitrogenous granular fertiliser, although he recommends that it should be used sparingly: too large a dose can weaken the stalks, which need to be strong to support above-average growth. He has been a keen exhibitor for some years, having once driven right across the southern half of the country to Nottinghamshire for a show offering a £500 cabbage prize. 'I won it,' he recalls with satisfaction, 'but the organisers went bust and the cheque bounced.' His smile expresses disappointment mingled with pride: 'But I'd still grown the biggest cabbage.'

George no longer distributes the seed of his giants. A year or two ago he sold the rights to Clive Bevan, who sells the seed alongside the other monsters in his catalogue – although under the arrangement George is allowed to keep a few back for himself. 'So nearly all these come from my seed,' Clive tells me, pointing towards the ten entries on the cabbage bench. Whether and how they are related to Scott's Giant Jac in Alaska is something on which more research is needed: certainly Scott will not tell me.

Joe, whose cabbage weighs 55 lb, has come fourth in the class. Only one of Peter's ill-fated crop has survived, and it makes only just above 46 lb. The Forteys are among the last exhibitors to arrive, only minutes before the deadline for staging, having also been caught in traffic jams. Their gamble in bringing their only cantaloupe has paid off, because there are indeed very few entries in the class this year: only four, in fact. So their little one, weighing just 7 oz, gains fourth place and a £15 prize – no matter that it will come in for some scorn when the show opens to the public next morning.

The showery skies and soggy turf have not prevented a large crowd turning out on Friday, the opening day. There is a strong array of attractions: sales of plants, garden equipment and local crafts; advice sessions with nationally known gardening experts; cookery demonstrations; and large quantities of food for sale. In the floral marquee a Welsh harpist adds some romance to the fragrant and colourful exhibits.

As always, the mammoth vegetables prove a powerful draw. I had observed at the Alaska State Fair that the attitude of visitors when they come across the giants is significantly different from the hushed reverence with which they tend to inspect the quality vegetable classes. The painstaking preparation that has clearly gone into staging the quality exhibits – the meticulous search for uniformity, the loving polishing of the skins of the onions, the careful combing of the roots of the leeks – confirms that they are the products of a ritual performed by totally dedicated disciples of a rigid cult. 'They look as though they've never been in the soil,' says one awed bystander, and she is quite right.

The giants have almost exactly the opposite effect on people. They are for the most part so ugly – the lop-sided squash, the knobbly swede, the parsnip with a mass of untidy roots – that the first emotion they suggest is laughter, the second incredulity. 'Why do they do it?' is a question asked just as often as 'How do they do it?'

The local paper, the *Western Daily Press*, reflects this in its coverage of the show on the opening morning. 'Invasion of the giant vegetables' is its headline, across a double-page spread dominated by a picture of Joe with his record parsnip. 'It looks like the alien baby from the sci-fi film comedy *Men in Black*,' reporter Tina Rowe observed (although to me it looks more like an octopus whose tentacles have got out of kilter). The smaller picture shows David Thomas, in a jaunty straw hat, caressing his winning squash. The pristine quality vegetables that occupy most of the shed are not mentioned in the report at all.

Some of the giant growers have shown that they are not hooked solely on size, picking up the odd prize in the quality classes. Alf Cobb, for one, has produced an all-conquering pair of marrows. The apples I saw Kevin gathering the previous day, entered in his mother's name, win first prize in their class, and she earns a second prize for a dish of blackberries. And three of Peter's carrots, entered in Mary's name, have come second in their quality category.

In classes for heavy and long vegetables there are prizes for the first five places. By entering nearly every one, Peter has managed to amass prize money of £1,280, as well as the £750 award for being the best giant vegetable grower overall. These are the classes in which he claimed one prize or more:

Heavy vegetables	£
Onion: first and second	170
Three onions: first and second	170
Squash: second and third	95
Two marrows: second and fourth	85
Leek: second and fourth	85
Potato: first and third	80
Marrow: second and fifth	80
Beetroot: first and fifth	70
Pumpkin: third	45
Swede: third and fourth	35
Water melon: third and fifth	30
Radish: third	20
Celery: fourth	15
Carrot: fifth	10

Long vegetables	
Beetroot: first and second	100
Runner bean: first and second	100
Carrot: second and fourth	55
Parsnip: fourth and fifth	25
Cucumber: fifth	10

When I congratulate him on these successes, he tells me he is especially pleased to have beaten Ian with his heavy beetroot – something he has never done before. He discloses, too, that he has won the heavy potato class ever since it was inaugurated three years ago, confirming the validity of his labour-intensive but effective technique of rooting in the soil around the young tubers and reducing them to one or two potatoes per plant.

Joe entered slightly fewer classes, so he did not hoover up so much lower-placed prize money; nonetheless, he came away with £870. Apart from the record parsnip and long carrot he picked up five more first places, two seconds, eight thirds, seven fourths and a fifth.

The Welsh contingent, nowhere near so prolific, fared less well. Ian's swedes and water melons won the top two places in their classes, his celery was second and third – beaten by the Forteys' – and his beetroot second and fourth. One of his parsnips sneaked into the rankings at number five but his carrots, radishes and cucumbers won nothing, and he had not thought it worth bringing any potatoes along. Still, winnings of £345 have certainly repaid some of his expenses.

The celery was the Forteys' only first prize-winner. They had three third places – heavy cucumber, long cucumber and long runner bean – a fourth with their mini-melon and fifth with a radish and a long beetroot. The beetroot represented the first time they had won anything with their experimental long roots, and their parsnip was only five inches short of Peter's fifth prize winner. Their prize tally amounted to £155.

Gareth and Kevin are not at the show on the first public day; they are both working. The other growers, though, are strolling along the aisles between the benches, checking on what classes they have won, comparing their efforts with their rivals' and exchanging gossip with acquaintances they might see only once or twice a year.

Occasionally, curious strangers approach them, asking the secret of growing such enormous stuff. I overhear Joe talking about his 14-lb radishes that took first and second prize and were some 4 lb heavier than Peter's best. (They are still a long way short of the phenomenal world record of 68 lb 9 oz, achieved by a Japanese grower.) What strikes me about Joe's radishes is that they have not forked much, but carry nearly all their weight in the main body of the radish. The others on the bench have all forked liberally. Most growers believe that the more they fork the heavier they will be; but that has not been borne out this time.

'I let my heavy parsnips fork, but I don't let radishes get legs if I can help it,' says Joe. Someone asks him how he gets them to such an 'incredible' size, and he says the growing medium is the most important factor. 'My mix is very light-draining and virtually soil-free, but I don't tell anyone exactly what it is. I riddle it down to make it extremely fine, so it doesn't inhibit any growth.'

As Peter stands alongside his winning 12-lb onion he is approached by a man who reads *Garden News* and has been following Medwyn Williams's experiment in growing onions hydroponically, using the same method as Gerald – who is not exhibiting here. Asked whether he thinks the technique will work, Peter is sceptical, observing that it all depends on getting the nutrient balance just right: a matter of trial and error that could take many years to resolve. The acid test will come in two weeks' time, when Gerald will take his biggest onion to Harrogate. Before that, though, many of the other growers have a date in Wales – home ground for Ian and the Forteys.

Chapter 10

Llanharry

The taxi driver taking me to Llanharry knows about the show, but does not think she will be going along. 'It's the kind of thing that men like to do, isn't it?' she observes disapprovingly. 'Growing that stuff you can't eat? I haven't got the time for any of that.'

Driving across Britain's motorway network in the holiday season is no fun, so I was relieved that I could make this trip by rail. A few minutes in a local train from the main-line station at Cardiff brings me to Pontyclun, a couple of miles from Llanharry. And it is easy to locate the taxi I booked, because it is the only car parked outside the small station: clearly this village show, confined almost exclusively to giant produce, does not attract visitors from as far and wide as the bigger events at Palmer, Shepton Mallet or, later in the month, Harrogate and Malvern.

Sitting among the low hills of the Ely Valley, just north of the M4, Llanharry dates back to pre-Roman times; the Bronze-Age skeleton of a man of the Beaker culture was discovered just outside the village not long ago. The Romans dug iron ore here and the industry survived in various forms until 1975, when the iron mine – the last in Wales –closed down. Overnight the village of 3,000 people was forced to adapt from a mining community into a commuter town serving the light industries of Cardiff, Bridgend and Pontypridd. It was largely Welsh-speaking until around 1900, when there was an influx of English mine workers, and over time their language came to dominate. Today Llanharry has two schools, one teaching in Welsh and the other in English.

The unlovely but functional Workingmen's Club was built in 1959, close to the centre of the village, primarily for men who worked in the mine. Many of them were keen gardeners, and a conventional flower and vegetable show was inaugurated by the club soon afterwards. In the 1980s, though, support for this show began to dwindle, with the number of entries going steadily down. That was when a group of men on the committee, including Bernard Lavery, went to the Abertysswg giant vegetable show, saw that it was a success and decided to start one of their own.

One of those pioneers was Philip Vowles, a former farm worker and gardener who has been the manager of every giant vegetable show here since the first, twenty-two years ago. By his account, it was he who brought Bernard Lavery into the club:

> I knocked on his door – he lived in the village – and invited him to join us. He was such a very good quality grower, one of the best I've ever known. He joined our committee, but he was always a bit headstrong – wanted to rule everybody, didn't want to run it as a committee. The rest of us wanted to keep it running as a committee, not a one-man band. That's what we do, and we never have any disputes.

(Later, Ian would make the same point to me more colourfully: 'Bernard was like a Jack Russell with a rat. But he was very good at persuading sponsors to part with their money.')

So Bernard went his own way, starting the national show that has now bedded down at Shepton Mallet. But the Llanharry event continues to thrive alongside the older one at Abertysswg, providing between them a focus for enthusiasts for the big stuff from a wide area of England and Wales, filling the gap between the bigger shows at the beginning and end of September.

Philip insists that there is no real rivalry between the two village shows.

I've always entered for Abertysswg – but not this year because I'm a bit down on my stuff. But I'll be up there supporting them. We always arrange that we don't clash: some years we're before them, like we are this year, and some years we come after them. But you'll find that Abertysswg is only half the size of this show, even though it was the original one.

Another who looks back to the time the show started is David Francis, the village historian, a former schoolteacher (Philip was one of his pupils) and president of the show committee. He recalls:

The old flower show was beginning to lose its impact. In other villages they've disappeared. The giant vegetables have kept this one going. It brings new people to this village and puts it on the map.

As my taxi drives up to the Working Men's Club on this sunny Saturday morning, I spot Ian and Joe in the car park, having just unloaded their vegetables and put them on the show benches inside the hall. Half a dozen tall sunflowers are lying on tables outside the entrance – the only non-vegetable class in the show, and the only one displayed outdoors. Joe and Carmel have again travelled here in company with Peter and Mary, after pre-5-a.m. starts and the usual rendezvous en route. Because there are not as many classes here as at Shepton Mallet, they were able to travel more comfortably in their cars, rather than bringing a van.

Joe tells me that neither of his vegetables that broke world records at Shepton Mallet has survived. The heavy parsnip is no longer sound enough to show, and the root of the long carrot snapped: an occupational hazard. There are no classes for long vegetables at this show, except for runner beans; indeed the only remaining event on the calendar that has classes for long root crops is Malvern at the end of the month, and Joe tells me he has one carrot left in the pipe to take there. Peter, who has now joined us, says he has saved the long carrot that he showed at Shepton and has another one growing.

Those growers who compete both here and at Shepton are showing many of the same vegetables as last week. There are just two classes without a Shepton equivalent – heavy rhubarb and cauliflowers. Peter has brought entries for both these new classes, as well as for most of the others, but as at Abertysswg he is sticking to his principle of making only one entry for each class, although he would be allowed two. 'I'm not here for the money,' he says. 'I'm a guest.'

By now Kevin and Gareth have arrived, again accompanied by Kyle. They have cut one of their disappointing crop of marrows but when they bring it to the bench they see it is smaller than both of Ken Dade's. Theirs has a hole in it, caused by the flower getting wet when it was being pollinated, setting back the pollination process.

'We've just got one marrow left for Malvern,' Kevin tells me. 'It's only between 30 and 40 lb at the moment but it may grow to a decent size before the end of the month if we have nice weather, although it won't be as big as in a normal year.' They have hopes, though, for their cucumber, beaten into third place last week by the redoubtable Alf Cobb, who is not competing here.

Inside the club's main hall, with its stage at the back and bar at the side, the vegetables are displayed on trestle tables, and the weighing and judging has begun. Nine of the twenty-eight classes are restricted to members of the club, and these are on separate tables at the end nearest the bar. There are also three quality classes – for onions, leeks and parsnips.

Philip's daughter Gail Wintle, the show secretary, supported by her eight-year-old daughter Emily, is keeping an efficient eye on all the preparations, so that everything is ready when the public are admitted in the afternoon. She tells me that the number and average weight of entries is slightly down on last year, no doubt because of the weather.

Nonetheless, the competition is still fierce – all the more so because of the participation of Richard Hope of Wigan, who did not go to Shepton Mallet. Richard, who won the prize for the biggest pumpkin on *The Great British Village Show*, has been a powerful presence on the giant vegetable scene for years. In 2003, here at Llanharry, he broke world records for the longest parsnip and beetroot, and those records still stand. I had telephoned him at the beginning of the year, when I was starting out on the book, with a view to asking whether I could track his progress as I have been doing with Ian, Peter, Gerald, Kevin and Gareth. He said he had problems with his back after an accident at work – now 63, he recently retired as a railway maintenance worker – and he did not know how active he would be this year; so we decided not to go ahead. Despite poor health, though, he has managed to produce entries in most of the classes here and appears to have done well. Another early riser, he has driven 200 miles in a car pulling a trailer. I talk to him just as the judging is coming to a close. He thinks he has won again with his pumpkin, which will earn him £100 – the biggest prize at the show. He also fancies his chances with the longest runner bean, heaviest rhubarb and tallest sunflower.

It looks as though they're edging out in front. It's good, seeing that I've given up fifty per cent of my growing area this year. I have a fairly large garden at home but I also had a big allotment where I grew giant cabbages and swedes; but I gave it up last year. I would have won the swede this year if I'd kept that plot, because

I had them over 60 lb on it. But I have limited space at home and I've only got them to about 30 lb this year.

This is not big enough to beat Ian, who has brought the swede he won with at Shepton Mallet.

Richard's winning pumpkin is less than half the size of the one that won at *The Great British Village Show*, which weighed nearly 900 lb.

Nobody's pumpkins this year are as big as they were last year, because last year was the nearest summer we've had to what they have in America, where they grow the really big ones. The pumpkins kept on growing right into October. That's unusual in the north of England where we come from.

He can see that he has no chance of winning here with his onions and leeks.

Peter's going to beat me. I've done my personal best this year but I don't have the set-up for onions – the light and that. With onions and leeks the people who grow under lights always have the advantage. I have a tunnel, but it isn't heated, and I don't really do a lot with it. I wish I could do the really big onions. They do them better in the north-east than the north-west, perhaps because of the sulphur from the coal. It kills a lot of fungal diseases on the vegetables.

He has a decent-sized cabbage, though, which he thinks could pick up second or third place.

Over the years I've had big cabbages. That man in Cornwall [Dave Thomas] has the best cabbages at present, and he says he's going to do some stem cuttings this year. In Cornwall they've got really good cabbage ground and conditions, and he's got the top strain at present – a really good strain.

Richard has been coming to the Llanharry show almost every year since it began in the early eighties.

They'd been going two or three years before I started coming. Then we did the garden festivals at Liverpool and Gateshead and places. We did shows at all the festivals on top of the other shows, which made them big years.

For the last six or seven years he has not gone to the national championships at Shepton Mallet because it is too far away.

Three hundred miles is too far for a four-day show. You have to stay down there, which is too much for me: I have too many commitments at home. I just come for the one-day events like this. It's a lovely little show, and it's the only one I do.

Richard has been into large vegetables for a long time.

I started doing giants about thirty years ago. Before that I used to grow quality stuff. I entered a local village show that was mainly for quality, but they had two or three novelty classes for the heaviest pumpkin and marrow. I was showing quality things like leeks and carrots but I looked at these pumpkins, and there was also a pair of cucumbers . . . I'd never seen anything like them – they'd win any of these shows today.

I thought it would be good to be growing something as heavy as that; so the chap said he'd give me some seed from his pumpkin. Before these shows started *Garden News* used to run their competition. There were about twenty or thirty classes. You had to send a photograph in, but it was a very haphazard way of doing it, because you could just get your mates to come and witness it and swear that it weighed so much. It was a bit dodgy – that's why a few Mickey Mouse records got passed, and there are one or two still going around now. [Richard is one of several growers who have nagging doubts about Bernard Lavery's 124-lb cabbage, which has stood as the world record since 1989.]

I started writing away to the winners in the *Garden News* competition and asked them to let me have some seed, and I started growing them. It's hard to get top strains from people nowadays, but I was fortunate and I managed to get quite a lot. Then you start breeding them yourself and saving your own seed. I found it a lot more interesting than doing quality vegetables. As soon as I started growing the big stuff I stopped going to the small shows and concentrated on the giants.

The judging is completed by 12.30, just half an hour before the public are admitted. Philip Vowles tells me there are 24 competitors, and between them they have brought along 166 entries – confirming Gail's assessment that numbers are down this year because of the terrible summer. He is pleased, though, that one or two local growers have competed successfully in the open classes against the national experts. The best local achievement is the winning 74-lb 5-oz cabbage grown by Llanharry's Alan Pantin, more than twenty pounds heavier than Richard Hope's, which takes second place.

Philip himself has not done at all badly. His 347-lb pumpkin came a respectable second to Richard Hope's in the open competition. 'There wasn't a lot in it, really – and mine looks nicer.' In the competition for members only, both his heavy marrow and his long runner bean took first prize. Alan Pantin is clearly the local champion, winning a raft of first and second prizes in the members' classes.

The public are due to be admitted at one o'clock, which just leaves me time to grab a good fresh cheese and onion roll from the bar, washed down with a pint of the sinewy Welsh bitter. Without the rival attraction of a rugby international, a knot of people have gathered outside the hall, waiting for the door to open, and by 1.20 p.m. nearly a hundred, including several families with children, have filed in to gawp at this year's crop of monstrosities. Some are first-time visitors drawn by advance publicity on the local radio station.

One regular attender notices immediately a distinct change in the atmosphere compared with previous years. 'It's the first year we haven't had to look at them through clouds of smoke,' she declares. The national ban on smoking in public places was introduced earlier in the summer, and there is no exemption for private members' clubs.

Some competitors have gathered near the stage to congratulate each other or commiserate. Gareth points out a curiosity in the results: this week Ken Dade's cucumber, which the Forteys defeated at Shepton, has beaten theirs. They are the same cucumbers, and both have lost a little weight through dehydration in the intervening week, but at different rates. So the narrow 2-oz margin that the Forteys' entry had over Ken's has been turned on its head, with Ken's cucumber now heavier by the same amount. There is, too, a minor controversy over Peter's winning heavy cauliflower, with some questioning whether it was sufficiently trimmed before it went on the scale.

Peter has also picked up first prizes for his beetroot (beating Ian again) and onion, and won one of the quality prizes with an exhibit of three parsnips. Joe has won with his heavy radish, carrot, leek and tomato. Ken Dade's heavy parsnip beat Joe's into second place by a few ounces. Ian came first with his swede and second with his beetroot, but disappointingly the Forteys picked up no first prizes at all, their best effort being that second with the cucumber.

Philip has listed the results on a whiteboard, comparing the weights achieved this year with those in 2006. The figures show that, even though entries are fewer this year, the weights are not universally lower. Six of the sixteen classes have produced heavier winners than last year – dramatically heavier in the case of Joe's carrot and Ken Dade's parsnip. Three that are significantly lower are Richard Hope's pumpkin, Ian's swede and Peter's cauliflower. Joe's leek, at just under 12 lb, weighs exactly the same as last year's winner.

The presentations are made at 3.30 p.m. David Francis, the president, makes a short speech, thanking the exhibitors and organisers, before handing out the cheques and trophies. Richard Hope wins the award for the most successful grower in the heavy classes – so that long journey from Wigan was worthwhile. Alan Pantin picks up the equivalent prize for local growers. When the raffle is drawn, Joe has the winning ticket for a hamper of vegetables, but he generously gives it back so that it can be won by somebody local.

At 4 o'clock the exhibitors start packing their vegetables away, with the greatest of care, in the hope that they will survive until next week's show at Abertysswg.

Chapter 11

Harrogate

For most of the summer I had been dreading Friday 14 September: the opening day of the prestigious show at Harrogate that represents the climax of the year for the elite onion growers of the north-east. Logistically, this threatened to be the most stressful day I would have to endure in researching this book. Well before noon I needed to be at the Great Yorkshire Showground in Harrogate for the weigh-in for the National Onion Championships at the North of England Horticultural Society's (NEHS) autumn flower show – one of the more lucrative of the season's heavyweight competitions in which prize money for the one class totals more than £1,000. This was the show that Gerald had been targeting with his hydroponic onions before being overwhelmed by technical setbacks.

Then, straight after lunch, I would have to be back in the car heading across the Pennines and down to south Wales, for the Saturday show at Abertysswg that I described in Chapter 1. To avoid two long motorway drives on the same day, I made for Harrogate on Thursday afternoon and stayed overnight at an hotel.

Queues of traffic are already forming near the showground entrances as I arrive just before the show opens to the public at 9.30 a.m. The weather has been kinder than at Shepton Mallet, and there is a festive air to the proceedings as I walk past the main gate and hear the Bourbon Street Roof Raisers launch into a lively programme of New Orleans jazz. I am making for Flower Hall 2, where the National Vegetable Society is holding its regional championships.

The onions are on a bench at one side of the hall. Strategically sited right alongside, Exhibition Seeds of Whitby, one of the leading suppliers of seeds for extra-large vegetables, has a stand with an impressive display of giant onions and leeks, manicured with precision. It is run by Keith Foster, an acknowledged expert in the field and author of two booklets of detailed technical advice for gardeners who want to grow their leeks and onions to maximum size.

The booklets are written in a hectoring, combative style and emphasise the importance of acquiring the right seed and providing the right conditions, which include heat and light over the winter. Foster warns that the growing of giant vegetables is an expensive hobby, and maintains that success simply depends on doing the right things at the right time. He discounts the importance of fertilisers: 'The condition you supply are the secret of large bulbs, not feed.' In the leek booklet he is more outspoken, asserting that the press coverage of shows is afflicted by 'middle-class snobbery', where exhibition gardeners are seen as superior to the often working-class vegetable growers.

Since the early nineteenth century, when many shows had separate classes for 'cottagers', the question of social class has always been a powerful undercurrent in competitive vegetable growing – and, indeed, in gardening in all its manifestations.

Staging at Harrogate had to be completed by 6.30 a.m.: serious growers turn into nighthawks on these critical days in the competition calendar. By the time I arrive about four dozen onions, some approaching the size of footballs, are lined up on the bench. The show secretary, Ray Orme, who has been doing this job for four years, reports that the number of entries is about the same this year as last. But he tells me there have been big changes over the last twenty years or so. Most obviously, the size of the winning onions has more than doubled, as a result of developments in the way they are grown, as reflected in Keith Foster's booklets. 'In the old days they grew them in the open, in their gardens,' Ray points out. 'Now they're all under cover, with artificial light and heat.'

The National Onion Championships originated with the National Kelsae Onion Festival, initiated in 1975 by seed merchants Sinclair McGill after taking over Laing & Mather of Kelso in the Scottish borders, the firm that introduced the Kelsae onion in the 1950s. The Kelsae is a hybrid, created by selective cross-pollination and improved over the years until it consistently produced onions weighing over 4 lb. The strain is prominent in the genetic make-up of all today's heavyweights.

The winning onion in that first 1975 championship weighed just under 5 lb. By 1983, when the competition was first held in Harrogate, that figure had risen by more than two pounds, and thereafter it rose exponentially, until by 1990 it was up to 10 lb 14 oz, then a world record. The record has been broken nine times at this show. In 1995 Mel Ednie from Anstruther in Fife, in the second of four successive victories, set a mark of 15 lb 15 oz that stood for ten years until overtaken by John Sifford's as yet unsurpassed 16-lb 8-oz giant.

All this from a vegetable that – to judge from images found in Egyptian tombs from around 2900 BC – evolved from a straggly plant with a bulb about the size of a modern shallot. It was said to have been the staple diet of the 100,000 labourers who built the Great Pyramid of Cheops. It is not hard to see how enthusiasts became hooked on developing that small bulb into something bigger; for its habit of growth is intriguing, its weight and girth being formed from tight layers of aromatic flesh formed at the base of its slender green leaves.

According to the *Cambridge World History of Food*, this layered structure was interpreted in ancient times as a symbol of eternity, which is why the Russians and others built their churches with onion domes, hoping they would last for ever. But the onion had lost any such divine status in western Europe by medieval times, when it was regarded as rough, common food, eaten raw by people who wanted to show that they could withstand strong flavours and did not mind adding to the noxious odours then prevailing in society – rather like today's young men and women who like to devour fierce curries after an evening in the pub. In *The Canterbury Tales*, Chaucer describes his ugly, lecherous summoner as being fond of garlic, onions and leeks, along with 'strong wine, red as blood'.

For a few years Sinclair McGill's Kelsae festival moved from venue to venue – including two years at Kelso itself – until in 1983 it found its permanent home here at the NEHS Great Autumn Show. The Society was established in Leeds in 1911 as a northern version of the Royal Horticultural Society, whose interests and activities at that time were focused on the south of England. Ten years later the NEHS held its first show in Harrogate, and most years since then it has organised spring and autumn shows in the spa town, growing steadily in size and reputation and drawing in many specialist flower and vegetable societies to hold their annual championships here.

In 1995 the show grew so big that it was transferred from the town's central exhibition halls to the Great Yorkshire Showground, a couple of miles away. It is tempting to call it the northern equivalent of the Chelsea Flower Show, but that would be misleading: it is bigger, in terms of the area it occupies, and a lot more down-to-earth. Where Chelsea is now increasingly dominated by designers letting their imaginations run wild on layouts and schemes that no ordinary gardener would ever aspire to, Harrogate puts more emphasis on the practical, while vying with Chelsea in the perfection of the flowers and vegetables it attracts.

The list of national champion onion growers from 1975 onwards, and of world record holders, shows that they have nearly all come from Scotland or the north-east of England. Peter is one of the few exceptions: he won in 1991 with an onion weighing 10 lb 9 oz, but has never managed to repeat that success.

So far, in my year with the giant vegetables, I had ventured no further north than Chesterfield. Harrogate therefore marked my first sustained encounter with the leek and onion aristocracy of the north-east, many of them former coal miners. They do not trundle their plump produce to the southern or Welsh shows I had attended so far, but fatten them up for their own regional contests, where the rewards are significantly greater.

Here, then, are a whole new set of dedicated growers to become acquainted with. Of the four I have been following, Gerald and Peter have entries here; but I do not at first see either of them among the enthusiasts who now, not long after the doors have opened to the public, mill around the bench admiring these weighty products of more than nine months of dedication, vigilance and loving care.

One of the first growers I meet is Jack Newbould, from Methley in Leeds, who has been coming to the show for twenty years and won last year's contest with an onion weighing 15 lb 9 oz. He also happens to be a long-time rival of Peter's, and is still angry at the way the Nottinghamshire man narrowly beat him in the contest for the three heaviest onions at last year's Dewsbury Onion Fair, through what Jack regarded as a sharp tactical manoeuvre. He is keen to give me his side of the controversy: 'Peter didn't put his heaviest one in with the single onions – where I'd have beaten him – but put it into his three for the three heaviest. It's not that I'm in it for the money, though I'm not a wealthy man, but I don't like to be beaten.' I shall learn still more about this simmering grudge when the onion road show returns to Dewsbury in a few weeks' time; but meanwhile Jack tells me his history as a grower.

A tiler by trade, he first came to the Harrogate show merely as an interested spectator. The ever-increasing size of the onions fascinated him and inspired him to try growing them himself. Some fourteen years ago he felt he was raising them big enough to compete with those he saw here, so he made his first entry. Those were the years when Mel Ednie dominated the scene, but Jack persevered and last year his determination paid off. Apart from taking the honours here, he won second prize – beaten by three-quarters of an ounce – at the big leek and onion show at Ashington a week later.

Like Scott Robb with his cabbages, Jack has bred his own strain, produced by swapping seed with other successful growers. He calls it MJL, after the three men who contributed seed to it. The M is for Mick Cook, another keen Yorkshire grower, the J for Jack himself and L for the legendary Billy Lamb, who has won this competition twice – in 2001 and 2004 – and whose stock is the source of the seed of many of the onions competing here today. 'I'm trying to improve my strain every year,' Jack says. 'It's a challenge, obviously. It's no good if you keep on growing seed from the same strain, because in the end it will lose its vigour. You need to cross it with a new strain to keep the vigour going.'

He is not going to break any records this year, partly because he moved house in January, about a month after the biggest onions have to be sown. He could not plant them in his new polytunnel until the end of April (he usually has them in by mid-March). 'It's been a real push to get to the show,' he confesses. 'I'm lucky to get any on the bench at all.' All the same, when the onions are weighed he will not be far behind the winners.

We get to talking about Gerald's ambition to beat the world record using hydroponics, and Jack tells me that he tried this method some eight years ago. He bought the equipment from a shop in Leeds, rumoured to be popular with those who use it for growing cannabis. But he encountered the same sort of problems that Gerald has, and he did not repeat the experiment.

What he and the others are seeking to achieve is the 18-lb onion – a pound and a half above the existing record – and he is confident that it will happen before long. 'It's certainly possible,' he maintains, 'but not with hydroponics. Last year I think I would have got to 18 lb easily if we hadn't had that very hot July. Nothing will grow at that heat.' This is a common hazard for giant onions. In his booklet Keith Foster notes that they resent temperatures above 75°F [23.9°C] and simply stop growing when it gets that hot. But the setback has not dented Jack's optimism: 'I hope I'll get the world record next year – by early August I'll know.'

Ray Orme is less dismissive of the hydroponic method. 'Gerald will get it right if he finds the right blend of nutrients,' he predicts. But he accepts that such a system needs constant monitoring. 'I went to visit a place in Cornwall where they were growing tomatoes hydroponically. The first thing I saw was blossom end rot.' Too much water can harm some vegetables as much as too little of it.

While most of the growers here are old friends, battle-hardened by their disappointments over the years, there are one or two fresh faces. Ken Ault from Doncaster, a first-time entrant, is mighty proud of his onion, although he knows that at around 10 lb 8 oz it will not be among the winners. 'It's the biggest I've ever grown,' he tells me. 'That's why I decided to bring it along and see how it measured up against the big boys.' He might still be in line to win something, though. He and three friends struck a bet at the start of the season as to which of them could grow the biggest onion. They each put £25 into the pot and get £10 back if they grow one big enough to put into the show. The rest of the pot goes to the winner.

I spot Mary Glazebrook among the crowd of onlookers. She and Peter had been up since 2 a.m. They arrived at the ground at 4.30 a.m., and, once they finished staging their exhibits, went back to the car to make up what sleep they could – which is why I hadn't seen them earlier. Peter has entered several quality classes in addition to the heavy onion. When he joins us he reports with some satisfaction that he has won second prize for his collection of three vegetables. He has also come first in the parsnip class, but he takes more pleasure in his second place with the collection – more prestigious and more hotly contested. He does not think he will win the onion weigh-in, though: to judge from appearances, Jack Newbould's biggest might just have the beating of his, as it did last year here and at Dewsbury.

Gerald's sole hydroponic onion is of respectable size but is clearly not going to take the top prize. In the quality classes his carrots – for which he has a high national reputation – have not won anything this year either, no doubt because of the disease that he was telling us about at Peter's open evening. His parsnips and quality onions are similarly unplaced. I look around for Gerald but do not see him. He is active in the National Vegetable Society and is probably hobnobbing with friends; or maybe sleeping in his car, like the Glazebrooks.

By 11.30 the scales have arrived at the end of the onion bench, and a white chain barrier has been put up so that onlookers cannot interfere with the work of the four officials charged with organising the weigh-in. First each onion is carefully tagged, so there can be no confusion about who grew it. Then it is trimmed by slipping a standard gauge (a length of pipe five inches long and three inches in diameter) over the leaves. All the foliage above the rim of the pipe is cut off. Finally the roots are cut away – and here the officials have to be careful not to slice off or fatally damage the root plate, because the growers will want to use this year's biggest onions to grow on for seed. Some of the more suspicious entrants are keeping a careful eye on the process, checking to see that no such damage is being done.

With half an hour to go before the scheduled start of the weigh-in, there is time for me to have a quick trot around the rest of the showground. By now the Bourbon Street Roof Raisers have been replaced by the equally ebullient Yorkshire Post Jazz Quartet. Overall this is a more enjoyable show than Shepton Mallet: friendlier and more compact, with less commercial huckstering. It is especially rewarding for enthusiasts of particular flower species, with nine specialist societies holding their annual championships here – including those for dahlias, fuchsias, chrysanthemums, carnations and gladioli. There is an exhibition of beekeeping and large displays of arts and crafts and regional food.

Back at the vegetable hall, the weigh-in is about to begin and the growers, mingling with interested spectators, cluster round the scales. There are two heavy onion classes – one for the cumulative weight of three onions, with a first prize of £75; and the big one for the single heaviest, with its prize of £500, plus an additional £1,000 if the winner breaks the world record. The three-onion entries go to the scales first, so that the event will reach its climax when the heaviest single onion, the big-money winner, is announced.

The master of ceremonies tries to raise the excitement level by giving a droll commentary on the proceedings, including one or two suggestive quips: 'They look a grand pair,' he observes, as two bulbous onions are brought towards the scales. Each is weighed individually, because the scales are not big enough to take three at a time. They are the kind of scales you see at greengrocers' shops, programmed to print out the weight in kilograms on a small ticket. After the weighing an official then uses a calculator to convert the result into pounds and ounces before the total is announced, along with the name of the grower.

The winning set of three onions, grown by David Williams from Durham, weigh in at 35 lb 7 oz – a respectable average of nearly 12 lb each. When the time comes to weigh the individual entries, the officials select the smallest first, so that tension builds up towards the end. The first, a measly 6 lb 7 oz, receives a round of polite applause, with just a hint of irony. Soon the poundage is into double figures, and Gerald's sole entry scores a fraction under 11 lb. This is far from disgraceful, but soon the weights are climbing above 12 lb and the competition is hotting up. The applause grows louder and more sincere.

Walter Stringfellow, the Wakefield grower whom, earlier in the season, Peter had tipped to take the title, comes up with a 12-lb 6-oz specimen: impressive, but still not quite big enough to win. Peter's onion makes exactly 13 lb and, to his surprise, beats Jack Newbould's by a good three ounces. David Williams's entry is just an ounce under Peter's, which holds the lead until the very last onion is put on to the scale.

'Barbara Cook from Knottingley,' intones the announcer. 'Thirteen pounds, five ounces.' A stocky, uninhibited woman, from the former mining district of West Yorkshire, Barbara lets out a cry of delight. One of a handful of women who participate in this traditionally male-dominated pursuit, she is the first of her sex to have won the heavy onion title. She has been a keen grower ever since she married Mick Cook (the M in the name of Jack's MJL onion strain), and for several years she and Mick have competed against each other in shows.

She poses with her onion for photographers, raising it above her head in triumph, while a clutch of newspaper and radio reporters form a ring around her. It quickly becomes apparent that she is not given to false modesty about her achievement. 'I had a feeling I'd win,' she says. 'After all, I came second last year – but that was with a bigger onion than this one.' Ray Orme pays tribute to her: 'Barbara has been trying to win it for years, and her perseverance has paid off.'

Asked what is now going to happen to the onion, she declares that she will take it home and grow it on for seed, in the hope of eventually producing something even bigger. 'The eighteen-pounder is the holy grail,' she declares. Although neither she nor anyone else will be getting close to that weight this year, she hints at greater things in just a week's time, when she will be going to the World Leek and Onion Championships at Ashington, between Newcastle and the Scottish border, where the top onion prize is £1,000. She suggests that she could spring a surprise: 'I hope I might have some even bigger ones next week.'

Peter is naturally disappointed at being pipped at the post, but the second prize is a handy £250, and he is sufficiently encouraged to consider taking another onion to Ashington to do battle with Barbara again. The snag is that he has not entered for the show yet, and thinks he might be too late. He asks me for the phone number of the secretary, Dickie Atkinson, so that he can ask about putting in a late entry. Even if his entry is accepted, though, he will not necessarily make the journey. There is a local quality show on the same day, where he would be almost certain to pick up a few prizes; and even though the money would be nothing like as good as at Ashington, he would avoid another impossibly early start and a long drive.

I should like to stay longer at Harrogate, strolling around the stalls in the sunshine, admiring the flowers and vegetables, listening to the open-air jazz, sampling Wensleydale cheese and other Yorkshire delicacies. But I must be on my way to Wales, for another night as a guest of my long-suffering friends near Builth Wells, before clocking in at Abertysswg on Saturday morning. I will be back up north before long to see whether Barbara can complete the north-eastern double.

Chapter 12

Ashington

Ashington is the home of the World Leek and Onion Championships, with their mysterious rules and generous prize money. At the start of the nineteenth century only fifty people lived there, but workers flocked to it after Ashington Colliery opened in 1867, and it went on to dub itself the largest mining village in the world. Now a sprawling town with a population of about 28,000, it is known in the football world for producing three exceptional international stars: brothers Bobby and Jack Charlton and their uncle, Jackie Milburn, who played in the 1950s. In the main shopping street an imposing statue of Jackie portrays him as he traps the ball, probably before starting one of his electrifying runs towards goal. Ashington also gained an improbable reputation in the art world for the Ashington Group of painters: untutored miners whose work became fashionable in the 1930s and 1940s.

The mine closed in 1988, and today the town's largest employer is an Alcan aluminium factory. The colliery site became a business park and a museum of mining, while the spoil heap (said to be Europe's largest) was transformed into the Queen Elizabeth II Country Park, dominated by a man-made lake that now supports large numbers of swans, geese and other water birds, as well as an enthusiastic corps of anglers.

Our hotel is at one end of this lake, and some rooms command alluring views across it; the rest overlook the car park. It operates as a pub as well as an hotel, and on arrival we immediately come face to face with north-eastern culture, in particular the engaging though at first impenetrable Geordie accent. Four fleshy men at a table in a corner of the bar make us immediately welcome: one proudly carries tattoos over every visible part of his body and, he assures us, over most of the invisible parts as well.

Next morning I drive two or three miles to the Northern Social Club, in a suburb called North Seaton. It is not the first time I have been here. In 1990, when I wrote regular gardening articles for the *Independent on Sunday*, I came up to report on this show – my first exposure to the giant vegetable cult. On the face of it, not much has changed in seventeen years. The show has just two classes – one for the heaviest onion and one for the largest set of three pot leeks, judged by measuring their critical dimensions rather than their weight. The prize money for the leeks remains unchanged at £1,300, but the onion prize has gone up from £750 to £1,000. The contests are still sponsored by Newcastle Breweries, and, to show their appreciation, exhibitors and spectators enthusiastically consume their products while admiring the giants.

The club has 2,000 members, a quarter of them women, and is housed in a nondescript but practical example of the brutalist architecture fashionable in the sixties and seventies, backing on to a small local shopping centre. The judging and showing procedure is unchanged since my last visit. As before, the onions are being collated in the concert room on the ground floor, ready for the public weighing ceremony at 1 p.m., while the leeks are being taken to the first floor saloon, where they will be measured and eventually displayed.

A few days earlier I warned Dickie Atkinson, the show secretary, that I would be coming, and as soon as I arrive I check in with him in his small office on the first floor. He gives me dispensation to observe the arcane and normally secret ritual of measuring the leeks. The door to the saloon is blocked off by a table, where a trickle of growers, their leeks wrapped in damp cloths for freshness, are waiting to have them formally accepted by the official sitting on the other side. He examines the leeks to see whether they appear sound: if not, he has the power to reject the entry. Having satisfied himself on that score he checks off the grower's name, marks his assigned number with a felt-tip pen on the leeks themselves and puts them in a holding area to await measurement.

Forty-six sets (stands, to give them their correct technical name) of three leeks have been entered this year. Robert Bell, who leads the team of three judges, says this has been an average figure for the last few years. Rereading my 1990 article I find that more than a hundred growers entered that year: so although it would certainly be premature to write an obituary for prize leek-growing in the north-east, it is patently less popular than it was – a victim, it seems, of changing social conditions in the area since nearly all the coal mines closed. On the brighter side, there are nearly sixty advance entries for the onion class – the highest for some years, and more than double last year's turnout.

While there is no universally accepted explanation of the popularity of growing leeks in the north-east, the most likely is the most straightforward one: that prevailing soil and weather conditions favour it – even if the legend that it was introduced by immigrant Welsh miners is more appealing.

Leeks have long lent themselves to romantic flights of fancy. In AD 540, St David might or might not have suggested that the successful Welsh defenders of the homeland wear them in their hats to distinguish them from the marauding Saxons. Whatever the truth of the matter, it became a tradition for Welshmen to wear a leek in their hat on St David's Day, the first of March. Shakespeare makes a meal of this conceit in *Henry V*, where Fluellen's cap sports a leek even though St David's Day is past. He forces Pistol to eat it as revenge for an earlier slight, and Pistol complies, although protesting that leeks make him feel 'qualmish'.

Like their close relatives, onions, leeks were portrayed in Egyptian tombs from around 3000 BC. The Romans probably introduced them into Britain, along with many other vegetables. The historian Pliny says Emperor Nero ate them regularly in the belief that they would improve his singing (so he might not only have been fiddling while Rome burned but trilling along as well), and his addiction earned him the nickname 'porrophagus', *Allium porrum* being the Latin term for the leek. Like many vegetables they were also thought to have aphrodisiac qualities: no doubt their shape had something to do with it.

Today's world of competition leeks is a complex one, riven by disputes and divisions that stretch back so far that their origins are all but forgotten. But the rivalries remain. In his book *How to Grow Giant Vegetables*, Bernard Lavery describes it as perhaps the most competitive category of all, rich in tales of sabotage and skulduggery, with reports of guard dogs, electric fences and shotguns being deployed to deter potential saboteurs. He concedes, though, that he has had no such problems himself, and I suspect quite a few of the stories can be dismissed as urban myths.

There are two distinct versions of the vegetable: pot leeks, the short and stubby ones, grown for weight and bulk; and long or blanch leeks, grown for elegance. The Ashington competition is confined to pot leeks and, although it is billed as the Foster's Lager World Open Leek Championship, it is not unanimously recognised as such. As in the world of professional boxing, different authorities have their own rival contests. The National Pot Leek Society's competitions have slightly different rules from Ashington, and those of the National Vegetable Society are different again, their judges placing more emphasis on quality than size. The Ashington show was begun in 1980 by a breakaway faction of the National Pot Leek Society led by Bill Rutherford, a revered name in giant vegetables. Because he was able to persuade Newcastle Breweries to put up the generous prizes for both classes the show was an immediate success, and every year it receives publicity in the local and national media. Bill is no longer an active grower, but he still comes to see the shows.

Robert Bell, who has judged leeks for twenty years, introduces me to his team. Tony Cuthbert is responsible for keeping track of the entries, taking them to the measuring table and making sure the correct weight is shown on the cards he places on them. Gary Bell, a cousin of Robert's, works out the cumulative weight of each set of three leeks on his calculator. In 1990 this was done using an old-fashioned ready-reckoner, specifically published for the purpose, but new technology has taken over. Each competitor is allowed just one stand, but they can enter another in their child's or spouse's name, and several do.

'We have to move on,' says Robert, 'because we want these doors to open to the public at four o'clock.' So he does not stop work while we talk, but explains what he is doing as he does it. The three have been there since nine, when the first stands arrived, and they can continue receiving entries until noon. The first measurement is a critical one because it determines whether the entry fits the standard criterion for a pot leek: that it must measure no more than six inches from the root plate at its base to the 'tight button' – the easily recognisable V-shaped point where the white outer skin begins to fan out into green leaves.

Robert takes the measurement carefully with a stiff ruler. If it comes to more than six inches, the specimen does not count as a pot leek for the purposes of competition. Sometimes a grower with a potential winner that marginally exceeds this measurement will carefully cut away the lower part of the tight button with a razor blade, hoping the judges will not notice; but an alert and conscientious judge like Robert will spot this quite quickly and disqualify the entry. He has found no such attempt at deception yet; but one of the three leeks he is looking at is a little over the six inch mark.

'We can't accept them, Gary,' he calls out. 'Put NAS on them – not as scheduled.' Then he turns to me: 'A shame, because they look nice quality; but if it's out, it's out. We try to get them in if we can, but you've got to be fair to the others.'

On the next leek, the crucial measurement comes to exactly six inches. Robert now has to mark the half-way point between the root plate and the tight button with a felt-tip pen, and measure the circumference of the trunk at that point, this time with a flexible tape measure. It comes to 18.6 inches. He shouts the figures to Gary, who feeds them into his calculator and, after some swift button-pushing, comes up with the cubic capacity of the leek. When the other two in the stand have been similarly measured, he adds the three figures together and announces the total. 'I double check because there's that much money involved in it that you've got to be sure you get it right,' he tells me.

Last year the winning stand came to 488.07 cubic inches, but three times in the last five years it has reached above 500. In 1980, the first year the competition was held here, the winner notched up just 215.78 cubic inches. This rate of inflation matches that of the onions at Harrogate, and similarly reflects more sophisticated growing techniques.

The measuring is not the end of the procedure. Robert now examines the three leeks to evaluate their condition and see how they have been treated, for they can be disqualified if there are obvious flaws, even though they have been initially accepted by the official at the entrance. He notes that some of the outer leaves have been stripped off and some are a little coarse, and there are a few wrinkles on the stem. All of this suggests that the leeks have not been freshly dug and might even have been shown at another show last week. 'The older you get the more wrinkles you get,' he says.

'Little bairns is bonny.' He puts his finger down in the root to see if there is a hole, another common flaw. He finds none, but there is a little rust. And one of the three has green veins coming down from the leaves. 'Sometimes that can't be helped,' says Robert. He allows the entry to stand – although if this were a quality vegetable show it would have lost many points for these flaws.

Some other leeks have been damaged by thrips or red spider mite – both hard to get rid of – or by snails. A few show some mottling on the leaves, a sign of potential trouble, and one has a crack. 'He's had rust there and tried to clean it off,' Robert explains, showing me some slight discoloration. If a leek has started to run to seed it is immediately disqualified, so some growers try to conceal this by cutting the seed head off – but again a good judge can spot this quite easily.

I leave the three to their task and go down to the concert room, where the onions are being prepared for weighing. I remember this room from seventeen years ago – a spacious, comfortable hall with a stage on one side and a long bar at a slightly higher level on the other, the space between them filled with round tables and chairs. The onions are being collected at a table in front of the stage. It is 11.30, half an hour before the deadline for submissions, but a good many of the sixty onions entered in advance have still to arrive. I see from the list that Peter did telephone Dickie and put his name down, but he has not yet appeared. Knowing his propensity to arrive at shows early, I suspect he has decided not to come here but to go to the local quality show instead, as he hinted when I saw him at Harrogate.

Suddenly there is a commotion at the door, and eight people march in with their onions. It is the West Yorkshire contingent, led by Barbara Cook, carrying hers in a strong canvas bag. Her husband Mick is with her, and I spot Jack Newbould among the others. Having deposited their precious vegetables on the table by the stage they gather around one of the round tables and fetch drinks. I ask Barbara what she thinks of her chance of doing the double. She is not too optimistic, fearing that the rule by which the onions are weighed here, with roots and foliage attached, might count against her. 'A lot of them are bigger in the top and neck than mine, and that's where they might win it,' she says.

Mick, a mining machine operator, tells me about his own onion breeding operation – the quest for the ultimate seed that he and Barbara have been conducting for the last twenty years. They diligently select seeds every year from the largest that he and his friends have managed to grow, and they sow them in the green-house at their Knottingley home. Over the years they have gradually produced larger specimens but only in the last three years or so have they felt confident enough to compete here, in this show of shows. Mick used to grow leeks as well, but he has now given them up so that he can put more effort into his onions.

At another table I join a group of growers from the Midlands and get talking to Frank Gregg, secretary of the Midlands Leek Society. 'I've been coming up here for twenty-three years,' he tells me. 'The onions have got bigger because nowadays it's all done with lights and under cover.' His society is based in the West Bromwich area and used to have a hundred members, but now it is down to around forty. It was started by a group of enthusiasts, many of whom had moved to the area from the north-east when the mines began to close. They organise their own show, but it is not as big as this one and the prize money nothing like as great.

Frank tells me with pride and sadness that John Sifford, whose 16-lb 8-oz onion still holds the world record, was a member of his society. John died early in 2006, a few months after setting the record. 'He'd have broken it again if he hadn't contracted this liver problem.'

Chris Mann, another member of the group, also knew John and bought some seed from him. He tells me that John was a canny competitor. 'He would come up to the bench and look around at the other onions on it, and if there were a few that looked bigger than his he wouldn't put his in. He was in it to win.' Chris, a builder, comes from Romsley, near Worcester, and was especially gratified to win the John Sifford Trophy for heavy onions at the Romsley Show.

A keen gardener for most of his adult life, Chris used to run three allotments until, as he grew older, he found the work too much. He raises his onions in a polytunnel in his garden. He enjoys coming up here because he has family connections. 'My mother was a Geordie, and a lot of my relations live fairly near here. But it's the first time I've exhibited here for a few years. My onions looked better this year than they have for quite a while so I decided to have a go. They were putting on two inches a week until the longest day of the year, and that's when they almost stop growing. After the end of June they don't put on two inches in a month.'

The public weigh-in is scheduled for 1 p.m., and just before that I decide to go upstairs and see how the leek measurements are progressing. This time, though, I fail to gain admission. The doors to the saloon are locked, and curtains have been pulled over them so that nobody can peer inside. Clearly the process has reached a critical stage.

Back in the concert room a set of scales has been placed in front of the stage, and the weigh-in is about to commence. The room is not full, and looking round it I gauge that the audience is largely made up of the growers and their friends. The number of onions actually submitted is fifty, which means that Peter and nine others who had entered in advance decided not to compete after all.

Rereading my account of the 1990 show, I see that the weigh-in was more of a production number then: a local comedian had been hired as master of ceremonies and was assisted by a glamorous young 'promotions assistant'. Today one of the club officials does the honours. 'Welcome,' he says, 'to the World Leek and Onion

Championships', and before there is even time for a suggestive quip the first onion has been carried to the scales.

It weighs 11 lb 12 oz and earns a ripple of applause – a precedent dutifully followed when every weight is announced, however unimpressive. Soon two have gone beyond 14 lb, and the competition begins to warm up. Walter Stringfellow's entry falls just below 14 lb, so he is not going to win a top award – although he might pick up something, for there are cash prizes for the first 35 places, ranging from £1,000 for first to £5 for 35th. Chris Mann's is only 9 lb 12 oz, so it probably will not qualify even for the lowest of the awards – but it is far from being the smallest, for one onion fails to make 6 lb.

Of the Yorkshire contingent, Barbara's onion weighs 13 lb 11 oz, slightly more than her winning weight at Harrogate but, given that it has the leaves and roots attached, the onion itself is probably smaller. The rule of thumb is that the roots and foliage weigh about a pound. Her husband Mick's is six ounces lighter, and Jack's an ounce or two below that.

The proceedings are interrupted briefly by a small muddle when one entrant's name and number on the onion itself does not tally with that in the entry book. Soon after that has been sorted out one of the largest onions goes on the scale. It has been grown by Paul Rochester of Seaham, County Durham, and makes 15 lb 6½ oz. The applause for this is the most enthusiastic so far, and as a succession of lesser specimens reach the scales it is clear that Paul stands a good chance of winning the top prize. He is challenged towards the end of the weigh-in by another entry from Durham, grown by Dennis Watson, but that is a crucial ounce lighter, and Paul is declared the winner. At the table where he is sitting with friends and fellow competitors, glasses are raised in congratulation.

When I join them Paul, a 44-year-old machine operator with a demolition company, tells me this is the first time he has brought an onion to this show. He has been growing them for just three years, inheriting the enthusiasm from his late father Wilfred, and raises them in a polytunnel on his allotment, a five-minute walk from his house. He acquired the winning onion as one of a handful of seedlings from a friend who had grown them from Billy Lamb's seed. He will take seed from it next year but will have to wait a further year to see whether it will reproduce an onion as big, or even bigger, to bring to the show in 2009. 'I knew it was going to be a big one through measuring it,' he tells me. 'It was 30.4 inches around and the biggest of the others was about 29. It was the only one that size so I didn't take it to Harrogate but waited for this show.'

One of the growing techniques that he omits to tell me about won him publicity the following week in the national press. Both the *Daily Express* and *Garden News* reported that he plays Glenn Miller tapes to the onions to get them 'in the mood' for growing out of their skins. 'I've got a tape player at the allotments with speakers close by,' Paul told a reporter, 'and every time I go down there I put Glenn Miller on. Even my leeks seem to be doing better.' (The leeks in question have won him prizes at the National Pot Leek Society's shows. He would have brought some here, but when he measured them they exceeded the six-inch maximum from root plate to tight button; perhaps the Glenn Miller music was too loud.)

Jack Newbould offers me a less fanciful explanation of why Durham growers tend to do well in giant vegetable contests: being nearer to the coast than he and his friends in West Yorkshire are, they benefit from the sea breezes and have fewer frosts. Then he introduces me to the most famous Durham grower of them all, the legendary Billy Lamb.

Without a doubt, my talk with Billy is the highlight of my day at Ashington. His seeds are part of the genetic make-up of the great majority of the onions exhibited here, and I have heard his name so often in connection with champion giant onions that when I finally meet him I feel the same sort of awe that I experienced years ago when, as a journalist, I found myself face to face with such as Muhammad Ali, Fred Astaire and Margaret Thatcher.

Billy, who is 67, comes from Easington Colliery in County Durham, where he worked as a miner until 1991. 'I was a chrysanthemum man first,' he tells me, 'and then I turned to leeks and onions.'

I've been exhibiting here for eighteen or nineteen years, with leeks as well as onions. I've won seven times here, the last time a couple of years back. But I've packed in the growing now, and I don't sell the seeds any more.

I come here to see my friends – it's just nostalgia in a sense. This is a fantastic show: I think it's the biggest entry [for onions] they've ever had. People who come to look at them don't appreciate how much time and money and effort it takes to produce leeks and onions good enough for this show. The layman doesn't realise the work that's put in.

I press him for the story of his seed. How was it that he, out of the scores of enthusiastic and knowledgeable growers in the region, came to be the supplier of choice for anyone who wanted to produce the very biggest onions?

The trouble is I don't know where the original seed came from. I'm often asked. It was given me by a friend. In those days most people grew Foster's seeds [that is Keith Foster, author of the leek and onion booklets, whose stall I admired at Harrogate] but this one was given me. I pre-selected the largest bulbs and grew them on, and as the years went on I got bigger onions. The biggest one I've ever grown was just short of 15 lb, which is smaller than the one that won today. So they're getting bigger all the time. People I know now are doing a better job than when I used to do it.

In the old days we used to send the onions away [sow the seed] on the shortest day but now they send them away in mid-October, and they've found that makes them grow bigger. They grow right on from October to the following September – it gives them that extra bit of growth, and that's why they're getting larger. Some still leave it until November. I ended up sending mine away on 25 November.

So what were the real secrets of his success?

Any good gardener knows that you need a good plant, and then you have to get the trench work and the soil right to produce prize-winning vegetables. It's not just the plant. The trouble is that heating and lighting are getting too expensive nowadays, so some people are moving from gas back to paraffin. And some of them have heated cables in the beds.

But the proof of the pudding is in the way I grew mine – a lot of top onion growers can't believe what I produced with what I've got. I've got no heated cables in the beds, and I struggle to keep the greenhouse at 48–50°F [9–10°C] – some of them keep it at 60° [16°C]. It depends on what people can afford.

I raise the topic of Gerald's and Medwyn Williams's attempts to grow giant onions hydroponically this year. Does Billy think the world record will ever be broken by a hydroponic onion?

They'll never get it right, for all that it's a water-cellular structured plant. For things like lettuce, hydroponics works, because the water can just circulate around. But for things like onions put in rockwool, or some substance that's constantly fed a quantity of water with the light on it all the time, you're stressing the plant, and it starts to go rotten or stops – and that's it.

Certainly the constant feeding of nutrients to the onions through the water goes against current thinking about how to make them into giants. Conventional growers put all the additives they think necessary into the compost before the onions or leeks are planted in it, and add hardly any extra fertiliser during the growth period. This is what Keith Foster recommends, and it casts doubt on all the colourful stories of growers feeding their plants with fertilisers based on secret formulas handed down from father to son.

I ask Billy why so many growers of giant onions and leeks are former miners.

In the north-east especially there wasn't much entertainment. After World War II the miners had gardens where they could afford to grow vegetables, and then they started to compete and have shows. The camaraderie of the miners at the leek shows was fantastic. Of course you also used to get back-biting between exhibitors, and some professional jealousy, but always the camaraderie was there. I did have a couple of leeks stolen a few years ago from my allotment but, touch wood, I think those days have gone when people steal other people's stuff.

And now that he has hung up his trenching spade, has it all been worth it?

For me it's a legacy. I've left something behind and I've worked hard to do it. My gardening is a hate and love relationship. I can spend hours in the greenhouse and then walk down the garden path and throw bricks at it. I'm that type of bloke. But I had seven good years here and at Harrogate, and that's something I can look back on.

As the onions are taken from the concert room up to the saloon, where they will be displayed to the public alongside the leeks, a disco begins on stage and more drinks are carried from the bar. Time for me to go and find some lunch and explore the town before coming back to discover the results of the leek championship.

In the car park quite a lot of the exhibitors are leaning against the wall, smoking. At the same time some are clearly bargaining and doing deals that culminate in plain brown envelopes passing discreetly from hand to hand. The atmosphere reminds me of the scene outside certain inner London underground stations on a busy Saturday morning. Here, though, it is not drugs being traded, but the seeds of prize-winning leeks and onions.

Selling seed has always been an integral part of these shows, even if it almost certainly breaches the strict rules on such sales enacted by the European Union. Billy Lamb is not selling any this year, but plenty of others are. My inquiries reveal that this year's top price for seed from prize-winning leeks and onions (i.e. those that won prizes last year) is £36 a dozen. That represents a colossal increase since my 1990 visit, when the going rate was just £4.

In town I seek out Jackie Milburn's statue, to pay my respects and to wonder whether any common factor links the achievements of Ashington's three supreme footballing sons with those of the men and women who spend the best part of a year nurturing very large vegetables to bring here every September. I conclude that there is no real link, unless you count perseverance, dedication and hard work, coupled with innate skill – or unless you accept Billy Lamb's explanation that miners never had much to entertain them in their spare time.

Back at the club, at just after four o'clock, the public and the growers have been let into the saloon to view the exhibits and see if their entries have won prizes. In fact every stand of leeks will win a prize of at least £10 – the award for all those placed between 40th and 50th. (With only forty-six entries, the £5 prizes for fiftieth to sixtieth places will not be awarded.)

Most people head straight for the bar for a drink to carry round with them as they cast a critical eye over the giants. Dickie Atkinson is a bit disappointed at the turnout of visitors so far. 'We don't get as many as we used to,' he sighs. 'There are too many other things going on of a Saturday – football, rugby and all that.' Certainly there do not seem as many as I remember crowding the room in 1990; but the show is open until 11 p.m. today and again tomorrow afternoon, so there is time for attendance to pick up.

In one corner of the room, where the top three stands of leeks are displayed side by side, there is a short queue of people determined to get a look at the very best. The £1,300 prize for the winning stand has gone to John Adcock, a civil engineer from Sedgefield – County Durham again – with a cumulative total of 528.54 cubic inches, only nine cubic inches short of the highest winning total ever recorded here. The man who achieved that record score in 2002, John Pearson from Hetton-le-Hole, has come second this year, with 506.62 cubic inches. A Hetton neighbour, M. Baxter, is third.

The visitors gaze at it all with an air almost of reverence – insofar as you can be reverent with a pint of Foster's in one hand. They certainly take it more seriously than some of the spectators at the southern shows, whose typical response is amusement mixed with astonishment. Here, when they see the plump leeks and onions ranged tidily on the display tables, people express a greater appreciation of how much accumulated effort and expense has gone into producing them.

After a while I leave and drive back to the hotel to get ready for dinner with Olga and the rest of my party. In the bar, in exactly the same place as the previous evening, are the four rotund men, including the one with the tattoos. They treat me to another friendly Geordie greeting.

When I met up with Olga and the others I found their sightseeing day had included a visit to a small village show which, being in the north-east, naturally had a class for quality leeks. They stayed to the end, when the produce was being auctioned, and came back laden with flowers, fruit and vegetables acquired by keen bidding. The haul included three prize-winning long leeks, and, back home a few days later, I commandeered one of these before it could be turned into soup, so that I could experiment with producing pips.

I followed the instructions Medwyn Williams had conveniently given in his *Garden News* column the previous week. I cut away the roots and most of the top, leaving a stump six inches long. (Six inches is clearly a mystical measurement to leek growers.) I peeled off the outer layers of the stump, reducing it to the same diameter as the root plate. I placed it in a pot of compost and left it outside, to be brought in when the first frosts were forecast.

If all went well, next spring a seed head would emerge and grow to some 4ft before producing flowers. I would then have to be ruthless and cut off all the flowers before they opened. Within a few days, according to Medwyn, the pips or grass would then emerge. I must leave them there until October, before planting them out in the hope of sweeping the board at the vegetable shows in 2009 – or at least of getting a few good meals out of them.

Chapter 13

Malvern

On the last weekend in September I am back among the softer landscapes and accents of the southern half of England. The last general show with a significant giant section is the Malvern Autumn Garden and Country Show, held at the picturesque Three Counties Showground at the foot of the Malvern hills, a few miles outside the pleasant Worcestershire town. One of the most popular shows in the calendar since it was introduced in the mid-nineties, it includes a major Royal Horticultural Society (RHS) flower show, and this year additionally hosts the peripatetic national championships of the National Vegetable Society (NVS). These two august bodies, though, like to remain aloof from the giant vegetable contest, which is run as a stand-alone annual event by the overall organiser, the Three Counties Agricultural Society.

The show attracts around 60,000 visitors over the weekend. Among its features is the World of Animals: contests and demonstrations involving horses, sheep, goats, pigs, dogs, ferrets and alpacas. Sadly, many of these have had to be scrapped this year because of restrictions on animal movements imposed in the wake of a small outbreak of foot-and-mouth disease in Surrey and a new cattle scourge, blue tongue, in East Anglia. Although the show opens to the public on the Saturday, the weighing and measuring of the giants is carried out as they are brought to the ground on Friday, between noon and 10 p.m. Olga and I arrive rather later than we intended, delayed by another of the natural disasters that have marked this accident-prone summer. The floods that swept through middle England subsided nearly two months ago, but some roads in the area are still closed because of weakened or absent bridges, and long diversions remain in place. Consequently it is quite late in the afternoon by the time we reach the showground but, when we do, we find we have not missed much of the action. In the large Harvest Pavilion, where the giant vegetables are billeted somewhat uneasily in the sidelines of the NVS quality show, we find Peter, Clive Bevan and Ray Davey – the chief judge here as well – chatting desultorily, waiting for something to happen. There has been an organisational glitch, and the scales provided by the show organisers are not fit for purpose. They are too big, designed for weights up to 3,000 kilograms – that would be a very large pumpkin even by today's inflated standards – and they do not record decimal points, essential in a close-run contest.

One piece of equipment you cannot do without at a giant vegetable contest is a set of working scales. Luckily Ray knows the firm that supplied them for the Shepton Mallet show, and he has been on the telephone: a set of smaller scales is even now on its way from Birmingham and should arrive at about 5.30. While we wait I relay to Peter the news and gossip from Ashington and tell him about my experiment in trying to produce pips from the prize-winning leeks that Olga bought at a local show. He is not too encouraging. 'They don't all work,' he warned me. 'They look OK until the spring, then they can start to go rotten.' Heigh-ho! I shall just have to wait and see.

Peter tells me he is not entering any of the NVS quality classes here because of the impossible logistics. Entries for the giant classes close at 10 p.m., to allow the judges to get some sleep after performing their weighing and measuring duties. But the NVS classes do not close until 6.30 a.m. tomorrow, and the judging happens later. This means that most of the quality competitors will dig their vegetables this evening, bring them in overnight and stage them in the small hours. Had Peter brought any from Nottinghamshire he would have had to dig them at least twelve hours earlier than that, and – as freshness is an important criterion of quality – he would have forfeited points and stood almost no chance of prizes.

The NVS exhibitors have not begun to arrive yet, but Peter tells me from his previous experience that when they do they are unlikely to walk the few paces across the hall to inspect the giant produce. 'A lot of the quality growers don't approve of the giants,' he says. 'And they especially resent the fact that our prize money is usually bigger than for their quality stuff.'

The reason for that apparent anomaly is that giant vegetables are much more likely to receive press coverage than the quality kind, so they are more attractive to sponsors. Here at Malvern, though, the difference is less marked than at other shows: the first prize for most classes in the giants is £30, compared with £20 in the qualities – although for collections of a number of quality vegetables in the same display the prize can sometimes approach £100. Peter is one of the very few serious competitors in quality classes who deign to muck in with the giant growers – and as such he is regarded as something of a maverick by the more conservative elements in the NVS.

The late arrival of the scales means that none of the heavy entries has yet been weighed, but the measurements for some of the long vegetables have been taken. In the long carrot class Peter has turned the tables on Joe with a root that stretches to 17ft 9in – six inches longer than his record-breaker at Highgrove last year. 'It's the longest one I've ever grown,' he says. 'It reached the end of the tube and started to curl back again. I shall have to add a foot or two to the tubes: the carrots seem to get longer every year.'

Yet Peter's is still some way short of the formidable 19-footer that Joe produced for Shepton Mallet. This week Joe can do no better than 14ft 5in and has to be content with second place; but he makes up for that with his long parsnip: 12ft 4in – more than twice as long as Peter's best.

Peter's long runner bean, at 29½in, looks as though it could be a winner, but he has not managed to grow a competitive long cucumber this year.

> I've had a bad year for cucumbers. You get good years and bad years. That's why I grow so many different kinds of vegetables: because you hope that at least one or two will come good. I put most of my effort into Shepton Mallet. This one's a bonus really – you just come here to have a nice weekend.

He has brought a pumpkin and a cabbage along, but the Cornish contingent has yet to arrive and his entries do not look anything like big enough to beat what they are likely to bring. He had a bigger pumpkin, he tells me, 'but it split, and the crack was so wide I could get my hand into it. I thought it would be judged unsound, so I brought a smaller one along. And my biggest cabbage started losing its outer leaves, because it's so late in the season.'

I spot Ian walking towards us, wearing a bright blue wind-cheater. While waiting for the scales to arrive he has been getting a sneak preview of the exhibition of vintage tractors, farm machinery and other devices that evoke nostalgia for early technology. Always a well-attended feature of the show, the display is organised by the National Vintage Tractor and Engine Club, the Historic Caravan Club and the Old Lawnmower Club – groups whose existence confirms reassuringly that giant vegetables are far from the only unlikely artefacts to command obsessive and (to some) inexplicable enthusiasm.

> It reminds me of my early days working on a farm. We had a thresher just like the one they've got there. Nowadays, with health

and safety, you can't have a threshing machine without guards on it, to stop young boys getting too close. In those days the boys would listen to the farmers and do what they were told. We didn't need any guards.

When I last saw Ian, at Abertysswg, he was in two minds whether to come to Malvern. He was indignant that the entry fees for the giant vegetable classes had been raised, without any commensurate increase in the prize money. In the end he could not resist the lure of competing in this, the last major giant show of the season. His heavy swede, marrow and carrot are in the queue to be weighed once the scales arrive, but his long cucumber has already been measured at a formidable 25½in. In the absence of Alf Cobb, who does not compete here, this looks as if it could be a winner – although Kevin and Gareth Fortey will be coming as soon as they can after work, and Ian knows they have a cucumber that will give his a run for its money.

Clive Bevan's cucumber is about an inch shorter than Ian's. He explains that he grows them in women's tights, and he has brought a demonstration pair along with him. As the cucumber grows the tights can expand in all dimensions. If you raise it in a sock or a bag, or anything with a fixed end, as soon as it touches the end and detects a trace of resistance it will lose heart and stop growing.

Because this is the last big show of the season there is an end-of-term feeling in the air as the growers congregate and compare notes. 'As soon as I get back I'll start ploughing in the tunnels to get ready for next year,' says the forward-looking Ian. I prompt him to reflect on this past season, and he declares it has been his least successful for twelve years.

I should have had four or five firsts at Shepton Mallet but I only had two. Partly it's because of the low light levels we've had. You can see the effects everywhere. A lot of oak trees around my place haven't got an acorn on, and the maize in the field next to the nursery went all yellow.

Not that he blames the weather entirely for his poor performance: he recognises that part of the fault must lie with his technique. 'I've got to sit down over the winter and have a long think about it.'

At 5.35 p.m., just five minutes after the promised time, the van carrying the scales from Birmingham backs up to the pavilion entrance. Ian and Joe help Ray set them up, and the weighing can begin. The tomatoes are put on first. I have noticed here and at the earlier shows that many winning tomatoes are green and unripe – a condition that would not be accepted in a quality class. I ask Peter why this is, and he explains that they weigh more when green; as soon as they ripen and start to go red they lose weight – so the trick is to catch them just as they are on the point of starting to redden. It is a close contest between his tomato and Joe's, with Joe coming out the winner by a bare three ounces, with 2 lb 7 oz.

Joe has two carrots of similar size. With each competitor allowed only one entry in each class, he does not know which one to submit. Ray lets him weigh both. The larger – and the easy winner of its class – weighs 7 lb 10 oz. Ian's swede makes 33 lb 14 oz. 'Last year I had one at 75 lb,' he says, 'but 33 lb is good for this year.'

Olga and I have to leave while the weighing is in full swing, because for the duration of the show we are staying with yet another accommodating friend near Hereford, and we have said we will be there in time for dinner. We shall be back in the morning to look at the results, but Ian says he won't be here: 'I've got a nursery to run – but I'll be back on Sunday to pick up the stuff.'

When I return on Saturday morning there is already quite a crowd of onlookers in the Harvest Pavilion. The arrangement of the exhibits is symbolic of the relationship between the NVS establishment and the giant growers. The NVS show, with many hundreds of entries, occupies most of the tent, with the giants tucked away somewhat apologetically in a corner. As Peter predicted, not many of the top quality growers, with their meticulously staged specimens, are deigning to drift down to inspect the rough and ready exhibits for which size means everything. Yet, as at Shepton Mallet, the giants are provoking rather more interest among visitors than the quality entries, even if they do not inspire universal approval. 'I don't see the point,' says one sceptical onlooker as he passes Ian's hideous-looking swede, its tangled roots curling like a Gorgon's locks. 'I say if you can't eat it, don't grow it.'

The first familiar person I run into is Dave Thomas from Cornwall. It took him four hours to drive here the previous evening and he arrived at around 7.30, after I had left. He has easily won the first prize in the squash and cabbage classes, as he did at Shepton Mallet, although to prove his fallibility he tells me his marrow came last in its category.

Unlike at Shepton, there are no separate contests here for pumpkins and squashes. Instead, they are lumped together in a single class. Dave has won it with the same squash he took to Shepton. Here it weighed in at 452 lb 9 oz – so it has diminished by a full ten pounds in the four weeks separating the two shows. It is almost three times as heavy as the biggest pumpkin, submitted by Clive Bevan's grand-daughter, Jessica Wright. Peter has come third. Dave's cabbage is also way ahead of the competition at 81 lb 9 oz – not quite as big as the 95-pounder he took to Shepton Mallet, but still more than twice as heavy as Peter's, which weighs a little under 40 lb.

All in all, though, it has been a successful show for Peter. He has won first prize in four of the eleven giant classes – heavy marrow and onion, long carrot and runner bean. The runner bean decision was extremely close, with Peter's less than half an inch longer than the Fortey brothers'. In another tight finish Kevin and Gareth's long cucumber pipped Ian's by three-quarters of an inch. Ian had his revenge, though, by comfortably beating their heavy swede into second place. Joe has done well, scoring first prizes with his heavy carrot and tomato and his long parsnip, while in the quality section Kevin and Gareth's mother took first prize for her cooking apples.

In the press office, a handful of gardening writers gather for a briefing given by Nick Vincent, Chief Executive of the Three Counties Agricultural Society. He is keen to talk about a new feature of this year's show, the Edible Gardens Competition, in which organisations were invited to design decorative kitchen gardens. The motive behind the initiative is to tap into current environmental concerns by encouraging the production of home-grown vegetables, reducing the notoriously large carbon footprint created by flying in, say, French beans from Kenya.

Whenever global warming is mentioned in this context I cannot help feeling guilty on behalf of the giant vegetable growers, whose carbon footprint must be as massive as the vegetables they are seeking to produce. Their extravagant use of light and heat, allowing the plants to keep growing through the winter, is about as environmentally unfriendly as you can get; and even if – despite popular belief – many of the vegetables are technically edible, realistically if they enter the food chain it is more likely to be through the bellies of cattle and pigs, or as part of the compost heap, than by direct human consumption.

That might explain in part the cool relations that exist between giant growers and the many conventional gardeners concerned with the environment. After the briefing I put the point to Stephen Bennett, Shows Director for the RHS and as such one of the most powerful people in the world of competitive horticulture. Although his term of office has seen the RHS develop closer relations with quality vegetable growers, he confirms that the Society prefers to keep its distance from the giant fraternity.

The RHS has nothing officially to do with giant vegetables. Personally, if they weren't here I wouldn't miss them, but we let them stay as part of the show because they're a popular attraction.

He does not, however, think that the Society can nowadays be accused of elitism, especially not with regard to vegetables.

When I first joined the RHS the impression was that we were all about clematis and camellias and had no time for vegetables. But I approached the NVS to see whether there were things we could do together. I must say they were surprised to hear from us; but our autumn vegetable show in London is always very successful.

Successful, yes – but it has no classes for giants.

We spend the afternoon looking round the rest of the show, packed with interest not just for gardeners but for anyone involved in country pursuits. We come away laden with purchases, including four small cloches that might allow me to have a stab at growing my own vegetables a bit larger than usual next year. There is music from Bev Pegg and his Railroad Skiffle Group, and I am only sorry we shall miss Al Boden with his Organic Hillbillies, scheduled for tomorrow.

I am especially impressed with the vegetable montage put on by Medwyn Williams's nursery, Medwyns of Anglesey, and I am lucky enough to bump into the man himself outside the Wye Hall, where the firm's stand is located. I introduce myself and tell him about the book I am writing. He discloses that, like Gerald, he will be making one last attempt at hydroponic onions next year – although later he would change his mind and decide to grow them all in the conventional manner.

Chapter 14

All Pumped Up

The Saturday of the Malvern show had been a seminal day in the history of giant vegetables globally. The stirring news from across the Atlantic was that the most prized world record of all, that for the heaviest pumpkin, had been broken – twice in one day, in the space of half an hour.

Coincidentally, this happened in the week that saw publication of the 2008 edition of *Guinness World Records*, in which a new record weight for a pumpkin had been acknowledged: 1,502 lb, set in 2006 by Ron Wallace from Rhode Island. Then on 29 September 2007, at the Topsfield Fair in Massachusetts – the venue for one of the many pumpkin weigh-offs held across the United States at this time of year – Bill Rodonis from Litchfield, New Hampshire, produced a monster weighing 1,566 lb. But only half an hour later Joe Jutras, a carpenter and a friend of Ron's, also from Rhode Island, produced a phenomenal 1,689-pounder to earn the $5,000 prize and a Guinness entry for 2009. (On the same day two other pumpkins at Topsfield weighed in at over 1,600 lb – one, shipped all the way from Iowa, only 27 lb lighter than Joe's.) It had been a phenomenal season for Joe, who had produced four pumpkins weighing more than 1,300 lb. He had to hire a specialist firm of contractors to devise a way of transporting them all to the show on a supersized flatbed truck.

In his book *How to Grow Giant Vegetables* Bernard Lavery

wrote that raising enormous pumpkins and squash 'has without doubt been the most fascinating and enjoyable part of my gardening career'. Perhaps unknowingly, he was echoing the view P.G. Wodehouse, expressed in his short story *The Custody of the Pumpkin*, that encapsulates the near-universal appeal of this lumpen vegetable: 'In a crass and materialistic world there must inevitably be a scattered few here and there in whom pumpkins touch no chord.'

Wodehouse put this thought into the mind of Lord Emsworth of Blandings Castle, who, after a series of misadventures, carried off the top prize at the Shrewsbury Agricultural Show, outstripping the specimen submitted by his old rival, Sir Gregory Parsloe-Parsloe of Matchingham Hall. The author did not reveal the weight of the winning pumpkin, nor the prize money it earned; but, as he was writing in the 1920s, both would have looked paltry compared with Joe Jutras's harvest. The phenomenal inflation of the pumpkin record over the last quarter of a century has been even more dramatic than that of the onion – and we are talking here not about a vegetable the size of a mere football, but one now approaching the dimensions of a small saloon car.

It is especially remarkable when you consider that until 1976 the record had remained unbroken for seventy-three years. Local pumpkin competitions had been held at fairs in the United States and Canada during the nineteenth century, but not until 1900 was the wider world introduced to the possibilities of growing this staple winter vegetable to fantastic sizes. That was the year of the Paris World's Fair, to which William Warnock, from Ontario in Canada, sent a 400-lb specimen across the Atlantic, to astonish visitors. It was then the heaviest pumpkin ever recorded, and the French Government honoured the achievement by awarding it a bronze medal and diploma.

In 1903, for the St Louis World's Fair, Warnock grew one three pounds heavier. Thereafter the record stood at 403 lb until 1976, when Bob Ford from Coatesville, Pennsylvania, won the US Pumpkin Contest in nearby Churchville with a 451-pounder. Four years later the record went back to Canada when Howard Dill, from Nova Scotia, achieved 459 lb, exceeding it the following year with a pumpkin weighing 493 lb 8 oz. Dill's name is still revered in pumpkin circles, for it was he who developed the Atlantic Giant strain of seed which remains prominent in the genetic make-up of today's monsters.

The really rapid pumpkin inflation began in 1984, when Norman Gallagher, from Washington state, exceeded the 600-lb mark at the second annual weigh-off of the newly formed World Pumpkin Confederation in Collins, New York. In 1989 the 700-lb barrier was breached, and the following year the magic number had climbed to more than 800 lb. Now the aim was to boost the top weight to four figures. This was achieved in 1994, since when it has been increasing regularly year by year to its present level, certain to be overtaken before long. 'I would think that 2,000 lb is not out of the question any more,' Joe Jutras told *The New York Times*.

The pumpkin originated in the Americas. Because our word for it derives from the Latin *pepo*, by way of the Old English *pompion*, some have assumed that it was known to the Romans. In fact *pepo* is their word for a melon. Although both are members of the cucurbit family and have similar growing habits, pumpkins as we know them were not introduced in Europe until sixteenth-century explorers had first clapped eyes on them in the Americas and been impressed both by their girth and by their virtues as an ingredient of warming winter stews. Their plentiful flesh saved the Pilgrim Fathers from starvation during those terrible early winters in their new home – which is why pumpkin pie features on the traditional menu for Thanksgiving Day at the end of November.

Pumpkins had long been a staple food of American Indians, having spread north from Mexico, where they were first cultivated at least 7,000 years ago. The climate of North America proved ideal for raising them to a large size. They grow so fast that they do not have to be sown until the cold winters are safely over, and then the warm days of late summer and early autumn ensure that they continue to gain weight until well into October. This timing, together with their satisfying bulk, led to the tradition of carving their tough orange skins into faces and lanterns to celebrate Hallowe'en.

As the monsters have grown ever more monstrous, public fascination with them has increased, confirming Lord Emsworth's notion that there are but 'a scattered few . . . in whom pumpkins touch no chord'. As Ron Wallace told a local college newspaper after he broke the record: 'It has been a thrill to watch the world of pumpkin farming evolve from a rural hobby to an internationally recognized art.' Both Wallace and Jutras – and their pumpkins – have appeared on nationally networked TV talk shows. And Wallace's 2006 world-beater was sold for $6,000, after which it went on display at New York's Grand Central Station and was then shipped to Japan for exhibition there.

A new spectator sport has emerged: blowing a giant pumpkin to smithereens. In 2006 a 1,300-lb specimen was spectacularly exploded on David Letterman's late night talk show (one flying chunk scored a direct hit on a camera). And a week after setting his world record, Jutras gave a 1,000-lb pumpkin to his local show so that it could be dropped from a low-flying plane and smashed to pieces, to signal the start of that year's pumpkin weigh-off.

Pumpkin-growing is becoming a big-money sport, as well. A seed from Wallace's record-holder changed hands for $850 (£425) – substantially more than the going rate for leeks and onions outside the Northern Social Club in Ashington. The dedicated growers who bought it were British: Ian and Stuart Paton, twin brothers who own a wholesale plant nursery near Lymington in Hampshire.

The benefits were quickly seen, because they used it in a cross that in 2007 set a new British record of 1,188 lb. So far British growers have not been able to match recent American weights; but the Patons are confident that within a few years they will be close to bringing the world record to Britain.

The entrance to Pinetops Nursery is unassuming in the extreme. On a minor road a couple of miles outside Lymington, a big sailing centre on the Solent, a jumble of low buildings surrounds an untidy yard where a few cars and vans are parked. It is the kind of higgledy-piggledy prospect that might signify the forecourt of a scrap merchant, or some equally unappealing enterprise.

It was not immediately obvious how to get in. My taxi from the station deposited me in the yard, and I tried the most obvious office; but it was locked and empty. A woman appeared from a building on the other side of the yard. Yes, Ian Paton was expecting me: 'Just slide that door open.' She gestured at what I had taken to be a blank wall but was indeed a sliding door, opening into the largest glasshouse I have ever entered. I stood for a moment transfixed. It reminded me of a scene from a pantomime I saw as a child (*Aladdin? Ali Baba?*) where someone knocked on an unassuming rock, whereupon it slid back and revealed a cave containing unimaginable treasures.

In this case the treasures were benches bearing row after row of potted lilies, being grown for garden centres to be ready for sale in time for Mother's Day. In a remote corner I saw a figure stooped over an empty bed, getting it ready for future planting. Ian glanced up, then came across to greet me. He told me I was looking at 30,000 lilies – 'but you should have been here before Christmas, when we had 100,000 poinsettias'. It must have looked like an endless bright red carpet. Ian said the glasshouse we were standing in stretched for two acres, and next to it was another the same size.

Ian and Stuart are 46 years old and they inherited the nursery from their father Derf, who still plays a role in running it. (Derf is a reversal of his real name, Fred, which he dislikes.) Steeped in horticulture from an early age, they were, like many children, attracted to pumpkins by the satisfying pace at which they put on the pounds at the height of the season.

Ian changed out of his working clothes and drove me to his house, so that he could call up pictures on his computer and log on to pumpkin websites as we spoke. Over the last few years the internet has become an indispensable tool for committed growers. The website *bigpumpkins.com* hosts hundreds of individual diaries, where enthusiasts tell of their triumphs and tribulations over the season. It has links to the Giant Pumpkin Commonwealth (GPC), an umbrella group formed a few years ago to co-ordinate the many major competitions and weigh-offs held in the United States and the rest of the world and to establish a common set of rules, so that new records can be confirmed and validated. Every official weigh-off now gets its results put on the web.

The website of the Atlantic Giant Genetics Co-operative (AGGC) is even more specialised and detailed, setting out not just the weights of the year's heaviest pumpkins but their pedigrees, including the weight and provenance of their parent plants. In this way the merits of seeds from each particular pumpkin can be evaluated – just as the value of a thoroughbred stallion can be judged by the racecourse performances of the colts and fillies he sires. 'Some seeds do perform and some don't – and some perform well above their own weight. That's what makes it interesting,' said Ian, as we read the latest league table.

You can see how fast weights are rising by looking at the results for last year. The top nine weights in the US were all above the previous year's record of 1,502 lb. So it's up for grabs. Stuart and I have always wanted to aim for the world record, and we're heading that way. That was why we spent so much on that single seed.

But the table also shows that their 1,188-pounder, while a British record, puts them at only eighty-sixth in the world rankings. What makes them think they can climb those eighty-five places in the foreseeable future?

You can't guarantee that it will happen for us next year, but it will happen over the next few years. It's becoming like a numbers game. We should have been much higher this year, to be honest. We could have got up to 1,400 lb if it hadn't been for an infestation of scarid fly – they're insects whose larvae chew away at the roots. It was a bit of a schoolboy error, and we should have spotted it earlier. We got rid of them but the damage had already been done.

I think we have a built-in advantage over the Americans in that they grow outdoors and we grow under cover. Last year we grew one pumpkin completely under cover and four partially under cover, and this year they will all be totally under cover. In America they get warmer nights than we do. You don't need it too hot in the daytime but night temperatures are the key: you don't want it to go much below 18°C, and this year it was down to 13° some nights in July.

As well as temperature, light is important. In a summer like 2007, when most days dawned dull, the quality of the light takes on extra significance.

We get very good light here – that was why Dad chose this spot to set up the nursery. We may not have the long days that they get further north, but the quality of the light makes up for it. I think England has got the ideal climate for pumpkins. Cornwall is even better than here – the light's better in Cornwall, and if they can get better growing facilities down there they could beat us.

The brothers are planning to build a new nursery just down the road once they receive planning permission to develop the present site. The new one would have more flexible heating, allowing them to give the pumpkins extra warmth in a poor summer.

By getting the best seed in the world we should beat the Americans under these conditions; but everyone's techniques are always improving. I've now got seeds from last year's top two pumpkins, and I'm going to cross them. That's where my confidence comes from. There's no doubt that the world record is going to come from Europe in the next few years, for the first time for many, many years.

So how and when did the twins' pumpkin obsession take hold? 'Both of us were interested in growing things,' Ian recalled. 'We started when we were about ten, and we used to get our pumpkins up to about 50 lb.' That seems derisory compared with today's four-figure numbers; but we are talking about the early seventies, when the world record was still only just above 400 lb.

After leaving school, the boys went to agricultural college to prepare them for inheriting their father's nursery. They also became heavily involved in an annual contest between gardeners in two local villages, Milford-on-Sea and Everton, to see which of them could grow the biggest pumpkin. This was the event that erupted in 2005 into a bitter public row between the two villages, putting an end to the competition and earning coverage in the national press.

The Paton brothers had become key figures in the contest. Although they competed for the Milford team, they supplied the raw material for both sides. Says Ian:

After a while I would sow all the pumpkins myself and give the plants to the growers from both teams, and the top ten would go to the weigh-off. Things began to get tense when the pumpkins got bigger every year – up to 100 lb and then to 200 lb.

In the early days he would sow the variety known as Hundred-weight – then the largest commonly grown. When Howard Dill developed the Atlantic Giant, Ian began to use that more potent seed instead. The winning weights quickly climbed to 400 lb and more – and this was getting too much for the Evertonians to handle.

As the pumpkins got bigger they started getting more difficult to lift. And there were fewer and fewer growers, because you need a very big garden to grow the big ones, and the average size of gardens is getting smaller. Youngsters don't have big gardens, so they couldn't come into it: and that was really the crux of the whole matter. Everton wanted to get back to growing Hundredweight, to make it easier; but our team, Milford, had no interest in growing them whatsoever.

If you are trying for the world record, as Ian and Stuart were, it has to be Atlantic Giant.

The show was getting better as the pumpkins got bigger, and we were making a lot of money for charity. We wouldn't have got so much coverage or so much money if we'd stuck to the smaller ones. . . . In the end Everton went their way, and we went ours. We asked them to come and talk about it, but they didn't turn up.

John Chaffey, an Everton painter and decorator who took part in the contests for more than twenty-five years, confirmed this:

Ian and Stuart were growing their Atlantic Giants under cover in their big nursery, so nobody else had a chance of getting near their weights. Anyway you couldn't move the very big ones on your own, and nobody had a big enough garden to grow them in. We used to grow Hundredweights up to 200 lb, which was about the biggest you can get them to grow to.

We still have our local village show, run by the Everton and Lymore Social Club. We don't usually get the pumpkins to more than 50 or 60 lb nowadays, because they're easier to handle. But we still enjoy it, and we still make money for the local hospital.

The two villages used to take it in turns to host the event. In 2003, when it was held in Milford, Ian and Stuart achieved the British record for the first time with a weight of 819 lb – but it was exceeded after just two weeks. In 2005 they grew one to just over 900 lb, but even that was not quite big enough to reclaim the record. The following year, though, they reasserted their supremacy with a 1,124-lb specimen, and last year they bettered that by 64 lb. It is worth remarking that the difference between the weights of their 2006 and 2007 record-breakers is greater than the entire weight of the pumpkins they took such pride in as ten-year-olds.

The abandonment of the Milford–Everton contests meant that the brothers had to hunt for an alternative venue to show their giants and have them officially weighed. They do not enter for the shows at Shepton Mallet and Malvern because they come too early, when their pumpkins are still growing, and the prizes are not large enough to make it worth their while to cut one off before it has reached its prime. They were considering entering the National Pumpkin Championship at Soham in Cambridgeshire, where there is a £500 prize donated by the seed merchants D.T. Brown. They would have won it easily – the winner was a comparative tiddler of less than 300 lb – but they learned that the top three growers would be obliged to give the sponsor 100 seeds from their prize-winners.

'I didn't want to do that,' said Ian. 'I give seeds away to anyone who asks but I didn't want to give them to a seed company, even though they were talking about giving them away themselves.' He had, after all, just paid hundreds of pounds for a single seed.

In 2006 they took their record-breaker to be weighed at a show in Romsey, north of Southampton, where they had scaffolding erected to support the scales. But the Romsey show was cancelled in 2007 because of the poor summer, so they entered a mid-October pumpkin festival at the Victoria Country Park in Southampton, organised by the Jubilee Sailing Trust. It was there that they had their latest British record confirmed, and the show was featured on the BBC children's television programme *Blue Peter*.

'There are no really big shows for pumpkins in this country, like the leek and onion shows up north,' Ian pointed out. That is why he and Stuart and four other growers got together to form a co-operative called XPG – eXtreme Pumpkin Growers – to affiliate to the Giant Pumpkin Commonwealth and create an official British weigh-off. Announcing this on *bigpumpkins.com*, Ian wrote: 'XPG is there to help growers where possible and share ideas. Oh – and to give our friends across the pond a run for their money.' He also hoped that the existence of the group would make it easier to gain commercial sponsorship for an official weigh-off.

Ian enters into the co-operative spirit by sharing his and Stuart's techniques with anyone who logs on to his grower's diary. Their method does not involve feeding the plants with the mysterious concoctions that are the stuff of so many giant vegetable legends (one grower was rumoured to be dosing his with Viagra), or playing them sweet music in the manner of Paul Rochester, the Ashington onion champion. Essentially, their secret is simple: expert and careful husbandry.

Every year the seeds are sown in early April in a good peat-based compost, under lights and at a temperature of 80–85°F [26.7–29.4°C]. Those that germinate will do so in four to five days.

Within two weeks they go into their final position in beds that have been prepared over the winter. Each plant gets between 600 and 800 sq. ft of space, to allow ample room for it to spread.

They put no fertiliser in the soil except for liberal quantities of farmyard manure. This contrasts with the technique used by other giant vegetable growers, who like to pack the soil with the nutrients they need from the beginning, and fertilise sparingly later. In America the top pumpkin growers mix a fungus (mycorrhiza) into the soil, which is said to establish a symbiotic relationship with the root system that strengthens the plant, helping it absorb nutrients and ward off disease. 'Imagine your whole garden just one happy campground of mycorrhizae, bringing nutrients to that pumpkin,' the lyrical Ron Wallace told *The New York Times*.

The Patons' method is more like that used by Gerald Treweek with his hydroponic onions. As Ian explained:

> We put nothing on apart from manure, then we liquid feed throughout the season. The plant doesn't want all that fertiliser the moment it's planted, even if you put slow release fertiliser in. We start feeding it with nitrogen feed and phosphates, but when the pumpkin starts to develop we go to a more potash-based feed, like a tomato fertiliser.

Again like Gerald, they set great store by checking and regulating the conductivity of the soil – in other words the amount of fertiliser available for the vegetables to take up.

> We take the conductivity every time we water, and adjust the feed to try to keep it at level two. We didn't use to do it every time we watered but we do now – that is one big way forward for us. We're putting in exactly what we consider the pumpkin wants, when it wants it. If you put all your fertiliser on at the beginning, you can't do that.

We water by hand a couple of times a week but always put the feed though the spray lines, and wash the leaves off with a little bit of plain water afterwards, so you don't leave any salt on the leaves. Watering by hand makes sure that you put water on to all parts of the root, where it's needed.

It has been calculated that the biggest pumpkins can consume 60 gallons of water a day at the height of their growing cycle.

Ian's 2007 diary on *bigpumpkins.com* provided a vivid account of the ups and downs of a growing season. The first April entry confirmed that the seeds were sown on the seventh, having first been soaked for twenty-four hours. The seeds are identified by numbers that indicate the weight in pounds of the pumpkin they were extracted from. So at the end of April Ian reported that he had successfully germinated five of the eight he originally sowed: one 998, one 1231, one 1068 and two 1502s. 'We lost one 1068 and two 723 seeds on germination.'

By mid-May Ian was already concerned about the weather, even though the really bad weeks were yet to come:

We've had cold nights for about a week now, and it does show, especially on the plants under the plastic cover. The foliage has a yellow tint which will go as soon as the warmer nights come back. We have put a plastic cover round the big patch to keep out most of the wind but still leaving it well vented.

Despite the low temperatures, the plants were developing faster than they had the previous year. A month later came the pivotal event in the season: the pollination. Until now the flowers had been covered to prevent them from self-pollinating, which would have meant a loss of hybrid vigour: 'If they pollinate themselves, they're really worthless,' said Ian. He reported in his diary that they crossed the 1068 with the 1231, the 998 with the 1068, one of the

1052s with the 998 and the other with the 1231. Pictures alongside the diary showed the female flowers swelling after their pollination.

At the beginning of July Ian told his readers, most of them on the other side of the Atlantic:

> The weather here in the UK has been absolutely appalling, and over the last ten days or so we have hardly seen the sun. All you see on the news is flooded homes and forecasts of yet more rain. All the hard work building a cover over the main patch is now paying off, as we are at least in control of the watering, but there is little we can do about the temperatures. . . . All the northern European countries seem to be locked in to the same conditions, and if the European record gets broken this year it will be a special achievement.

A week later:

> We're not sure if the 998 has become our first real casualty of the year. On Sunday we found some shallow cracks in the skin and dots of sap coming out of the skin on the top of the fruit. We're guessing that it has something to do with the two hot days after so many cold ones. . . . For the moment we are going to keep it on the plant, and we got to pollinate another female this morning. Oh the joy of pumpkin growing!

Cracking, or splitting, is one of the principal hazards of the undertaking, and is often caused by over-watering in hot weather.

In the diary Ian meticulously recorded the progress of each plant, its increase in weight and girth over the summer weeks. Some prospered, while others fell by the wayside. By late August, like every other vegetable grower in the country, he was becoming ever more frustrated by the unhelpful weather. He resorted to irony:

First of all I have to say the weather over here is fantastic – if you're growing parsnips or winter cabbages, that is! The temperatures have been down to 10°C [50°F] at night. . . . Extreme measures have been taken with the 1231 to try to get it back on track. This week we filled in both ends of the tunnel and made a roll-up vent on the side. We then plugged in five hot-air heaters but found we only have enough electricity to run them on one bar. Never mind, we are 4–5°C warmer than outside, and if the now HOT pumpkin looks like it has potential, we have more cunning plans to keep the temperature up as we get into September.

A week later they discovered the infestation of scarid flies, but a month after that, with less than three weeks to go until the Southampton show, three of the giants were showing winning potential.

Most of the pumpkins are nearly fully grown now, but all are still putting on the pounds. The 1231 has put on 104 lb in the last two weeks, and after day 78 tapes 710 lb. The 1502 has only put on 15 lb and now tapes 862 lb. And finally the 1068 has put on 32 lb to end day 94 taping 986 lb.

By 1 October the 1068, crossed with the 1231, had attained the 1,000-lb mark, and this was the one that, twelve days later, took the new British record. Said Ian:

The growers' diary on *BigPumpkin* is good for us, because you can see at a glance where you were last year and compare it with this year. Thousands of growers from all over the world log on to the site. It's all about the skill of growing, really. It's like onions: it's about the seed, sure, but you also have to have skill, because onions can go rotten quite quickly. I used to grow big onions, but some local tearaways broke into the greenhouse and destroyed them all. I'd been after the world record, and I'd spent so much time on them that I got disheartened and didn't try again.

So it is the pumpkins alone that essentially take over his and Stuart's lives every summer. In his talk with me, and in his online diary, Ian was remarkably forthcoming about their methods. He answered all the 'How?' questions – but not the all-important 'Why?'. What precisely is the attraction of raising these temperamental and outrageously inflated vegetables?

All his other answers came readily and fluently, but this time he paused for an uncharacteristic length of time. 'Well,' he finally ventured, 'it's not for the money, that's for sure. The prizes are quite small. But then when you're making something grow that can put on 50 lb in one day – well, it's just fun.'

Chapter 15

Dewsbury

The onion fair at Dewsbury has a long tradition, but it had fallen by the wayside until revived by the enterprising Kirklees Council, the authority covering Huddersfield, Batley and a large swathe of West Yorkshire. The fair has only four open competitive classes – two of them for quality onions: one for the heaviest and one for the three heaviest – but because the prize money is good it attracts a select coterie of the leading specialist growers from the north-east, as well as Peter and Joe from the Midlands. In addition there are four classes restricted to Kirklees residents, offering smaller prizes.

Dewsbury prides itself on having the largest and one of the oldest outdoor markets in Yorkshire, with two market days each week. A ballad of 1614 mentions 'a market of great note' there, but this was allowed to decline until it was revived by the Duke of Leeds in 1740. Some time after that the onion fair was inaugurated. A directory published in 1853 says it was held annually on the last Wednesday before 10 October. Schoolchildren were given a half-holiday, while farmers and smallholders occupied the market place for the day, selling mainly onions but other produce as well. As dusk fell the market was lit by naphtha flares, so that the fair could continue into the night.

Through the twentieth century Dewsbury Market thrived and gained a new lease of life from the arrival of a sizeable Asian community in the town. The onion fair, though, was discontinued in 1992. Then, in 2005, the Council relaunched it as part of the celebrations of the fiftieth anniversary of Dewsbury's twinning link with Besançon in eastern France. It was such a success that it was decided to restore it as an annual event, a means of bringing new customers into the market; and the traders' association was persuaded to fund prizes totalling £2,000.

On the north bank of the River Calder, Dewsbury, along with its neighbouring towns and villages, developed as a centre of the woollen industry after the Industrial Revolution. The architectural writer Nikolaus Pevsner, in the West Yorkshire segment of his monumental *The Buildings of Britain*, dismissed the town as 'large textile mills huddling close together, workers' housing and little else'. (That was written in 1959: today, with the mills long closed, some of these buildings are considered gems of industrial architecture.) In the 1830s Patrick Brontë, the father of the literary sisters, was a curate in Dewsbury, and today's most notable native is Betty Boothroyd, the former dancer who became the first woman Speaker of the House of Commons.

The railway line from Leeds, built in 1848, runs above the valley and gives a bird's-eye view of the roofs of the dark stone terraced houses and factories. From the station visitors walk to the town centre and market place down a steep hill opening out into a broad square in the shadow of one of the rugged former mills, now a large children's clothing shop with apartments on the upper floors. Here rows of stalls sell clothes, household linens, kitchenware and food, catering for both Asian and Yorkshire tastes. The onion fair occupies two stalls near the centre of the market. Alongside them the town crier, in a Dickensian costume, is ringing his bell and summoning people to where a hammock is slung, filled with hundreds of onions. Market-goers are invited to guess how many are there, and the nearest estimate will win a prize.

When Olga and I arrive in the middle of a warm, sunny Saturday morning, Peter and Joe are already there. Joe has not entered any of his own produce this time but has come with Peter to help him carry his onions from the car, set them out and give him any moral support he might need. This was the scene of the unpleasantness with Jack Newbould last year, and it would be no surprise if hostilities were resumed. Joe tells me that he has been going through the complicated process of registering with *Guinness World Records* the heavy parsnip and long carrot records that he achieved at Shepton Mallet. Nowadays it is all done on the internet.

> You have to tell them first that you are trying for a record and they give you a claim number. Then when you've done it you have to have it confirmed by the judge at the show. Then you send it in, and they're supposed to acknowledge it. I haven't heard back from them yet – if I don't hear I'll go down to London myself.

Maria Wilson, the Council's events officer and the fair's principal organiser, preparing to log the entries as they arrive, tells me that eight leading growers have entered for the national classes, and there has been a good response from local gardeners in the restricted classes. Her priority, though, is not what the fair means to the competitors but what it means to market shoppers, some of whom might seldom venture beyond the town into the countryside: 'When these very big onions are shown in a public space, people can see them who wouldn't normally go to vegetable shows.'

The senior elected member of the Council on hand is Ken Sims, whose responsibilities include regeneration. He explains why the council has revived the onion fair:

> It all ties in with the growing interest in farmers' markets. We're seeing more interest in fresh fruit and vegetables and home produced goods. We have a very diverse population here, and I think that makes for a better market. The onion fair is something

they can all come and enjoy. I love it myself: I wonder what special brews they use to get the onions to this size.

Among the assembled growers I am glad to come across Vin Throup from Keighley, a notable veteran of the leek and onion scene and winner of countless prizes over the years in both quality and giant competitions. He carried off the Harrogate onion trophy five times between 1986 and 2002. He is not competing in the giant categories here – he has not grown anything big enough – but has brought three dressed onions for one of the quality classes. He is disappointed to discover, though, that they will be disqualified: they just exceed the upper weight limit for their class of 1.5 kilograms (3 lb 5 oz).

> It used to be that you could have them as big as you liked. The same happened to me last year when they were too big – but they said they were going to change the rules for this year, and they haven't.

A local grower explains that the reason for the upper limit is to give a chance to the ordinary hobby gardeners, who might not have the heating or lighting equipment necessary to grow really large onions.

Still, Vin has not entirely wasted his day. He has brought some seed with him and is finding plenty of takers at £6 a packet – somewhat below the top price at Ashington. Peter has also brought some seeds to sell to anyone who asks. In the past he has had trouble with the EU regulations stipulating that only certified seed can be sold. He used to run advertisements in *Garden News* some years ago but they eventually refused to accept them, and he had a cautionary visit from a man from the Ministry of Agriculture. Still, he has noticed that Gerald Treweek now advertises in the same weekly paper, so he might try again.

Peter is unimpressed with the way the show is organised, and has made some notes for Maria suggesting improvements. Although the official closing time for entries is 10 a.m., people are still bringing stuff in after that. Peter has taken advantage of the lax regulation by not yet setting his onions out on the stall, keeping them instead in boxes underneath. He says this is to protect them from the sun in advance of the weigh-in, because once they start drying out they gradually lose weight. All the same, his reluctance to put them on display until the last minute is provocative, because it is precisely what caused the disagreement with Jack Newbould last year. Jack twigged that he was waiting to size up the opposition before deciding which onion to put in the single class and which in the class for the three heaviest. Whereas at Harrogate the major prize went to the heaviest single onion, here the position is reversed: the prize for the three heaviest is £500, as against £200 for the singleton.

Jack has by now arrived, along with Barbara and Michael Cook. Living locally, they can afford to cut it fine. The trio are clearly disgruntled when they see Peter's onions still lurking in boxes beneath the stall, with Joe standing guard over them. 'He's hanging back to see if he can beat me with a single onion,' Jack tells me. 'If he can't, he'll put his biggest in with the three to make sure he wins that.'

The judges are going to weigh the local classes first, with the grand weigh-off for the national heavy classes scheduled for noon. A set of electronic scales is brought to the stalls at around 11 o'clock but it does not work, because the voltage is wrong. A replacement set is borrowed from a helpful trader selling fruit and vegetables. It takes a while to set it up, and there is a delay before the judges can start the weighing. When they do, it is clear that they are going to be strict in interpreting one of the rules of the competition, that the onions should be 'sound all round'. A few of them look as though they are turning soft and are summarily eliminated.

The scale weighs in kilograms, and a calculator is used to convert the result into pounds. It soon appears that the schedule is slipping: it is 12.30, with the sky beginning to cloud over, before the judges are ready to move on to the national classes. The town crier circulates in the market, ringing his bell to attract spectators. 'Do you like onions, madam?' he asks one bewildered shopper. 'You wouldn't need many of those to make an onion stew, would you?' When the woman gets to the stall she admits to being impressed. 'How would you grow a thing like that?' she wonders.

Having had the chance to see what his Yorkshire rivals have brought with them, Peter has decided to stake his all on the triple class, as Jack had anticipated, and the tactic pays off. His three onions total 39 lb 13 oz – more than two pounds heavier than Barbara's second-placed trio, which are again two pounds above Jack's.

Barbara turns the tables on Peter in the single class, with a 13-lb 2-oz specimen, three ounces lighter than her Harrogate winner. The stern judges disqualify Peter's entry because of soft patches on its surface that have already drawn some barbed criticism from Jack and Barbara. Jack tells me that his heaviest onion was similarly flawed, so he left it at home. The best one he brought picks up the second prize, marginally beating Michael Daley, a crane driver from Howden, near Goole.

Peter takes his disqualification philosophically. 'I wouldn't have won, anyway,' he says. Nor is it the first time it has happened to him: his biggest onion similarly fell foul of the judges at Harrogate in 2005. Despite this setback, he has come off best of all the exhibitors here in cash terms, due to his £500 prize in the triple class. Barbara is not far behind him, with a total of £400 for her second and first places, while Jack comes away with £250 for his third and second.

As soon as the awards have been made, the exhibitors begin to remove their onions. This seems perverse. If the competition is supposed to be for the edification of shoppers and visitors, the onions should surely be on display until the market closes later in the afternoon, as happens at other shows. In the event they have been on the stalls for little more than two hours. Peter and the other exhibitors agree that their giants ought to be exposed for longer – but the organisers have asked them to take them away and they are not going to forfeit the chance of an early start to the drive home.

Olga and I explore the market food stalls and come away laden with local specialities – tripe, cow heel, rabbit, kippers and parkin. Thus burdened, we find the hill up to the station seems a lot steeper than it did on the way down.

Chapter 16

The Alchemist

Certain growers have become legends in the giant vegetable community. When I met Scott Robb in Alaska in August he repeatedly mentioned John Evans, an Irishman who moved there in 1990 and started trying to break world records, inspiring Scott and other local growers to do the same. I was eager to meet him myself.

John has an inquiring mind, of a scientific if unorthodox bent, and was constantly looking for ways of maximising the potential of the produce he grew. He and his brother now market a liquid soil additive based on the secret formula he developed to feed his champions. Although he has moved away from competitive growing in recent years to concentrate on the fertiliser business, he still holds the world records for the heaviest broccoli and carrot. He left Alaska in 2006 to return to his native Ireland.

When I phoned John to propose a visit he was enthusiastic. I arrived at Cork airport on a wet, dark afternoon to find him waiting outside the terminal in his people-carrier. A short, wiry and energetic man with a white beard, he began his story almost as soon as we set off on the 75-minute drive south-west, through persistent rain, to his farmhouse at Drimoleague, ten miles inland from Bantry Bay.

Born in Ireland to Welsh parents, he spent most of his childhood in Wales before training as an engineer. Gardening was in his genes, though:

It goes back to my grandmother, who lived in Brecon and was always involved with the soil. When I was in the garden with her I was like a little puppy: I would follow her everywhere, and she would tell me what to do. Then my father let me have a little bit of land in his garden, and I grew flowers and took them down to the market every week to earn pocket money.

He was already fascinated with the chemistry of gardening, the mysterious influences that make plants thrive in some conditions and languish in others.

What intrigued me – one of the fundamental things that really got me – was compost. My grandmother had a huge compost heap, at least 50ft long and 15ft wide. She grew marrows and cucumbers on part of the heap, and they were enormous. When you compared them with those grown on ordinary soil, you saw the difference. And that got my attention.

Everywhere I've been I've gardened: I'm a gardening nut-case, absolutely nuts about it. It's in my family's blood. My grandfather [another John Evans] was a forester who went plant-hunting in the Himalayas, India, China, South America.

His grandfather's stories about his travels and adventures made John restless. In the early seventies he inherited some money from a great-aunt, bought a one-way ticket to Bombay and spent two years on the move, including an epic bicycle trip across India. In 1973 he met and married Mary, a young American woman, and in 1975 they moved to her home state of Minnesota, where he further pursued his interest in the soil.

I grew fabulous gardens there, starting them from scratch. That was when I started developing my techniques. I realised that most gardeners don't know a lot about gardening. They just look at the plant and the fertiliser. When you do that you're already a loser, because unless you have the foundation you won't succeed. You have to feed the soil, not the plant.

After three years in Minnesota the couple moved to a ranch in Montana, where he learned to coax plants to grow in adverse conditions.

Terrible soil there, extremely acidic, a kind of gumbo-type clay. [Gumbo is a soil common in the western USA, that gets mushy when wet.] The spring near the ranch was part of the volcanic system of Yellowstone National Park, ninety miles away. We couldn't drink it because there was sulphur in it, and because of that we had to water the garden with water from the washing machine and dishwasher.

In less than two years John and Mary moved on again, this time to Phoenix, Arizona.

My life in gardening has nearly always been in extremes. We had extreme heat in Arizona, extreme cold in Alaska. In Arizona they told me I couldn't grow tomatoes because they would burn to death. I grew fabulous tomatoes. You name it, I grew it – peaches, plums, apricots, kiwi fruit, almonds, all the citrus. I had a grape vine 33ft long. I grew some huge vegetables too: I had them at the front of the house, and people would slow down in their cars. Neighbours would come to me for advice.

Then, after ten years, they left Arizona 'because of crime, gang warfare and atrocious schools', and went to Alaska.

The adaptation going from Arizona, where the temperature sometimes went up to 120°F [50°C], to Alaska was a big challenge. Down in Arizona it was mulch, mulch, mulch, to keep everything cool. Up in Alaska it was about getting exactly the right conditions to warm the soil; so I devised what I called super-raised beds. Once in place they were never tilled but I put compost and stuff on top of them to heat them up. You need different techniques for different places.

Until then John had been growing for quality rather than size. Alaska was where the giant vegetable bug took hold.

It was by accident, really. Everything I grew seemed to be doing well, and then in 1991, my first year there, I went to the state fair. When I looked at the giant stuff on show in that first year I was disappointed. I thought – this is large? Some of it was no bigger than my own.

I was always talking about gardening, and somebody dared me – they said why don't you bring some of your vegetables to the state fair? I'd been in gardening most of my life and I knew I could grow large vegetables if I wanted to. I love challenges, and this was really a wonderful challenge. So next year I entered for the quality and the heavy classes. Altogether I got 11 first prizes and 21 ribbons [rosettes] in that first year.

The following year I grew this giant swede – rutabaga – and it was 53 lb, and in 1993 I got the world record for broccoli. It was a hassle because Guinness didn't have a category for broccoli then – Bernard Lavery had pretty much set down the criteria, and he didn't grow it. So I got together with Guinness to work it out.

Once John decides to pursue an interest he likes to immerse himself in it and to intervene where he sees room for improvement. That is why his early relationship with the organisers of the Alaska State Fair did not run smoothly.

I was having a lot of problems with the fair when I got there. I trod on a lot of toes. I took a record from a senator's wife, and that was badly viewed. A lot of people who had records didn't like me coming in and virtually wiping them out. It's a very closed community, and I hurt people's feelings a bit. And then I started scrutinising their record-keeping, and it was atrocious. Some of their records didn't correlate – ounces being mixed with grams, etcetera. I helped them get their books together.

At first I thought the superintendent had a grudge against me. When I first took my world record carrot in she threw it out. Because of all the split roots she said I must have planted 20 carrots and put them all into one. I said how come they were all coming out from the same stem, then? I had to get an agronomist in to tell her it was a single carrot. She was qualified for flowers but didn't know as much about vegetables.

It was also undiplomatic of him to be dismissive of the fair's central event, the giant cabbage weigh-off.

I was never very interested in cabbages. I thought: everybody is doing cabbages, I'll do something else. I didn't approve of it. I thought it should be an amateur thing for children and all that. I grow the big stuff partly because children are attracted by it. I know children who don't know that carrots come from the ground and who've never eaten a raw carrot.

So when they introduced the $2,000 prize for the cabbage weigh-off I refused categorically ever to be a part of it. The whole point of it is entertainment, and to see what you can achieve. Once you start getting big money it goes against the spirit of a state fair. A few dollars for a prize, to help your heating, is fine, but when you start going into the thousands of dollars range it seems wrong.

He paused and reflected: 'Everybody has their own way of looking at life.'

Another matter on which John challenged received wisdom was the basic question of why vegetables grow so big in Alaska. It is not, he insists, primarily a result of the long hours of daylight in summer.

> That theory is all wrong. The key to Alaska is the soil. There are volcanoes all round, and that means there are a lot of minerals. They've got really good quality humus [organic matter in the soil], and that's what makes everything grow. When you have a seed it's like a child. If you put the right minerals into it, the genetics are elevated to produce a better-quality plant. That suggests to me that it's the soil rather than the sun that's important.
>
> The daylight is, if anything, too intense there. The plants go into extreme stress until the end of June. Plants like to sleep. For example you can't grow corn in Alaska, because there's too much light; and there are certain onions that you can't grow, because they have to have a certain amount of sleep time at night, otherwise they don't do anything. Do you hear of any giant vegetables in Scandinavia? No. Sweden and Norway and Finland are on the same parallel as Alaska, and they don't grow them. Everything is the soil.

John has a flair for engendering publicity and, despite his clashes with the fair's officials, he helped raise the profile of the giant vegetable competitions. One of those attracted to participate was Scott Robb.

> Scott was in Alaska when I arrived, but his main thing then was potatoes. It wasn't until the late nineties that he started to compete in the giants and started getting the awards. I know he

has air-conditioning, heating coils in the soil, and everything like that. I want to see the plant doing it naturally.

For a few years he and Scott were fierce rivals: Scott once did a radio interview and joked that he had John's garden under surveillance.

'And throughout all this time,' John continued, 'I was developing my microbial soup.' That is his name for what he later marketed as Bountea compost tea, a product based on his theory that it is the interaction of microbes and minerals, rather than man-made chemicals, that induces plants to grow.

Here he broke off the narrative because we had reached his house. The rain had eased enough for us to venture briefly into the garden, with what on a clearer day would be ravishing views of the surrounding hills. A horse grazed peacefully in an adjoining field. John and Mary had been in this house for only a year, and he had yet to develop his vegetable garden fully, but he had some young carrots and parsnips and a crop that he told me was wheat-grass, marketed in health food shops as a mineral supplement. 'Fifteen pounds of wheat-grass is equivalent, nutrition-wise, to 350 lb of juiced vegetables.'

Back inside, over a cup of strong tea, he picked up his story. He had been about to reveal the secrets of the microbial soup – or at least as many of them as he thought prudent. He explained first how he came to direct his thoughts towards such matters:

Back in the late seventies I was listening to a gardening adviser on the radio. He said there was no need to use garden chemicals but just get everyday things, such as ammonia, beer, chewing tobacco, baby shampoo. Between them they would act as fertilisers and insecticides.

I started experimenting with that kind of thing for a while and played around with minerals – granite and so on. I knew that wherever there's volcanoes there's always very good land. I've always had a knowledge of what's underneath the soil, and I've made very few mistakes. I started to realise quite early on that it isn't about chemicals; it's natural organisms that need to flourish in abundance to keep in balance. The whole idea is balance and recycling. Live microbes live off dead microbes, and they all keep going in this cycle all the time, staying in balance.

Microbe, an unfashionable word today, was introduced in Victorian times to describe any extremely small organism (the first use recorded in the *Oxford English Dictionary* was in 1881). In a rationalist age, the concept of invisible entities that could critically affect the health of plants and people was controversial at first. It was derided by sceptics like George Bernard Shaw, who, in *Too True to be Good*, represented a microbe on stage and had a doctor engage it in conversation, observing: 'Patients insist on having microbes nowadays. . . . When there is no microbe I invent one.'

Nowadays, though, microbes are called micro-organisms, and their existence is accepted by nearly everyone. John went ahead eagerly with experiments to perfect his soup.

The concoction isn't all mine. I consulted various agronomists and other experts. They all had their little silver bullets, and I tried to pull them all together. I've worked with every kind of natural hormone, acetone, calcium carbide, methanol, hydrogen peroxide: you name it and I've done it. I got some of them from companies that normally supply them only to universities.

Then he got to hear about *terra preta*. The words mean 'dark earth' in Portuguese and describe a type of exceptionally fertile soil in the savannahs of the Amazon basin that scientists believe was man-made some 4,000 years ago – which would make it the world's first known manufactured growing compost. They have come to this conclusion because it contains charcoal and shards of pottery vessels. The charcoal was probably produced by a technique named slash and char – a variant of the more common slash and burn, but using lower temperatures for the burn – and the presence of pottery suggests human intervention.

The effect of the charcoal is to encourage the growth of mycorrhizal fungus. This is the substance that the most successful American pumpkin growers, such as Ron Wallace, now routinely mix with the soil to coax their giants into still more excessive growth. The theory is that in Brazil the fungus reproduces itself, spreading from the charcoal and pottery mix to the surrounding soil, where it is constantly renewed.

'The point is that the soil builds,' was how John put it. 'It never goes away. It's because charcoal sequesters the carbon dioxide from the atmosphere. It's a perfect haven for microbes.' He bridles at any suggestion that feeding the soil in this way cossets the vegetables or amounts to taking short cuts to success.

I challenged myself in many ways – not allowing the plants to have too much soil area and putting them in different situations, sometimes in extreme conditions. I wouldn't pamper them. Sometimes I wouldn't water them for a while.

In growing plants you have to discipline them, like children. You can trick the plant into doing things. The most important thing is to get a good root ball, so you want to suppress as much as possible any upper growth, and you want a stocky plant – low growth and a robust stem. When you see that, you know everything is going into the root system. That's pretty much the key.

In Alaska he grew most of his produce in two polytunnels and a conservatory.

I had a greenhouse, but it got blown away. I used heat in the greenhouse and the conservatory, but not in the tunnels. I'd start them with heat and some lighting, but I spend less than most giant growers on utility bills and equipment. We have to be environmentally responsible.

The plants need 70°F [21°C] to germinate and the outside temperature was 40° below. But as soon as the seedlings got up to about two inches, depending on the plants, then I would put them under stress as much as I could, withdrawing water and getting them down to about 40°.

The nutrients will work at some temperatures, not others. If you put a plant under stress it will use its survival tactics. If the conditions are cold it has to go searching for nutrients with its roots, and that builds up the root system. Then, when the root system has built up, the soil and outside air get warmer, and they start to grow fast.

John is dismissive of many of the accepted practices of gardening and maintains that he can detect early in a plant's life whether it is responding to his unique treatment.

When I feed them with my soup the vegetables get a sort of gloss on them. They shine. Everybody says so. I've never read a gardening book – I think they're complete garbage, and you can quote me on that. I have reference books for diseases and pests and so on, but basically that's it. You can take all the conventional wisdom of gardening and you can throw it out the window.

He wants his vegetables to be tasty as well as large.

My purpose is both quality and quantity. I've grown up to 21 lb of potatoes per plant. I had Brussels sprouts fork into two stems from the same root, and I grew peas with thirteen to a pod [the normal average is eight or nine]. I had tomatoes breaking their supports down with the weight – and that was outside, with no heating. And I once had a Swiss chard that grew to over 9ft tall.

My stuff helps keep the soil a bit warmer in the very cold weather, like compost heating up. My world record celery survived even when the temperature went down to 23°F [minus 5°C] at night. The friction from the bacteria warms the soil. I put tomatoes in early in May, when there was still a frost in the soil. I took the soil up from 42° to 83°F overnight. It makes them start growing earlier in the spring and last longer into the autumn. That's the added benefit, and it's part of the key to giant vegetables.

The proof of his theories, he believes, lies in the results he achieved.

I thought that to get credibility for my mixture I would go on a mission to get as many awards as I possibly could, to prove that it actually works. That was one of my ulterior reasons for going after the Guinness records.

In 1993 he grew a 35-lb broccoli that has still not been exceeded. Five years later he surprised even himself when he broke the record for the heaviest carrot.

It had been a very hot summer with lots of rain, and I saw that the carrot was bolting: starting to go to flower. I wrote it off and ignored it for a couple of weeks, thinking it would never grow a really big root if it was using up its energy on the flowers. Just prior to the fair I went over to it. Because I'd been ignoring it I hadn't seen how wide it was. As I gently scraped the dirt off it got wider and wider and wider and I took a tape measure across. It was eleven inches.

I got my youngest daughter out to hold the leaves while I got a spoon and a brush and excavated the carrot as though it was an archaeological dig – it took us forty-five minutes to take it out, and not one of the side shoots broke. She was patient enough with me to bring it all out and wash it down. It weighed three ounces less than 19 lb and beat Bernard Lavery's record by about four and a half pounds.

By 1999 John was ready to launch Bountea on to the market as a liquid concentrate, sold principally by mail order. The business is now well established and is run by his brother from a base in Colorado. 'Demand for the stuff is going through the roof,' John said. 'Foreign aid groups have taken it up. There's a big demand in Malawi, and it's being tested in China and Japan.' He was also selling it from a stall it in his local market, along with some of the vegetables he grows using it. 'I had a zucchini plant with about forty zucchini on it, and last week I took some enormous ones to the market and sold them as marrows. I also make a lot of zucchini cake and carrot cake.'

John remains controversial. Not everyone is convinced of the effectiveness of his microbial soup. Scott Robb said: 'I think he thought that Bountea was the silver bullet, the answer to it all, from healthy soil food, to nutrients, to fungicide, to pesticide. I think he thought it was going to do everything for him. It won't.'

John is used to such doubters.

I've been ostracized and ridiculed for it. My father-in-law, although he was raised on a farm on Long Island, said: 'How come you're doing it the hard way, John?' I told him it wasn't the hard way but I wanted to build up my soil.

Initially these gardeners think I'm nuts; but when they see the results they say they can see there's something in it. Basically, you could call me an alchemist.

Chapter 17

The Showman

The legendary Bernard Lavery lives with his second wife and their five young children in a sprawling house on the edge of Sutton St Edmund, a village on the flat, featureless Lincolnshire fens made unsightly by a scattering of plain grey barns, mostly involved in intensive poultry rearing. It is not far from Spalding, where his early giant vegetable shows were staged; but he no longer has any connection with the hobby that effectively took over his life for a decade. He does not even do much work in his garden: it is far from the meticulously cultivated plot that you would expect from a man who once had such a way with plants.

He moved to this part of the country from Wales in the nineties. At first he spent the summer living here in a caravan while his wife remained out west – an arrangement that no doubt contributed to the breakdown of his first marriage. Before he retired from competition in 1996 he had accumulated 25 world and 37 British records.

A friendly, bear-like man, he explained the hold that giant vegetables once exerted over him: 'At its prime, when a giant pumpkin is going really well, it will grow two inches in circumference in a day. Every morning when you get up the first thing you do is not to put the kettle on but go out and take a look and see how big it is today. Only then do you put the kettle on.' He believes that there is no definable limit to the size of pumpkins or any other vegetable that will be grown in the future: as in athletics, records are there to be broken, and then broken again.

Why, then, did he abandon growing giant vegetables competitively when he was still under 60 – an age when many people begin to get serious about gardening? In 1996 his life took an unconventional turn: Sheikh Zayed, the ruler of the Gulf state of Abu Dhabi, having seen his name in the *Guinness Book of Records*, invited him to redesign and look after the gardens of his palace. The offer came at a time when Bernard was beginning to feel disillusioned with the giant vegetable movement, which had for him never been simply a sport or pastime but involved a more altruistic motivation as well.

At the end of the day, when I packed it in I considered that all my ambitions had failed. When I started breeding giant seeds and had my own range of seeds in the shops, my ambition was to have sponsorship so that I could export the seeds – or even give them away – to poor countries. If you put ordinary seed in good ground you get good results. If you put giant seeds in poor ground you get normal-sized vegetables. Certainly you'll get something worth eating out of it, without any trouble.

My aim was to start these strains of seeds and produce them on a mammoth scale for Third World countries, and this would help relieve starvation in some parts of the world. I approached nearly every seed company in the UK and America, but nobody followed it up, so I gave it up. I was very disheartened towards the end, and I still feel aggrieved about it. There are certain things that people have missed the boat on, and this was one of them.

There was no doubting his sincerity in promoting this project, even if the science is suspect. Just because a seed produces very large vegetables in perfect conditions, it does not follow that it will produce anything worthwhile in a less favourable growing environment. Giant vegetables are not necessarily high yielding, and for developing countries the total yield is more important than the weight of an individual item. They are not genetically modified but the result of selective breeding, very much a hit-and-miss undertaking. And some very big vegetables have structural weaknesses: the Atlantic Giant pumpkin, for instance, is more prone to rot in the rain than the smaller Hundredweight variety. Large onions also are vulnerable to too much moisture.

All the same, his failure to interest seed companies depressed Bernard, and when the Abu Dhabi offer came he accepted it with enthusiasm and some relief. In Abu Dhabi his principal achievement was to create four giant glasshouses, replicating the four seasons of a temperate climate, transferring the fruit, vegetables and flowers from one to the other at the appropriate time. The difficulty was to keep the greenhouses cool, not warm, and he had to devise a lighting system that mimicked the changing day lengths; but he succeeded in his aim of ensuring that the Sheikh had fresh fruit for breakfast every day of the year.

Then in 1999 Bernard had a serious heart attack and returned permanently to England, where he now lives in retirement. 'I sit and relax – I have to because of my heart,' he said. 'I'm a very lucky chap: I'm 69 years of age and I've got a new family and I'm still here. OK, I'm not growing giant veg, but I've been there, I've had the T-shirt on and I enjoyed every minute of it.'

One record likely to stand for a while yet is his 124-lb cabbage. 'Scott Robb has been trying to break my cabbage record for donkeys' years,' he said. 'The last photograph he sent me showed that he had a plastic tunnel and he had the ground covered with plastic. He said he'd beat my record, but he didn't.'

The hazards of getting such enormous specimens to the display bench are underlined by Bernard's insistence that his record cabbage was not the largest he grew that year. He had hired a crane to lift the really big one on to the truck that would transport it to

Alton Towers, and BBC television cameras were on hand to record the event.

> We lifted it up in a sling but it slipped out of the sling and broke. So we couldn't take it, and we had to have my number two, which broke the world record even though it was eight pounds lighter than the one that was damaged, and we must have left five pounds on the ground with the leaves that broke as we unloaded it.

Although in his prime he was certainly a go-getter, sweeping all before him, Bernard now says that winning and breaking records is not the be-all and end-all of competitive horticulture. 'Of course, it's like all sports – you don't do it to come second. But you've got to enjoy what you do, and if you get too competitive the fun goes out of it.' Gradually his old records are being broken, but he is philosophical about it:

> It's like a heavyweight boxer. He might have three world championships, but in the end someone will come along who's better. If you can't take a beating, don't bother in the first place.
>
> My advice to anyone doing it is: enjoy yourself, and don't care about anybody else. If you've grown something 100 lb this year, then don't worry about Joe Bloggs down the road but try to grow something 101 lb next year. Try to beat your own record. Otherwise you'll end up like other people in giant veg who are very bad sports and get very bitter when they don't win. It's brilliant when you can get top of the tree, but not everybody can be top of the tree. If there were only winners there would only be one in each class, and then you wouldn't have a show.

This isn't a philosophy that he has developed since he retired. He was expounding it while he was still active. In an interview in the *Independent* he told Jim White:

A lot of showmen are very secretive about their methods. I think a gardener who takes his secrets to the grave has wasted his life. If I can tell someone how to do something and they come back and beat me, I'm more proud of them than if I won everything myself.

That was in 1995, the year he published *How to Grow Giant Vegetables*, a book that is still used as a guide by many growers.

White asked him the perennial question about sabotage and theft. The legend of jealous gardeners creeping down to the allotments with axes or acid sprays on the eve of a show, to spoil their rivals' chances, is a recurring one. Bernard replied that it had happened to him only once, when he was still in south Wales: someone broke into his greenhouse and snapped off all his cucumbers three days before a big show. His initial anger quickly subsided into resignation.

Speaking to me twelve years later he said that he had only once allowed himself to become so obsessed with the risk of sabotage as to spend the night before a show sleeping with his prize specimens.

I used to grow a lot of stuff over at a local farm, and one night just before the show I slept over there. But I swore I'd never do it again; I was crippled for about a week through sleeping in the shed. From then on I thought: let them get on with it. . . . Some people have a very jealous streak in them, but I fortunately don't.

If he did have any angry confrontations with rivals, he has deliberately excised them from his memory: 'I try to remember all the good things in life and not the bad things.'

Chapter 18

Things Can Only Get Bigger

By mid-October the show season was over. There were two reasons for going back to Newark towards the end of the month, three weeks after the Dewsbury show. I wanted to ask Peter how he thought his year had gone, what lessons he had learned from it, and whether he planned any changes to his techniques and strategies for 2008. He had also promised to take me to see Alf Cobb, the 91-year-old widower who broke the world record for the longest cucumber at Shepton Mallet but was unable to attend the show in person.

Peter picked me up from Newark station on a balmy autumn morning, and drove us the three miles to Holme, the village where Alf has spent his entire life and where his family has lived for 170 years. He lives on his own in Clematis Cottage, a large hundred-year-old red brick house with a more modern extension, some 300 yards from the farm where he used to work as a stockman. He was born during the First World War in the house just across the road, next to a former smithy, and in 1961 he bought his present place, with its two acres of land, for £1,400. His son is building a house on the part of the garden nearest the road, but there is still plenty of space for Alf's vegetables.

The garden boundary is about 100 yards from the east bank of the River Trent, protected by a flood bank planted with willows: there were elms there once, said Alf, but Dutch elm disease killed them off. Alf is a little deaf but spry for his age, although he was complaining about a pain in his right arm that ruled out any strenuous gardening for the time being.

Before we got down to talking about cucumbers, Peter showed him the results of a soil test on Alf's garden. When Peter was last here he had taken some soil away and sent it to a laboratory, together with some from his own garden. The results showed that Alf's pH level – the measure of acidity and alkalinity – was a little lower than Peter's, indicating an acid soil; but the level of nutrients was high. 'I put all the nutrients and fertilisers at the top of the soil rather than digging them in,' said Alf,

> because when you water you wash them down to the roots. But the secret is in the soil and the preparation. This is a light and quick-draining soil here, not sticky; it's a kind soil to work. I dig the rows and put the manure and compost on top, so the water flows through it. I do that in the autumn or winter: if it wasn't for my bad arm I'd probably have done it by now.

He sometimes improves the soil with leaf mould from a nearby wood, and Peter remembered going with him a few years ago to collect some for himself. 'That really was hard work,' he recalled. Alf continued:

> I hand-pollinate all the cucumbers and put them on cordons – you've got to cordon them – and I take all the side shoots off. I limit each plant to one or two cucumbers, and I give them a lot of water. I water them every other day and get up at five in the morning to do it. That means that the soil starts to get warmer not long after the water has been put on, as the heat begins to build up. If you do it at night they stay cold all night. I put the fertiliser on separately but only feed them towards the back end of the season, in August.

It was Peter who inspired Alf to join the giant vegetable circuit – a venture that won him many column inches in the gardening press and even in national newspapers as he captured records. His photograph appears prominently in the 2008 edition of *Guinness World Records*. 'The first time I showed was at Spalding,' he reminisced. 'Peter had a tomato there, and it went wrong, and he gave me some of the seed from it.' Among his collection of trophies are two cups from Spalding shows – for the heaviest radish in 1996 and the biggest cucumber in 1997.

Before venturing into the heavy stuff, Alf had competed in quality classes at local shows. He began doing that after he retired from the farm, where one of his tasks was to prepare the cattle for agricultural shows and take them there. It was something he loved doing, and he continued for some time after he had officially retired from the farm.

I was looking after the cattle and showing them until I was past seventy. I used to love showing – clipping them and shampooing them – and I won a lot of prizes at local and national shows. I had four hundred cattle to look after. One year I got champion and reserve at Collingham, Flintham and Southwell, all in the same year. But then my farm stopped showing cattle. There used to be a lot of little farms around here – horses and a few milk cows and orchards – but they've all gone now, been built over.

So his strongest motive for entering vegetable shows was to fill the competitive void left when his life with the cattle ended. And when Peter introduced him to the giant contests, he decided that this was where he would concentrate his efforts.

I got my first cucumber seed from Bernard Lavery. For the competitions I only grow cucumbers, radishes and potatoes, although I still grow a range of vegetables for the kitchen. The secret is in turning over the soil and preparing it properly. I spend a lot of time on that, although it's hard work at my age. I start the seeds off in the first or second week in April. I give them heat but no artificial light. I had a new polytunnel this year, and the year before I had to get a new greenhouse, because the old one blew down.

I grow about forty cucumbers every year, some in one tunnel and some in the other. I don't get any help with the digging. I'll go on doing it as long as I can, but it gets harder and harder every year. All the time I was married I grew my own vegetables: my wife never bought any. I grew everything we needed.

We went into one of his two tunnels, where about thirty cucumbers – bright orange, some flecked with green – were laid out on a central bench, including the record-beater from Shepton Mallet. To an inexperienced eye it was hard to tell the difference between those grown for length and the heavy ones. The beds along either side of the tunnel were empty except for some marigolds, grown there to keep the aphids away.

He had promised to give Peter some seed from his biggest cucumbers. Peter once held the record for the longest cucumber, and he gave Alf some seed then; so now Alf was returning the favour. They both eagerly sliced some of the cucumbers in half, lengthwise – but they were in for a letdown. The majority of the seeds appeared to be empty husks that had not swelled, as they would have if they had been fertile. Some of them were on the borderline: Alf and Peter would not be able to tell whether they were viable until they had dried them out.

'A bit disappointing, isn't it?' was as far as the stoical Alf would go towards expressing his feelings. Peter pointed out that some of the cucumbers were on the green side and probably not quite ripe, which would explain why their seeds had not developed properly.

If he was right, it meant that they would have grown even bigger given more time – confirming his view that the Shepton Mallet show is scheduled several weeks too early.

'It's been a bad year for setting seed anyway,' Peter remarked. 'Alf got away with it but I didn't, I think because it was too dark to set the seed properly. Alf might have got his away that crucial bit earlier, when the weather was still reasonable.'

Alf let me taste a chunk of one of the cucumbers he had cut open. It was excruciatingly bitter: this is certainly not one of those giants that are good to eat. In the other tunnel some out-of-season potatoes were putting on growth, and Alf hoped they would be ready in time for Christmas – not for show, but for eating. 'It isn't good soil for growing potatoes,' he reported. 'King Edwards don't do any good at all here – they want a heavier soil. They did better on the farm, where there's good clay land.'

Back in his living room, alongside his framed Guinness certificates, was a photograph taken when he was much younger, showing him standing proudly next to a prize bull. 'It was the best one we had,' he recalled. 'Charollais crossed with an Aberdeen Angus. We bought him in Yorkshire and he won us two fatstock prizes.' Gratified as he was by his cucumber successes, he still hankered after his cattle.

Peter drove me to his house, where our arrival coincided with a delivery of fertiliser that neatly illustrated his ambition to go for even bigger and better vegetables in 2008. It was a product he had not tried before. Called Antagon, it came from Belgium, cost £60 for 25 kilos and was said to add bacteria to the soil – something John Evans would approve of. The picture on the sack suggested that it was used on golf courses and other sports fields, where, said Peter, it helped combat fusarium wilt in the grass. A grower called Ivor Mace, who wins prizes for quality onions, told Peter it also works against a similar fungal disease that attacks leeks and onions. As Peter explained,

> When you lift your onions the roots should be white, but some of mine are pink, and that suggests a fungal disease. By mixing some of this Antagon into the barrels I hope to stop them getting the disease. But I'm only going to put it in the barrels where the onions were clean this year.

So he is using it as a preventative, not a cure – and, in his methodical way, he has put a white marker on the 'clean' barrels to avoid any confusion.

Before we started our tour of the garden we sat down for lunch. Mary produced some tasty sandwiches, including one made from a heavy tomato that matured too late to be a contender in any of the shows. When we headed out into the garden it was the tomatoes we made for first, and Peter showed me one that was especially large and knobbly:

> It's the best one I've grown all year but it's too late – it should have been as big as this in August. It's as if June and July never happened. Some of my giant cauliflowers aren't ready even yet, and I was trying to time them for the two Welsh shows.

There were plenty of other ripe or ripening vegetables in the garden to confirm that it had been a year for late developers. Several pumpkins were thriving on his large compost heap at the bottom of the adjacent hay field. 'One of them has grown to about 200 lb. It's the biggest I've had.'

Nearly all the remaining marrows were destined to be thrown on to the compost heap, after Peter had taken seed from the two biggest. And there were still plenty of long runner beans in evidence:

I've had one grow longer since the shows – it would have won a prize, although the pheasants have been pecking it and making it go rotten. It's 32in long – longer than the one I won with at Shepton Mallet, Abertysswg and Malvern. Richard Hope beat me at Llanharry, but that one would have beaten him – although he might also have a longer one by now, of course.

Looking ahead, Peter showed me the leeks that he had planted in pots with the aim of growing pips from them. (I noted with concern that they had put on significantly more growth than the one I planted after Olga bought it in Northumbria.) 'I put them in after the shows, and they're making roots, and hopefully they will survive the winter, although most years I lose quite a few,' he said. The ones he planted a year ago had now produced their grass, on the top of their long stalks, after he took the seed flowers off in the spring. Some were already showing signs of swelling just above their miniature roots, and he would be taking them off and potting them up in a matter of weeks. 'November is about the right time. Nobody grows leeks from seed if they're going to show them: they don't come early enough, and you don't know what you've got.'

Next we came to the onion seedlings, which were methodically labelled with their source. A few of the labels said Sifford – obviously a reference to the late John Sifford, whose 2005 world record weight of 16 lb 10 oz has yet to be exceeded. I asked Peter to explain.

A friend in Birmingham reckons he got a bulb from Sifford the year he broke the record (he did give some bulbs away to his friends). And he reckons that this was the seed from it. He only gave me about ten seeds, and I put seven of them in, and I've got three-and-a-half plants – so I doubt if they're any good at all, actually. But you've got to try, haven't you?

Some others were labelled as coming from Billy Lamb's strain.

They're from a 13-lb bulb I had last year, a nice high one. The ones with blue labels are from the 13½-lb bulb that I showed at Dewsbury. It wasn't such a good shape but it weighed heavier. They're new seed and they're vigorous. If you keep them for over a year the vigour seems to go from them. They really need to be fresh.

He customarily lets his biggest onions run to seed, and he had several of them ranged in a shed, placed upside down in crumpled plastic bags, with the weight that each of them reached marked neatly on the base. They were upside down because he was draining them from the neck, making it more likely that they would survive the winter. This was yet another experiment.

I'm trying to get the moisture out of them before I store them away and try to make them produce seed next year. This is what Billy Lamb says he does to them but I've never done them like this before. They'll stand like that for another month and I'll take them into the barn, where it's nice and dry, and start them off again in January or February, when they should start to shoot.

At first Billy only let me have six plants, so I only had two or three to put down. This year I've got more to put down because I've got more big ones. If I can get more of them through the winter by doing this, so much the better. The big ones don't keep very well in any case.

It would be two years before those seeds produced what he hoped would be prize-winning onions, but the next year's crop had already begun their life cycle These were the ones that he started off a few days earlier under 24-hour light and heat. Again he was planning to challenge the received wisdom.

Traditionally they should stay in here for six weeks, but I think five weeks is long enough. Then they go into the heated greenhouse. You can put leeks under lights too, but I don't think they need it. I might put a few in here – maybe half a dozen – just to see how they like it. This box will be going through to the end of January. The trouble with sowing early is that you need to keep them going through the winter, and you have to repot them again and again.

We came to the cabbage seedlings next:

These are some that I saved from one of the cabbages that went to seed. Out of the six or seven I planted, four went to seed early. And these others are seed that I got from George Rogers in Cornwall – but so far the new seed is doing a lot better than the older. It's looking a lot stronger.

He was letting some of that year's root vegetables go to seed, with a view to bolstering his stock. He had never tried this with beetroot and swedes, but he likes to keep experimenting. 'We'll have to see how it goes,' he said uncertainly.

There was not much else to see in relation to the following year's potential champions. The long carrots would be started off in January or February, most of the other stuff later in the spring. He would again be placing his drainpipes both in his shed and leaning against an outside barn. The only difference seems to be that the ones grown indoors develop a little faster.

My long carrot at Malvern came from the pipes standing outside, like the one I showed at Highgrove last year. Both shows were late in the season. The long carrot I took to Shepton Mallet came from in the shed. I think Joe's was longer than mine because he had left it in for two years and it was still going. They might go to seed but they still grow.

Meanwhile Peter had been improving his infrastructure. He let off a smoke bomb in the greenhouse to sterilise it and modified the interior to keep a smaller area heated, so saving energy. He designed a space where he would bring the onions when they emerged from their 24-hour heat and light box. A light would be directed on them here for eight-and-a-half hours every day initially, increasing by half-hour increments up to eleven hours in March, just before they were due to be planted out in their final containers. And, now that the tunnels were empty, he had taken the covers off some of them to let the rain get in, adding a bit of zest to the soil.

'My next project is to take two trees down,' he told me, in case I assumed there was going to be any let-up in activity over the winter. 'The one in the front of the garden takes a bit of light from the front tunnel.'

Before driving me back to the station, Peter gave me a sheet of paper. On one side he had listed ten points that summed up the 2007 season and, on the other, twelve resolutions for 2008:

Thoughts on 2007 growing season

1. Extreme weather – hot and dry April; cold, dark and wet June and July; good autumn.
2. Vegetables requiring flower to fruit did no good at all – i.e. marrows, melons, cucumbers.
3. Trying to grow too many kinds.
4. Cannot cope with quality vegetables when giants start.
5. Failures this year of normal bankers – e.g. melon – but won prizes with some for first time: swede, beetroot.
6. All growers suffered.
7. Onion weights generally down but I was slightly higher.

8. Good show results but I lost the world record for long carrot. Weather suited leeks.
9. A lot of travelling to 13 shows but we enjoyed them and the weekends away – good weather at all of them.
10. I liked the wins; meeting other growers; swapping notes, vegetables, etc.

Thoughts on 2008

1. Try to cut down on kinds grown.
2. Concentrate on giants.
3. Go all out for heavy onion.
4. Enter same shows but no more.
5. Limit quality vegetables to August.
6. Reduce barrels of parsnips and carrots and consider covering some.
7. Erect second small onion tunnel.
8. Remove two large trees over the winter.
9. Plan for another garden open evening (or evenings).
10. Apart from giants at Shepton Mallet, try to enter fewer classes at each show.
11. Aim to grow heavier leek if correct strain acquired.
12. Set up more water collection and irrigation.

I suspected that, in contrast to the majority of New Year resolutions, most of these would be kept.

When I got back from seeing John Evans in Cork I found an email from Kevin in Cwmbran. He and Gareth and Ian had been invited to London at the beginning of November to take part in a new television show for Channel Five called *Cooking the Books*. I went along to watch.

'They asked us why we couldn't come in on the Underground,'

said Ian, unloading a giant water melon, beetroot and courgette. 'I said that if we tried to carry my 130-lb water melon on to a train, people would think it was a bomb. It would cause a riot.' He added that he had last been in a TV studio in 1994, when he had taken one of his giants on to the BBC's children's programme *Blue Peter*.

After chef Paul Rankin had demonstrated how to stuff a chicken with lobster, it was time for the giant vegetable slot. Ian had grown the featured water melon, but it was mutually agreed that Kevin, younger and more media-friendly, would be the one to talk about it.

As it was carried on to its table, Jeremy Edwards, the presenter, asked Kevin how heavy it was.

'Ten stone' (only a small exaggeration).

'A ten stone melon!' Jeremy cried, and we in the audience, at a signal from the floor manager, applauded vigorously, with one or two whoops.

Jeremy asked the secret of growing produce that big.

'Good seed, good weather, good luck,' was Kevin's succinct reply.

We said our farewells in the lobby. Kevin went to fetch the car, and Gareth said that they planned to spend the rest of the afternoon at the Natural History Museum before driving back to Wales; 'No point in wasting a trip to London.' Later in the week, back at home, they had scheduled a meeting with a representative of Welsh Water, to try to make some progress on the drainage problem in their tunnel.

Ian, meanwhile, would be getting his beds in order for next season's planting. But first he had some unhappy news to give me: he no longer featured in *Guinness World Records*. His 51-lb 9-oz beetroot, which had won him a place in the 2007 edition, had been not just exceeded but pulverised by Piet de Goede, a Dutch grower, who produced one weighing a scarcely credible 156 lb 10 oz. I had been warned of this disconcerting development by

Scott Robb while I was in Alaska. He told me disapprovingly that, according to what he had heard, the Dutch monstrosity was in fact industrial sugar beet, very different from domestic beetroot: and a Dutch report of de Goede's triumph, which I picked up on the internet, confirmed this. According to the Guinness rules, only domestic vegetables should be eligible for the records.

I made sympathetic noises to Ian over this seeming injustice. Just a year earlier a photograph of him, proudly brandishing his beetroot above his head, had dominated the vegetable page of the Guinness book. Now he was a non-person, all traces of his feat expunged. It was no consolation that Alf Cobb, his friendly rival, was now pictured in his place, wielding his record cucumber. Fame is fleeting. Every season, one man's triumph is another's disappointment.

Speaking of disappointments, the giant leek that Olga had bought at the Northumberland show, which I was growing on to produce pips, survived until the first days of January, when it gave up the ghost. It had not been looking well for some time. Peter had warned me that this might happen, and if there is one thing I have learned during the year, it is how to take setbacks in your stride.

When I telephoned Gerald just before Christmas, I was pleased to discover that, after this frustrating year with his hydroponic onions, he was far from disheartened. 'I'm a little bit more optimistic than when we last spoke, to be honest,' he declared, 'and I'll tell you why.'

He had now come to the conclusion that there were four principal problems with the method as he practised it last year, and he was taking steps to address them. I already knew about two of them – the balance of the nutrients he fed the onions, and how often he delivered the feed. The third issue was related. Gerald believed the onions were getting too much moisture direct to the roots; the short but sharp flow of water can damage the roots and encourage them to rot. He thought this could be addressed if he changed the method of delivery of the nutrients, as well as the frequency.

So far I've been pumping up from the bottom into the roots. I've been to see Simon [from Aquaculture] and I've asked him to make me a system that will drip-feed from the top. That way I'm not disturbing the roots, am I? And I'll do it just once a day – they don't really need as much water as I've been giving them.

As for the nutrient level, Simon's advice was to lift it in the early stages of growth and drop it right down when the weather warmed up.

The fourth problem was the excessive heat in the middle of the sunniest days. Although there were comparatively few of those last summer, it needs only one or two days when the temperature climbs to the high thirties Celsius to put excessive strain on the onions and halt their growth. 'One day in June it got up to 39°C. That's far too high. Some of the onions just stopped in their tracks.'

Gerald was going to tackle this by adapting his greenhouse so that two panels of glass could easily be removed, allowing the hot air to escape. He had also asked Simon for a larger humidifier, to stop the tips of the onions drying out in the heat, and he planned to fit green netting over the roof to provide shade. 'Ideally I should install an air-conditioning unit but the problem with that is the running cost. But if I can keep the temperature down in those other ways I can still break the record.'

He sowed the seed on 1 December: 'They were very large seeds, from my own 11 lb onion.' He was growing six hydroponically and fifteen in a commercial John Innes compost. For 2008 he made a further change to the initial growing medium. He was dissatisfied with the rockwool plugs he experimented with the previous year because they retained too much water, and this again encouraged the roots to rot. So this time he was using the peat-based Jiffy plugs that can be bought in garden centres.

After three weeks the roots had already started to emerge. The six hydroponic onions were potted on just after Christmas into 3½-in pots filled with a smaller version of the clay balls he used last year, which he thought would encourage stronger root growth. 'I think that with hydroponics I can grow an onion up to 18 lb,' he enthused.

When he telephoned me in mid-April, as I was in the last stages of preparing this book, his confidence was undented. 'One of them has got eighteen leaves,' he told me. 'There's been a little tipping but not as much as last year. They look really healthy.' He had put the onions into the hydroponic system in the third week in January and he still had them under lights.

On Simon's advice he was using a stronger mix of nutrients, taking the conductivity level up to 21, whereas he kept it at 14 for most of last season. (This went against the view of Medwyn Williams, who attributed his failure with the system in 2006 to setting the conductivity level too high.) The smaller clay balls meant that the roots were absorbing the nutrient more quickly, and he was changing it every week instead of every fortnight. A humidifier and a fan had been installed in the greenhouse, as well as more efficient shading on the glass, to keep the temperature down on the hottest days. Gerald was willing to move heaven and earth to produce a world-beating onion.

'I'm really, really optimistic,' he declared. 'I'm absolutely sure I'll break the record this year.'